Mona Lisa
in
Camelot

MONA LISA in CAMELOT

how JACQUELINE KENNEDY *and* DA VINCI'S MASTERPIECE CHARMED *and* CAPTIVATED A NATION

Margaret Leslie Davis

DA CAPO PRESS
A Member of the Perseus Books Group • New York

Printed in the United States of America.

Design by Pauline Brown
Text set in 10.75-point Caslon

Library of Congress Cataloging-in-Publication Data

Davis, Margaret L.
Mona Lisa in Camelot : how Jacqueline Kennedy and Da Vinci's masterpiece charmed and captivated a nation / Margaret Leslie Davis.
p. cm.
Includes bibliographical references.
ISBN 978-0-7382-1103-9 (alk. paper)
1. Leonardo, da Vinci, 1452–1519. Mona Lisa. 2. Onassis, Jacqueline Kennedy, 1929–1994. 3. Art—Exhibitions—History—20th century.
I. Title.
ND623.L5D35 2008
759.5—dc22
2008019767

Published by Da Capo Press
A Member of the Perseus Books Group
www.dacapopress.com

10 9 8 7 6 5 4 3 2 1

For the Women's Literary Society

Contents

Author's Note

I started this book with the intention of writing a history of the triumphant American exhibition of Leonardo da Vinci's Mona Lisa. Early into my research, however, I discovered a surprise: First Lady Jacqueline Kennedy had been the mastermind behind the 1963 exhibition, which was made possible only through her alliance with National Gallery Director John Walker and her adept international diplomacy.

Sent as a personal loan to the President and Mrs. Kennedy by the French government, the famous painting arrived in the States on December 19, 1962, where it was exhibited in Washington, D.C., and New York for fifty-two days. Nearly two million Americans, for many their first visit to an art museum, stood in long lines for a chance to see a masterpiece created in the early sixteenth century. As if engaged in a religious pilgrimage, visitors traveled great distances and waited for hours, ready to embrace the Mona Lisa, a harbinger of a transcendent new era.

The visit of the Mona Lisa produced the greatest outpouring of appreciation for a single work of art in American history and pioneered the phenomenon of the blockbuster museum show. It was one of the most daring, elaborate art exhibitions ever staged, and the painting's unlikely, romantic journey to America captured the imagination of the world.

What follows is a true story. The principal events take place over the course of two years beginning in March 1961 and ending in the spring of 1963. Jacqueline Kennedy mustered the full force of her influence as First Lady to bring the Mona Lisa to America, all the while drawing on her innate understanding of symbols and image crafting to infuse the exhibition with a sense of history, drama, and pageantry. The Mona Lisa's controversial visit also served vital national interests at a decisive moment in U.S. history, and "*La Joconde*," as the painting is known in France, was transformed into an icon of freedom at the height of the Cold War.

The painting's successful debut awakened a passion for culture that had been dormant in the national psyche during the provincial postwar years, and the sensational exhibit ignited a national love affair with the arts. In his emotional speech at the closing ceremony at the Metropolitan Museum of Art, John Walker acknowledged that the great achievement of the exhibit was not how many people came to see the Mona Lisa, but rather that the painting acted as a catalyst. Her visit, he said, "stirred some impulse toward beauty in human beings who may never have felt that impulse before."

Part One

The Art Enthusiasts

Jacqueline Kennedy looked closely at the eight paintings by Paul Cézanne displayed for her on easels arranged in a wide row. At her side was National Gallery Director John Walker, standing with his arms crossed, beaming like a proud father. He nodded knowingly as he watched her select the most exquisite of them all: *The Forest* and *House on the Marne*.

The new First Lady had learned that a group of magnificent Cézannes had been bequeathed to the White House but for unknown reasons had ended up at the National Gallery. Not long after the inauguration she telephoned Walker and asked to see them. Walker wasn't surprised to hear her lay claim to the Cézannes. After all, he had known Jackie since she was a child.

The extended families of Jacqueline Bouvier and John Walker had moved for generations in the same wealthy, socially connected circles of New York City, East Hampton, Newport, and the sprawling estates of Virginia. Walker was a lifelong friend of Hugh D. Auchincloss, Jackie's stepfather, and Walker often visited Merrywood, the Auchincloss estate. The forty-six-acre wooded retreat overlooking the Potomac River in McLean, Virginia, had been Jackie's home since 1942. Although she was a sophisticated urbanite who enjoyed elite company in the world's great cities, she often returned to the countryside and seashore.

"I always love it so at Merrywood—so peaceful—with the river and the dogs—and listening to the Victrola," Jackie once told her stepbrother, Hugh D. Auchincloss III. "I will never know which I love best—Hammersmith [Farm] with its green fields and summer winds—or Merrywood in the snow—with the river and those great steep hills."

It was only natural that when Jackie's mother, Janet Lee, took her teenage daughters to Washington, D.C., for cultural enrichment, they would call on John Walker for a personal tour of the National Gallery. Walker noticed that Jackie's interest in art was more than casual for a girl her age; she was drawn particularly to the works of the great French impressionists, including pictures by Renoir and Monet. Walker understood why the vivid landscapes would appeal to a quiet, studious youngster who had grown up loving the outdoors.

In a handwritten thank-you note following one guided tour, Walker detected more than proper etiquette from young Jacqueline. He saw a real interest in art and a surprisingly heartfelt resolution. "I'm still floating on air after my idyllic afternoon at the Gallery—those few hours made it worth staying in Washington for the entire summer," Jackie wrote Walker. "I came away in an absolute frenzy of excitement, and resolved (oh please let me keep the resolutions this time) to go back nearly every day—and read and read—and write things about the paintings I love."

The earnest adolescent who had once strolled about the National Gallery with such joy was now the First Lady and had summoned Walker to assemble the Cézannes for her—paintings that he knew she would love.

As head of the National Gallery, Walker had a proprietary interest in the Cézannes. Not only did they provide him pleasure because of their superb quality and place in art history, but he had also personally taken a hand in seeing to it that they came to the Gallery. In fact, he'd assured their arrival by a ruse that he later admitted was somewhat ignoble for a museum curator, but he felt it was urgent that the paintings come into his care as soon as possible.

Had it been anyone but Jackie Kennedy who wanted them, he would have barred the door to their departure. Instead, he arranged a private viewing at the Gallery, where he displayed the eight master paintings so Jackie could pick the two she liked best.

Her selection was not dictated solely by her instinct as a connoisseur, but came as well from an emotional connection with the outdoor scenes Cézanne had created. *The Forest* was painted with summer colors of blues, greens, and yellows, layered against the strong dark hues of branches and trunks of trees lining a path that invited the viewer deep into the painting. *House on the Marne* was also a statement of vibrant color, with strokes of alizarin crimson, burnt sienna, and traces of yellow offering a glimpse of a cottage along a riverbank. The rich colors were repeated in the reflections of the smooth, glassy water.

Walker was pleased, but not surprised by Jackie's strong eye. She had been educated at the best private girls' preparatory schools, where exposure to the cultural arts was encouraged. As a Vassar College student, she had continued a similar curriculum that had been bolstered with extensive travel, in which she spent her junior year studying at the Sorbonne in Paris, a life-changing experience that had shaped her adult tastes.

When she returned from Europe, "she was no longer the round little girl who lived next door," an old friend said. "She was more exotic. She had become gayer and livelier." Blanching at the prospect of returning to Poughkeepsie, New York, to be "a little girl at Vassar again," Jackie chose instead to live with her mother and stepfather at Merrywood so she could complete her college degree in the nation's capital at George Washington University.

At Jackie's request and under Walker's direction, on May 3, 1961, her two Cézannes were packed and taken to the White House. The paintings were meticulously hung with wires from the crown molding and displayed on the walls of the Green Room, one of the three parlors located on the first floor.

It was the first of the White House state rooms that Jackie planned to refurbish. Furnishings in the neoclassical Federal style had been chosen for the parlor in the 1920s, but unhappily most of the pieces were reproductions. Per Jackie's exacting instructions, the Green Room would undergo a dramatic makeover, and the vibrant landscapes of Cézanne's French countryside soon became the fresh new highlight of the historic presidential parlor.

Even before Jackie carried away John Walker's two prized Cézannes, she had volunteered to use her station as First Lady on his behalf to promote the interests of the National Gallery. Less than eight weeks after the inauguration, on March 19, 1961, she appeared before a national television audience on the CBS program *Accent*, where she joined in the celebration of the Gallery's twentieth anniversary. "It seems almost like a birthday for me, too, because my love of art was born there," she said.

At the age of thirty-one, the First Lady had a regal carriage and a high-pitched breathy style of speaking that projected an aura of sophistication and extreme femininity to the nation's television viewers. They were drawn by her large hazel eyes and impressed by her poise and confident manner.

"I remember as a young girl my first visit there with my mother and sister," she told the audience. "It was then I first discovered one of my greatest delights—the deep pleasure experienced in looking at masterpieces of art and sculpture."

She urged parents and teachers to encourage children to visit the National Gallery. "In the coming years," she added, "I am sure that my children will come to know the Gallery. After all, a child of any age gets his own message, his own very important emotional response from looking at a work of art." The best way to learn to appreciate art, she said, is "by using your eyes, by focusing your whole attention on a work of art to try to understand the message the artist wants to convey."

The museums of Europe had accumulated collections over the centuries, but in the short span of two decades the National Gallery had been built upon the contributions of such American men of wealth as Andrew Mellon, Samuel H. Kress, and Joseph E. Widener. "To me it is one of the country's greatest cultural assets," she said. "I am always proud to hear the impression it makes on visitors from abroad who come to admire the treasures collectors have given the Gallery in just twenty years."

Seated behind a varnished table bearing a vase of freshly cut white flowers, Jackie spoke earnestly to her audience. Her dark coiffed hair and the light-colored dress created a striking figure that resonated on the screen. "It is here for one purpose and one purpose only," she said of the Gallery, "for all of us to enjoy."

Following her remarks, the television cameras cut to John Walker in the National Gallery ready to take the audience on a brief tour of the museum's masterpieces, including the uncompromising image of "Mrs. Yates" by famed American portraitist Gilbert Stuart, Renoir's *Girl With a Watering Can* and Jacques-Louis David's commanding 1812 portrait of Napoleon. "We have one of the best-balanced collections in the world," Walker said.

"Other galleries are stronger in certain periods and artists, but they don't touch the range we do."

With infectious enthusiasm, Jackie invited White House guests to view the two Cézannes displayed in the Green Room. She announced that she would rotate the paintings periodically, so that all eight of the Cézannes, once owned by American expatriate and collector Charles A. Loeser, would eventually be hung in the public rooms. Those paintings not on view in the executive mansion would stay at the National Gallery.

When Loeser died in the 1920s he bequeathed the pictures to the United States to be hung in the White House or in the American Embassy in Paris. President Truman, however, rejected the pictures in 1952 for the White House, and when the embassy was unable to properly display the prized landscapes, they landed in Washington under the protective care of John Walker, then chief curator of the National Gallery. With two of the Cézannes now gracing the walls of the Green Room, Jackie assured Walker they were widely admired. "They have brought beauty, indeed greatness, to our walls," she said, "and are the focus of many appreciative eyes."

Always attuned to the feelings of wealthy art donors, Jackie wrote to Matilda Loeser Calnan, Loeser's daughter, who lived in Florence, and invited her to come and see the Cézannes. That summer, Philippa Calnan, representing her mother, arrived in Washington to meet the First Lady and see for the first time these master works that had been acquired by her grandfather now being beautifully displayed on the silk-damask walls of the Green Room.

"Mr. Loeser is one of a number of important collectors to present treasures, lovingly collected during a lifetime, to the President's House," Jackie announced through the office of her social secretary. "It is hoped that their pride in the White House will serve as an example to other collectors, so that one day this much loved house will be as great a repository of historical and beautiful objects as any other official residence in the world. It is with great pleasure that the Cézannes are welcomed."

On May 5, 1961, a mesmerized nation watched in awe as the one-ton Mercury spacecraft named *Freedom 7* streaked to an altitude of 115 miles as astronaut Alan B. Shepard became America's first man in space. A feeling of optimism boosted the national mood as man and spacecraft safely splashed into the Atlantic Ocean. Scientists had given the mission only a 75 percent chance of reaching the prescribed arc, but former navy test pilot Shepard performed with cool aplomb, thereby launching John F. Kennedy's manned space program on its winning trajectory.

Late that morning, Jackie was told that John Walker had suddenly been taken ill. Doubled over in pain, he was rushed to a nearby hospital where doctors ordered emergency surgery. The sudden attack frightened Walker's staff, who regarded the long-limbed and scholarly director as a formidable figure. Jackie asked White House Social Secretary Letitia ("Tish") Baldridge to telephone Walker's office and keep her informed about his condition. The nature of Walker's illness was not disclosed, but he may have suffered a ruptured appendix.

As soon as he was out of danger, Jackie immediately dispatched a message: "I am delighted by the reports you are coming along well after your operation," she said. "I am sure you are suffering from *ennui* as much as the pain lying there in the hospital. Knowing your energy, if they give you a month in which to recuperate, you will probably accomplish it in three weeks.

"Hurry back to our midst. Not only does the Gallery need you, but we need you at the White House. The Cézannes are the hit of all time you will be sorry to hear," she teased. "I will send you Millard Fillmore in return to cheer up your hospital room."

The following morning a handsome arrangement of fresh-cut flowers appeared at Walker's hospital bedside. Jackie despised stuffy formal arrangements and insisted that the bouquet contain no stiff snapdragons or gladioli. "These flowers were to have gone with Mrs. Kennedy's letter by hand yesterday!" Baldridge scribbled in the note attached to the bouquet. "The astronauts threw us into an utter state of confusion—so forgive the distaff side's inefficiency. We are all waiting for you to get well soon."

Almost immediately following the inauguration of John F. Kennedy, Jackie had announced her plans to make the White House a "showcase for great American art and artists." She shared with President Kennedy the belief that art was a great unifying and humanizing experience. To her mind, art was not a distraction in the life of the nation, but rather a testament to its very quality of civilization.

As White House advisor Arthur Schlesinger astutely observed, Jackie's response to life was aesthetic rather than intellectual or moralistic; in 1951 during her senior year at college, she had won *Vogue* magazine's *Prix de Paris*, a writing contest that awarded the winner an internship at the popular fashion magazine and a year in Paris. In her essay Jackie said that the three men in history she would most like to have known were French poet Charles Baudelaire, Irish playwright Oscar Wilde, and Russian ballet impresario Serge Diaghilev.

If she could be the overall art director of the twentieth century, she wrote, "watching everything from a chair hanging in space, it is their theories of art that I would apply to my period, their poems that I would have music and paintings and ballets composed to."

Her preferences in music, literature, and painting reflected the tastes of a well-born woman with demanding standards. An amateur painter, she collected eighteenth- and nineteenth-century drawings in addition to the contemporary works of American modernist painter Walt Kuhn. She was a frequent concertgoer who counted the works of British composer William Walton among her favorites, but she also harbored a great affection for the romantic music of the nineteenth century and was a self-proclaimed "balletomane." Among her favorite American authors were Henry James, Nathaniel Hawthorne, and Ernest Hemingway, and she was drawn in particular to biographies depicting the lives of historic figures.

"She had a fantastic desire for historical knowledge," observed Tish Baldridge, who knew Jackie since their days at Miss Porter's School and Vassar College, "and she was a sponge once she learned it."

Jackie's admiration for all things French was also widely known, including the fact that she preferred the French pronunciation of her given name. Jackie's sister Lee declared, "Louise de La Vallière and Madame de Lafayette were her heroines," referring to the mistress of King Louis XIV and one of France's most famous female novelists. Jackie had a degree in French literature and was captivated by the fiction of André Malraux, author of *La Condition Humaine* (Man's Fate), which won the *Prix Goncourt* literary prize and elevated Malraux to global attention. Malraux's thought-provoking books made a profound impression on her, remembered one close friend, who said Jackie knew the author's works "inside and out." He was one of the exceptional figures and truly original minds of the era, and Jackie was powerfully drawn to his ideas about culture, humanity, and social justice.

In fact, when plans for an official presidential trip to Paris in 1961 were underway, Jackie expressed her hope to meet the flamboyant writer and social critic who was now France's cultural minister. Jackie confided her interest to Nicole Alphand, wife of the French ambassador to the United States and a member of Jackie's inner circle. At forty-four, Paris-born Nicole, the most powerful hostess in Washington, deftly combined sophistication with politics at her extravagant embassy parties. One Kennedy insider described her as an "authentic French beauty," who was charming, intelligent, and one of the best-dressed women in the world.

"She had a long conversation with me in which she expressed her ardent desire to meet André Malraux," Nicole remembered. "Her dearest wish was to hear her favorite author comment on the master art works she already knew." Nicole communicated Jackie's interest in an introduction, and Malraux "immediately gave his accord." Arrangements were finalized for a meeting in Paris during the much anticipated official springtime visit.

Alas, the careful planning was undone by an overwhelming tragedy that threw plans for the meeting into doubt. On May 23, Malraux's two sons, Gauthier, twenty-one, and Vincent, eighteen, were killed in an automobile accident. The young men had been studying for exams at a friend's home in the south of France and were returning to Paris when the Alfa Romeo sports car they were driving was hit by a speeding car. Malraux, appearing in news photographs pale and gaunt, took the bodies of his sons to the medieval church of Saint-Germain de Charonne in Paris and, after a religious service, the boys were buried beside their mother Josette in a nearby cemetery.

Upon learning of the death of Malraux's sons, Jackie immediately contacted Nicole and Hervé Alphand at their home in Paris.

"Monsieur Malraux must not feel obligated to keep his promise," Jackie told them.

On May 31, 1961, the Kennedys arrived in the French capital to find cheerful mobs of well-wishers. The alluring couple enchanted throngs of Parisians—the crowd was estimated at half a million—who chanted "Vive Zhack-ee" and "Kenne-dee" along the flag-draped city streets. President Kennedy, who spoke mediocre French, reveled in the attention and ignored formal protocol by dashing away from his police escort to wade into the crowds of giddy onlookers.

As the presidential motorcade neared the French palace, plumed guards on horseback marched nearby blowing their trumpets. Kennedy's personal secretary, Evelyn Lincoln, recalled that the President looked proud as he walked by the side of President Charles de Gaulle reviewing the guard of honor during the arrival ceremonies.

That afternoon, crowds packed the sidewalks in pouring rain to see both presidents visit the Tomb of the Unknown Soldier. Kennedy was dripping wet when he returned to his palatial quarters at the Quai de'Orsay, where one window looked out across the Seine toward the Champs Elysées. "He asked me to get a towel and rub his head," Lincoln said. "I could tell he was in a good mood."

Jackie's star power also proved irresistible. Beautifully regal, she impressed onlookers by answering questions from reporters in superb French. White House Press Secretary Pierre Salinger had arranged an interview with French National Television before the visit, and the program provided an early glimpse into the lives and personalities of the Kennedys. Jackie conversed in fluent French for fifteen minutes, covering a wide range of topics, including her interest in the arts and her love of Paris. She told viewers that she was a "daughter of France," and that culture was her passion and "French taste her ideal." The interview was broadcast the night before the Kennedys' arrival, and, according to Salinger, was a factor in the tremendous reception they received.

Progress on the diplomatic front, however, was harder to come by. War veterans Charles de Gaulle and Kennedy exchanged congenial pleasantries during discussions, but the Frenchman, unpersuaded by Kennedy's promise that the United States would defend western Europe, refused to back off from plans to develop independent nuclear weapons. De Gaulle demanded that the American president support France's nuclear ambitions—so that France could be equal with the United States and Great Britain in a coalition to oversee strategic planning for Europe.

According to Kennedy aide Theodore Sorensen, the seventy-year-old French head of state was "irritating, intransigent, insufferably vain, inconsistent and impossible to please." Yet de Gaulle found himself taken with Jackie, who chatted with him in her "low, slow French" during lunch in the Elysée Palace. Reports from Arthur Schlesinger said de Gaulle barely touched his food, deeply engaged with Jackie in such archaic topics as "Louis XVI, the Duc d' Angoulême and the dynastic complexities of the later Bourbons."

Jackie, de Gaulle told her husband, "knew more French history than most French women." She further ingratiated herself by giving the French president a letter written by George Washington to Louie-Marie, Vicomte de Noailles, a French aristocrat who played notable parts in the American and French revolutions. (It had been acquired for her at great expense by her friend Jayne Wrightsman, wife of the oil magnate.)

As President and Mrs. Kennedy greeted dinner guests in the long receiving line at the Elysée Palace, two shadows appeared in the doorway. "We were taken over by a profound emotion," Nicole Alphand remembered, as Malraux and his wife quietly joined the line before fading into the crowd. Somehow, the grieving father set aside his pain to perform his duty as Minister of Culture. "Mrs. Kennedy was deeply moved at his appearance, and an enduring friendship began," recalled Arthur Schlesinger.

The following day, Malraux was Jackie's guide for a tour of Paris's cultural highlights. As camera bulbs flashed in quick succession, the minister escorted her through the Musée du Jeu de Paume so that his guest could see the impressionist masterpieces painted by her favorite artists. Malraux thought he knew which canvasses would most appeal to her, and he lingered in front of her favorites, lecturing animatedly about works by Manet, Renoir, and Cézanne.

In fact, Malraux had painstakingly prepared for Jackie's cultural tour. At the Jeu de Paume, he had instructed workers to move William-Adolphe Bouguereau's enormous nineteenth-century canvas *The Birth of Venus* (depicting the transportation of Venus from the sea) to be in proximity with Édouard Manet's reclining *Olympia* so that Jackie could enjoy the two nudes: the studied mythological Venus and the all-too-real courtesan, side by side. During the First Lady's visit to the Musée National du Château de Malmaison, Malraux steered her to the portrait of Josephine (crowned empress of France in 1804) and expounded on her tumultuous relationship with Napoleon.

"What a destiny," Jackie said. "She must have been an extraordinary woman!"

Malraux was smitten with his celebrated guest, and in photographs in the Parisian press he appears captivated by the American First Lady. The feeling was apparently mutual. "Jackie bewitches, simpers, and bubbles with sophisticated banter" alongside her French escort, noted one writer. In addition to sharing literary and cultural interests, they also shared a quick sense of humor. "What did you do before you married Jack Kennedy?" Malraux asked her. "*J'ai été pucelle*" (I was an innocent little virgin), she answered.

The conversations between Jackie and Malraux in Paris focused on Malraux's theories about the value of cultural heritage. At moments the minister would nod his head in response to his companion and grunt the word "*oui*," but invariably he would launch into another long discourse. It was characteristic of Malraux to raise his voice and gesture broadly to make a point. He rarely engaged in small talk and indulged his talent for rhetorical questions and piercing critiques. He grew bored easily and was quick to show his irritation.

But Jackie found his personality quirks amusing, and it was no secret that she was captivated by him. Letitia Baldridge observed that Mrs. Kennedy held Malraux in such esteem that she developed a palpable "intellectual crush" on the vivacious French minister. She acknowledged their intellectual synergy, saying that Malraux in many respects became Jackie's most important cultural mentor: "She listened to him and wrote to him. Malraux was her prize."

To be sure, the magnetic Malraux with slick black hair and dark eyes had a voracious intellect coupled with great bravery. In World War II he had been captured by the Germans, and following his harrowing escape, had fought with the French Resistance. Decorated for his service, Malraux emerged from the war as a close ally of his brother-in-arms Charles de Gaulle. *Time* magazine reported that the earthly alliance between Malraux and General de Gaulle was akin to the linking of Jupiter with Prometheus.

In 1958, President de Gaulle had appointed Malraux as France's first cultural minister. Since the reign of Louis XIV, the French state had assumed the administration of culture to be part of a government's duties, organizing a vast body of institutions that Malraux later would lead. Although the new minister had his sharp detractors, in general his countrymen had cheered his audacious initiatives as a sign that things were at last beginning to change in the "stuffy realms" of French museums.

As reported by the *New York Times*, Malraux's fans—along with millions of tourists—applauded him for the scrubbing of Paris and the cleansing of the age-blackened stones of the Louvre. Thousands of important buildings and monuments had been cleaned on his watch, and according to news reports, the octagonal Place de la Concorde—the handsome public space between the Tuileries Gardens and the Champs-Elysées—now gleamed a pale ochre, the enormous Corinthian columns of the Madeleine were suddenly baby pink, and the Louvre no longer "tattled of neglect."

According to biographer Jean Lacouture, Malraux worshipped the fine arts, but he loved glory even more, and he wanted painting, architecture, and sculpture to amplify the renown of France through lavish exhibitions and daring international exchanges. With this in mind, it's easy to see why the most art-conscious of all First Ladies found him so intriguing.

De Gaulle saw to it that the Kennedys were generously entertained, and the finale to the visit was a banquet at the Palace of Versailles in Louis XIV's dramatic Hall of Mirrors. The ceiling frescoes had recently been restored and were lit for the first time. The couple were the center of attention among 150 guests who enjoyed a six-course banquet served on Napoleon's gold-trimmed china. De Gaulle conversed in French with Jackie, who occasionally paused to interpret for her husband. The evening's entertainment was the Paris Opéra Ballet, who performed in the powder blue and white theater built for King Louis XV. For Francophile Jackie, the evening spent among the finest accouterments of French culture was overwhelming. "I thought I was in heaven," she said.

In keeping with the occasion, Jackie wore a gown from the collection of French designer Hubert de Givenchy that was made of white silk embroidered with multicolored flowers. A celebrated Parisian hair stylist, Alexandre, created a look for Jackie that was inspired by her interest in the style and flair of Louis XIV's mistress. He showed Jackie's thick dark hair to dramatic advantage with a tambourine-shaped ornament set with five diamond pins. The French press raved (*Charmánte! Ravissante!*) over her stylistic choices.

Following the President's final meeting with the French leader at the Elyseé, where he had paid his farewell call on de Gaulle, Kennedy's cortege returned to the Quai d'Orsay. The *Garde Républicaine* lined up in white breeches and dark blue coats and delivered a roll of the drums as the Kennedy limousine appeared behind a coterie of motorcyclists. Despite de Gaulle's austere public persona, the French leader had somewhat warmed to the new American president. At the conclusion of the trip, Kennedy told journalist Cyrus Leo Sulzberger that as he departed, de Gaulle turned to him and assured him, "I have more confidence in your country now."

"Not since Queen Elizabeth visited Paris in 1957 have Parisian newspapers packed their pages with so many bouquets," the *New York Times* wrote of Jackie's triumphal Parisian visit. Her superb skills as a linguist had allowed her to serve as the translator between de Gaulle and her husband, which "solidified Mrs. Kennedy's position as the pivot on which French-American relations were strengthened."

Winning the adoration of the citizens of France was no easy task. Arthur Schlesinger noted that as much as the Parisians liked President Kennedy and cheered him in the streets, it was his wife whom they came to adore. "Her softly glowing beauty, her mastery of the language, her passion for the arts, her perfection of style—all were conquering the skeptical city," he stated. "This was a good deal more than the instinctive French response to a charming woman. It had the air of a startled rediscovery of America as a new society, young and cosmopolitan and sophisticated, capable of aspiring to the leadership of the civilized peoples."

At the end of the whirlwind interlude, President Kennedy delivered one of his most memorable *bon mots* as the state visit came to a close: "I am the man who accompanied Jacqueline Kennedy to Paris, and I have enjoyed it."

After the cultural hugs and kisses, Jackie bid adieu to Paris. Minister Malraux had made a deep impression. "He spoke of the larger purposes of culture to society," she told one friend as she reiterated Malraux's conviction that government should assist in efforts of culture outside the museum, a distinct view that Jackie would utilize in her own future projects as First Lady. "Culture is the sum of all the forms of art, of love, and of thought," Malraux held, "which, in the course of centuries, have enabled man to be less enslaved."

On the President's return to Washington, Arthur Schlesinger asked Kennedy about his impressions of Malraux, the adventurous author of *Man's Fate*. The President said wryly, "He was far more interested in Jackie than in me—which I perfectly understand."

Several weeks later André Malraux sent Jackie a copy of the book *Le Louvre et les Tuileries*, a compendium of the history of the Louvre. The elegant volume evoked memories for Jackie of her visit to the Louvre in 1952 as a twenty-three-year-old student majoring in French literature. The gift brought to mind her pleasure on first encountering some of the world's most celebrated artworks works, including Alexandros of Antioch's ancient Greek statue of

Aphrodite, *Venus de Milo*; Delacroix's robust painting of the July revolution of 1830, *Liberty Leading the People*; and, of course, the renowned Mona Lisa by Leonardo da Vinci.

In her courteous, breezy letter of reply, Jackie sent the cultural minister one of the books he had written. "Now for all your thoughtfulness you are to be rewarded by being asked to do an annoying thing," she wrote Malraux on June 21. "Would it be too much trouble to ask you to sign it and return it? I am forwarding it to you through your Ambassador, grandly via the diplomatic pouch, since I was afraid it would be lost in the ordinary mail." (Jackie's sister, Lee Radziwill, had presented her with the book as a gift for Christmas seven years earlier and it had strong sentimental value.) Malraux sent the volume back to Jackie via the French Embassy with his bold autograph scrawled in thick black letters across the dedication page.

Inspired by her trip to the French capital, Jackie began poking through the White House storage rooms and announced her determination to transform the executive mansion into a "museum of our country's heritage." The White House was not Versailles, but it too was an important icon in human history. Dressed in a pair of blue jeans and an old sweater during her frequent missions to uncover lost art and furniture, "she looked like the Queen of Rummage sales," Baldridge recalled.

White House chief usher J. B. West said that he watched with delight as Mrs. Kennedy roamed the mansion, discovering new treasures and removing horrors. "If there's anything I can't stand, it's Victorian mirrors—they're hideous. Off to the dungeons with them," she said laughing.

"Everything in the White House must have a reason for being there," she told journalist Hugh Sidey of *Life* magazine. "It would be a sacrilege merely to 'redecorate' it—a word I hate. It must be restored—and that has nothing to do with decoration. That is a question of scholarship.

"When you read Proust or listen to Jack talk about history or go to Mount Vernon, you understand. I feel strongly about the children who come here. When I think about our son and how to make him turn out like his father, I think of Jack's great sense of history."

The children's rooms were upstairs above the north entrance, and Jackie pointedly made them lively living spaces—not extensions of the formal White House. John Jr., who was born shortly after the 1960 election, had a miniature version of his father's well-known rocking chair along with his playpen and canopied crib. Toy soldiers, planes, tanks, and trucks were on hand to play with. His sister, Caroline, three years older, had a fireplace in her room and twentieth-century paintings on the walls selected by Jackie from the White House collection. Among them was *Fourth of July* by American folk artist Grandma Moses.

Jackie asked the Library of Congress to send her everything in its files about the White House's colorful past—more than forty volumes of records—which she studied in detail. She then set out to acquire donations and loans of museum-quality paintings, drawings, and sculpture. Fourteen prominent Americans, including John Walker, were lured into joining her White House Fine Arts Committee, which she established on February 23, 1961. Henry Francis du Pont of the Winterthur Museum and an authority on Americana was named committee chairman.

In her irresistible persuasive style, she prodded her restoration committee into action. "At last we have a list," Jackie told John Walker. "I do hope we will be able to find lots of generous people soon so that by early Fall we will have something wonderful to show." The hallmark of the new upstairs was to be art on every wall—paintings, water colors, and original art at every turn.

By late summer, Jackie had somehow convinced James Whitney Fosburgh of the Frick Collection to chair the new Special Committee for White House Paintings, an adjunct to the Fine Arts Committee. "It is my greatest hope to acquire permanently for the White House all the finest from this country's past," she told him, citing "the crying need" for good American pictures.

In a deft act of arm-twisting, Jackie even managed to persuade wealthy publisher Walter Annenberg to part with his newly acquired portrait of Benjamin Franklin (the only picture the founding father had posed for), painted by Scottish artist David Martin in 1759. "I've been told that you have a magnificent portrait of Ben Franklin," Jackie said. "You, Mr. Annenberg, are the first citizen of Philadelphia. And in his day, Benjamin Franklin was the first citizen of Philadelphia. And that's why, Mr. Anennberg, I thought of you. Do you think a great Philadelphia citizen would give the White House a portrait of another great Philadelphia citizen?"

Annenberg, who had purchased the picture for $250,000, told her that he needed time to think about it. One hour later he called back to say he would give up the portrait because it belonged in the White House. When the Franklin picture was delivered, Jackie placed it above the fireplace mantel in the Green Room where it joined the two Cézannes donated by Charles Loeser.

The superb portrait was the first important work acquired for the White House's permanent collection, and it was followed by other pictures, including Childe Hassam's flag-decorated rainy street painted in 1917, and a magnificent still life painted by Rubens Peale. Jackie's selection of Fosburgh turned out to be fortuitous, and before Jackie would leave the White House, more than 150 paintings, including several life-sized portraits of early presidents and other extraordinary drawings, prints, and pieces of sculpture, became part of the permanent collection.

On December 5, 1961, President Kennedy formalized the administration's commitment to the role of the arts in national life when he asked August Heckscher, the talented director of the research foundation known as the Twentieth Century Fund as well as the former Arts Commissioner of New York City, to serve as his Special Consultant to the President on the Arts.

The author of the groundbreaking treatise *The Public Happiness*, Heckscher based a claim for federal support on his belief that public support of the creative arts could act as an "antidote to the boredom and alienation of modern industrial society" and that promotion of culture was essential to "true progress for the nation."

It was Jackie who had initiated the appointment of a special White House "arts czar," and she welcomed Heckscher's new voice. She had confided to Rhode Island Senator Claiborne Pell, an avid arts supporter, that she had engaged in conversations with André Malraux about the idea of an American version of the French Ministry of Culture and "what kind of shape" it could take and "what was realistic" for America. She and Pell had discussed who the best person to take on the job would be and how Congress could help.

Jackie was appalled at the billions of dollars spent by the Pentagon while not one cent went to a national ministry of culture. "No support of the museums on a regular basis, no educational television—all these things troubled her," recalled longtime friend Vivian Crespi. "She was a great influence on Jack in that regard.

She did not want this known, she did not seek credit for any of it, but she discussed it with him."

Years later, Jackie explained her viewpoint. "The arts had been treated as a stepchild in the United States," she said. "President Kennedy and I shared the conviction that the artist should be honored by society, and all of this had to do with calling attention to what was finest in America, what should be esteemed and honored." To their way of thinking, the centuries-old tradition of public support of the arts embraced in Europe was one of the missing ingredients in American life.

Heckscher said at times Jackie resisted her emerging role as the nation's de facto ambassador of culture, and Tish Baldridge tried to cover for her when the requests became too much of a burden. "We are bombarded every week by requests of this nature," Baldridge confided to Heckscher, "every piano prize, art exhibit, charity concert, from Alaska to British Guinea. So we have to be tough and 'Neigh' [*sic*] all of them. Sorry!"

Heckscher found that Jackie was determined to keep a private life as she found herself becoming the representative of a "bright flame of cultural interests." The First Lady was strong-willed and protective of her time. "She was an original and difficult to decipher," one close friend observed. "She might be warm one day and freeze you out the next; she did this to everyone, even her closest friends. She could charm the birds out of the trees at times; and then there were almost hermetic periods, when she refused to leave her room, reading, corresponding."

"Sometimes she seemed to draw back as if she didn't want to get too much involved in all of this," said Heckscher. "The public had the impression, for example, that Mrs. Kennedy was doing an enormous amount for the arts, was busy every moment. But Mrs. Kennedy herself was much too wise to be busy every moment promoting the arts. She would do one thing with superb taste and it would have a tremendous impact."

The new year of 1962 opened with fireworks and resolutions. On January 5, *Time* magazine named President Kennedy its "Man of the Year," and his sturdy face depicted by Italy's famous painter Pietro Annigoni graced its cover. For three days in mid-December, Annigoni had been secreted into the Oval Office to sketch the President's portrait. *Time* described Kennedy's coming of age:

> Personality is a key to the use of presidential power, and John Kennedy in 1961 passed through three distinct phases of presidential personality. First, there was the cocksure new man in office. Then, after the disastrous, U.S.-backed invasion of Cuba (in White House circles, B.C. still means Before Cuba), came disillusionment. Finally, in the year's last months, came a return of confidence—but of a wiser, more mature kind that had been tempered by the bitter lessons of experience.

Making note of the new social order that pervaded the "New Frontier" (the term used to describe the administration's exuberant and idealistic vision), the news magazine observed that the Kennedy style came like a hurricane to Washington:

> For a while, the problems of the world seemed less important than what parties the Kennedys went to, what hairdo Jackie wore. Seldom, perhaps never, has any President had such thorough exposure in so short a time. John Kennedy is acutely aware that he, and he alone, sits where the decisions have to be made—and there are plenty yet to be made. Berlin remains a city of chronic crisis, and Kennedy faces choices far harder than that of sending fresh troops down the Autobahn. He has yet to get down to making the final but necessary decision to go

> ahead with nuclear testing in the atmosphere. Other problems lie ahead in Southeast Asia, in Congress, in NATO, in the United Nations. With full realization of what he faces, and the experience of the year behind, Kennedy speaks today of the uncertainties of statecraft.

On a brisk, cold Valentine's Day in Washington, a somewhat nervous Jackie told White House chief usher J. B. West: "I'm going to be a television star, what do you think?" Late that afternoon she performed with steady self-assurance in the broadcast of "A Tour of the White House with Mrs. John F. Kennedy," hosted by veteran CBS correspondent Charles Collingwood.

In the program, Jackie invited viewers to tour the White House as she moved from the state rooms on the first floor to the historic rooms upstairs. Attired in a two-piece maroon wool suit with a cableless microphone and a small transmitter hidden in the bodice, she spoke to the audience completely from memory and conveyed an astounding grasp of presidential history and American decorative arts.

In the Lincoln Bedroom, Collingwood asked Jackie to describe the "detective work" that had resulted in new discoveries. "Yes, these two chairs are an example of that," she said smiling. "We found one at Fort Washington, which is the storehouse; so battered, all the stuffing coming out. But we just thought it looked of the Lincoln period so we dragged it home. And we found from an engraving that it was. And then out of the blue a Mrs. Millard Black of Arlington sent us an exact pair. And then a Mrs. Burton Cohen from New Jersey sent us some Victorian green and yellow

Morris velvet and it was just enough to cover the two chairs. So here they are, Lincoln's chairs."

As fifty-six million Americans tuned in to watch the program, the First Lady articulated her vision of the White House as not only a place for the President to work and live "but also as a pilgrimage for every American, a showcase for art and culture, and a place of national pride."

Keenly aware of the symbolic importance attached to the President's official residence, Jackie launched an imaginative initiative to publish a White House guidebook. Proceeds from the booklet's sale to the millions who toured the executive mansion would be used to fund the restoration and purchase furnishings and art works located by the Fine Arts Committee. Jackie had first visited the White House as a tourist with her mother and sister in 1941 and distinctly remembered her frustration that no booklet or fact sheet was available to explain what she saw or to answer her questions.

Unhappy with the slow progress and disappointed with the text compiled by the National Geographic Society and the newly formed White House Historical Association, Jackie turned to John Walker to give her his truthful opinion of the booklet's contents. Uncertain if Jackie wanted the text to be intended for the general public or the intellectual elite, Walker quizzed her on exactly what she had in mind. "This must be scholarly—and not talk down to the public—then they will learn from it," Jackie replied.

"I have never seen a case in politics or books—where talking down did any good—it just bores people." She wanted the book to be something the White House Historical Association could be proud of and that historians would admire. "It shall be something that Berensen, Uncle Lefty and Arthur Schlesinger would want to read," she told Walker, referring to art authority Bernard Berensen, book collector Wilmarth Lewis, and Harvard-educated Arthur Schlesinger. She added that she would be forever grateful if Walker could "eliminate the purple prose."

"What I would really love—and haven't dared ask you as you have been so unbelievably helpful already—but that is—if you would write an introduction.

"I feel so blackmailing to even ask you to do this—maybe you think it is too pathetic and commercial—so if you can't I will understand perfectly—but I will keep my fingers crossed and breath held until I hear from you—if you won't do it, I will get an irresistible urge to have 6 more Cézannes from the National Gallery!

"I'll understand and appreciate anything you do—as I always have in the past—you have always been so incredibly kind to me."

Walker found it next to impossible to refuse her request and reluctantly agreed to undertake the difficult task of retooling the text and writing a new introduction to create a guidebook that would be appreciated by millions for years to come.

Unbeknownst to Walker, Jackie had already persuaded busy presidential aide Arthur Schlesinger to contribute his brain power to the project. She told Schlesinger that she found the text "ghastly—uncoordinated and conceited." She wrote to him that he was the only person in the world who could make the guidebook live up to its promise. "I would be so grateful if you could polish it up a bit—with some stirring phrases," she said. Following a short list of suggestions, Jackie added that she must have a "marvelous closing sentence worthy of Euripides."

The final guidebook with Schlesinger's input and Walker's fine touch featured dozens of color photographs and offered a perceptive overview of White House architectural, decorative, and presidential history. But before Jackie's booklet could be published, Walker had to locate forty thousand dollars to pay for the printing costs. (He only managed to do so with a personal loan from Paul Mellon, son of the National Gallery founder.) In short order, the book's first printing of 250,000 copies sold out within three months and Walker was able to pay Mellon back.

On the day of the book's debut, Jackie expressed her deep appreciation, telling Walker, "At last our guidebook is a reality! I can never thank you enough for all you did to make it possible."

Over the years Walker had watched Jacqueline mature from a young girl into a self-confident woman who was making a determined effort to work out for herself a meaningful sense of aesthetics and a philosophy to guide her thinking and her work. He had been happy to be an early and oft-consulted mentor. In the months after the election, he had no way to know that he would soon be replaced by a more assertive, more charismatic—indeed, more outrageous—consultant. He and his star pupil would come to have sharp differences about the role of art in national life, and as a result, his frustration would nearly overwhelm him.

Nearly a year had passed since the celebrated presidential trip to Paris. Over the ensuing months, various invitations had been extended to Cultural Minister André Malraux to visit Washington. Several invitations, including one to speak at the Seattle World's Fair, had been extended but rebuffed as "too provincial." Despite other well choreographed overtures, Malraux declined, prompting officials to note that a meaningful "official flavor" must be attached to the visit. One confidential State Department memo noted that Malraux would expect "full red carpet treatment," including White House visits and tours of principal cultural institutions.

According to the official files, it was only after Jackie expressed her personal interest in Malraux's visit that the minister acquiesced and agreed to visit Washington in May, 1962. "He was deeply touched at Mrs. Kennedy's interest," noted one entry. Once the dates for the visit had been formalized, Jackie scrambled to action. It was a tall order to entertain properly the visiting dignitary who put so much stress on the quality of cultural attributes, and the First Lady spent five weeks meticulously preparing for the minister's arrival. "She was a completely disciplined creature," Baldridge recalled. The formal state dinner in honor of Malraux would be fresh and imaginative and executed with high style.

As the date for Malraux's arrival drew near, Jackie turned to John Walker to set up a special tour of the National Gallery for the morning of Friday, May 11. "Mrs. Kennedy is dying to personally take Malraux around the gallery," Baldridge wrote Walker. "Do you have a listing of works in the galley, so he can check off the ones he wants to see, and a short-cut tour can therefore be designed. She is so excited about Minister Malraux's visit this is all we seem to be working on these days!"

As Jackie continued to fuss with the painstaking preparations for her special French guest, she and the President hosted a state dinner on April 29 in honor of the Nobel laureates of the Western Hemisphere. In many respects it was a dry run for the forthcoming Malraux *soirée*. Inside the gold-curtained East Room, actor Frederic March, in his deep, rich voice, read excerpts from Sinclair Lewis's *Main Street* and passages from an address by soldier-statesman General George Marshall in which he had outlined the plan to save Europe from economic ruin after the war.

The dinner fully revealed Jackie's "taste in telling touches," wrote Hamish Bowles of *Vogue* magazine, noting the highlight of the evening was the result of Jackie's request to Mary Hemingway, widow of the Nobel laureate, for permission to read from the master's work. Mrs. Hemingway hunted through her husband's unpublished manuscripts to find the perfect passage to be read publicly for the first time.

Attired in a Grecian-styled sea foam green gown with one bare shoulder, Jackie moved among the distinguished guests, assuring that it would truly be a night to remember for each of them. Tish Baldridge recalled that President Kennedy, looking "fit, relaxed and handsome," basked in the company of American icons such as poet Robert Frost, astronaut John H. Glen, Jr., and Nobel Laureate Pearl Buck. Author William Styron later described the Kennedys' uncommon aura: "Jack and Jackie actually shimmered. You would have had to be abnormal, possibly psychotic, to be immune to their dumbfounding appeal. Even Republicans were gaga."

In his toast to the assembled guests, which in addition to laureates in the arts included scientists Linus C. Pauling and Dr. Robert Oppenheimer, President Kennedy raised his glass and famously said: "I think this is the most extraordinary collection of talent, of human knowledge that has ever been gathered together at the White House with the possible exception of when Thomas Jefferson dined alone."

A Whispered Promise

At the age of fifty-five, John Walker was the second director of the nation's most important gallery, the National Gallery of Art in Washington, D.C., which housed America's greatest collection of art. The only child of a prominent Pittsburgh family, Walker had forged ties to the British aristocracy through his marriage to Margaret Gwendolen Mary Drummond, the titled eldest daughter of the sixteenth Earl of Perth. He and Lady Margaret, stars of the social scene in Washington, frequently entertained prominent guests at their Georgetown home.

Tall and lean with handsome chiseled features, Walker was known for his intellect and his humorless manner. His dashing good looks and social airs ably served his career, and, by all accounts, he was exceedingly charming. His great love of museums had originated when, as a boy, he was stricken with polio. When he lived in New York City to receive treatment, his mother used to drive him up and down Fifth Avenue in an open barouche for the healthful benefits of fresh air. "I am one of the few people to have been driven around New York day after day in his pajamas," Walker said.

When he felt well enough, Walker was allowed to steer himself in his wheelchair through the halls of the Metropolitan Museum. There he found his first love—a blonde girl in an empire dress attributed to artist Jacques-Louis David.

"My curiosity about the works of art became increasingly intense, and the only way I could satisfy it was to read," he said. "All my tedium and loneliness had vanished. I had found my profession. I wanted to be a curator."

After graduating summa cum laude from Harvard in 1930, in good health, Walker studied for the next three years with Bernard Berenson at Villa I Tatti. In 1935 he was appointed professor of fine arts at the American Academy in Rome.

A "confirmed esthete," Walker condemned exhibitions mounted for casual viewers and the public at large. "I was, and still am, an elitist," he wrote in his memoirs published in 1969. He believed museums should be places of enjoyment and enlightenment. "I am indifferent to their function in community relations, in solving racial problems, in propaganda for any cause," he said. He preached an understanding and respect for quality; he measured the success of a museum by the importance of its collection and the harmony of its display—and never by the number of its visitors.

He further frankly admitted that his supreme pleasure was buying great art with "other people's money" to hang on the walls of the National Gallery. Walker's close ties with America's wealthiest families—the Mellons, Carnegies, and Fricks—permitted him access to sublime works of art and helped his quest to gather important pictures. And the wealthy clearly warmed to his robust intellect, charm, diplomacy, and persistence as they relinquished their masterpieces. It was no accident, Walker once said, that the undertaker and the museum director arrived simultaneously.

Walker's favorite time of day was after the museum doors closed and the public disappeared. In the late evenings he would transform into a regal prince strolling through his own private palace, with the high vaulted ceilings, marble corridors, and galleries designed solely for his pleasure. All the paintings and sculpture—the high achievements of human genius—existed for no one else. "Can life offer any greater pleasure," he asked, "than these moments of complete absorption in beauty?"

On May 11, 1962, a pack of press photographers waited outside the National Gallery's massive bronze doors to capture the precise moment Jacqueline Kennedy would arrive to greet Minister André Malraux. At 9:30 A.M., the presidential limousine pulled to the curb along Constitution Avenue, and Jackie stepped out of the car and paused to pose for the photojournalists. Attired in a three-button, cream-colored wool suit with three-quarter sleeves and white gloves, she wore a jewel-encrusted brooch near her left lapel, a handsome panther bracelet designed by Cartier, and patent leather low-heel pumps.

Smiling with satisfaction, she kissed Malraux's right and left cheeks in the European fashion, then gave a warm greeting to Mrs. Madeleine Malraux. Walker, who'd been anxiously waiting, bolted out of the front door and raced down the steps to clasp Malraux's hand vigorously and fondly embrace Jackie.

It had been almost a year since Malraux had taken the First Lady on his tour of the Musée du Jeu de Paume to view the works of the master impressionist painters. Now it was her chance to return the favor. Photographs of that morning show Jackie in an exceptionally happy mood as she went out of her way to accommodate the photographers and lingered outside the museum. Her French dignitary responded in like fashion. Even though Malraux refused to smile for the cameras, he could not conceal his pride: one photograph with Jackie was worth a thousand statements to the press.

The two art lovers toured the Gallery as John Walker expounded on important pieces and their historical significance. As planned, Walker escorted the group to see the museum's first public display of its recent acquisition, *The Copley Family*, a monumental portrait by American Colonial painter John Singleton Copley. Walker had purchased the picture through the Andrew W. Mellon Fund. In what Walker called "the most important group portrait by an American artist," Copley painted a warmly emotional portrait of himself with his family.

Malraux stood with his hands folded behind his back and listened intently. But soon he stepped out of the role of guest and took on the role of lecturer, explaining the artist's work to his hosts. As the group stood gazing at Copley's enormous canvas—seven-and-one-half feet wide and six feet high—Malraux shared his observations about the seemingly patriotic motive inherent in the picture, which was painted in 1776. "Some paintings are in the Gallery because they belong to humanity," he said, "and others because they belong to the United States of America."

Malraux and his entourage strolled through the Gallery as the minister pointed to objects and discussed their merit. As he examined each piece, Jackie and Walker waited for his reaction. He paused to study a Byzantine painting of the Nativity by Duccio di Buoninsegna from about 1308. One photographer captured him in a contemplative moment in front of a work by fifteenth-century Italian painter Fillipo Lippe.

At first John Walker found Malraux's rapid highbrow discourse on the museum's works of art annoying, but as the morning came to a close he found himself surprisingly captivated by the colorful intellectual, whom journalist C. L. Sulzberger had described as a brilliant, fast-talking "combination of orchestra conductor and stage manager, a sort of super P. T. Barnum."

According to *Paris Match*, a leading French weekly news magazine, at some point during the tour Jacqueline Kennedy, in a quiet aside to the French minister, broached the topic of the international significance of great art. "You should lend us some of your art works," she told him. "I would love to see the Mona Lisa again and show her to Americans."

Malraux reportedly replied, "I'll see what I can do."

Malraux's cerebral comments on the Gallery's prized objects were quoted in newspapers across the globe, from London to Paris to Berlin. In the States, the front page of the *New York Times* put it succinctly: "Malraux Takes Over National Gallery Tour: Explains Works to Mrs. Kennedy and Museum Officials."

In the final moments of the staged event, Walker succumbed to the charms of the loquacious French minister, telling the world press with a smile, "I learned a great deal about the Gallery today."

As Malraux posed for photographers in front of the imposing Copley canvas, it was clear that his visit straddled the worlds of art and politics. Combined with the presence of the popular First Lady, the simple museum tour became a vivid international drama, and the widespread media coverage created the illusion of Franco-American solidarity. Malraux's artistic day trip, thanks to his genius for publicity, had brought attention to the French regard for culture—but Malraux would top himself when he next returned to the National Gallery on the night of January 8, 1963.

At 11:00 A.M., the Malrauxs said their goodbyes as they departed for the French Embassy, where the minister rested in his suite. At 1:00 P.M., his driver took him to the nearby Sheraton-Carlton Hotel, where Malraux attended a stag luncheon hosted by the Overseas Writers Club, a group that consisted of a thriving membership of diplomatic reporters that had formed following the Versailles Peace Conference in 1921.

Over the decades guests had included many secretaries of state and important visiting dignitaries. One member observed that access was the club's main business, as journalists and diplomats connected with one another for mutual benefit. "Trust was currency" at the group's prestigious monthly luncheons, and the general rule for speakers was off the record or deep background with no attribution. When calls came from an Overseas club member, officials were quick to answer.

Malraux was in lively form in front of the all-male assembly. He talked across an array of disciplines and engaged in a "torrential discourse" on politics, culture, and the plight of man. The previous Sunday, the minister had been featured in a lengthy profile in the *New York Times* in which journalist Curtis Cate expounded on Malraux's momentous role: "If France's culture was imperiled by bureaucratic paralysis, bourgeois complacency or public apathy, what man was better fitted to play the role of providential savior than the revolutionary author of *Man's Fate*, the romantic man of destiny with the pale Napoleonic brow?"

The American journalists gathered in the ballroom of the Sheraton-Carlton were transfixed by the passion of the celebrated writer, war hero, and Resistance fighter. Following Malraux's stirring forty-five-minute homily, the room was opened for a session of questions and answers.

First on his feet was veteran reporter Edward Folliard of the *Washington Post*. Folliard had prepared his question far in advance, and at long last the moment had arrived. Folliard told Malraux of an old dream that the French minister had the power to make true. The dream he explained, was that the masterpiece of Leonardo da Vinci—the Mona Lisa—might someday be exhibited in America. "Wouldn't it be a wonderful thing if the Mona Lisa could be shown in the National Gallery?" he asked. The room fell silent as the group waited for the reply.

The question gripped the minister's full attention—the idea of sending the painting caught his fancy. After all, Jackie had mentioned this very thing to him during their tour of the Gallery that morning. Malraux responded that he didn't know why this could not be accomplished. "Perhaps a loan could be arranged," he said. "France feels that these masterpieces belong to mankind—that she has no copyright on them."

Malraux then added his hope that in the next five years Americans could see many of the master artworks from France's great museums. The room burst into roars of laughter when Folliard suggested that President Kennedy would be only too happy to assign a regiment of U.S. Marines to protect the Mona Lisa if Malraux would permit the masterpiece to travel to America.

Folliard was regarded with respect and affection by his fellow journalists. "Tall and gangling, he had an intense prying look that often was transformed by a broad, boyish smile," observed one *Post* reporter. He dressed in three-piece vested suits, wore a dark felt fedora on the back of his head, and pecked out an avalanche of front-page stories with two fingers on his manual Smith Corona typewriter. At the age of sixty-three, Folliard accompanied President Kennedy almost daily, covering the White House and national news for the *Post*. Folliard filed hundreds of Kennedy-related stories, and his front-page features covered the gambit of the White House news on Khruschev, Laos, Berlin, civil rights, the space race, the Supreme Court, the UN, NATO, and the atomic bomb. The reporter and the President's press secretary, Pierre Salinger, were frequently at odds over Folliard's tough form of probing journalism.

Folliard was even known to frequently wander into Salinger's office for discussions both on and off the record. "Here's a question I'm going to ask your man today," he would say. "You had better have him ready for it."

Known by his nickname "Eddie," he had covered the White House since it was occupied by Calvin Coolidge. He had traveled with King George and Queen Elizabeth in 1939, filing daily reports for the *Post*, and during World War II he had been at the front lines with the Ninth Army during the Battle of the Bulge and reported from Paris on VE-Day. He had recorded some of the greatest newsworthy moments of the twentieth century, including the flight of Charles A. Lindbergh.

Folliard's idea for the Mona Lisa's trip to Washington originated in 1935, when he was dispatched to Pittsburgh by the *Post* to interview Andrew Mellon, the wealthy financier and former Secretary of the Treasury who had served under Presidents Harding, Coolidge, and Hoover. Folliard spent hours with Mellon during the course of several interviews in which the eighty-year-old "Pittsburgh Croesus" with the snow-white moustache revealed engrossing details about his collection of rare masterpieces, which included works by Raphael, Titian, Van Eyck, and Botticelli.

Mellon held forth on his deep-rooted desire to build a magnificent national museum for fine art—an American Louvre. Mellon had begun plans for a National Gallery of Art in the 1920s. "From a Hollywood standpoint, Andrew W. Mellon is a very unorthodox millionaire," Folliard told his readers in the *Post*. "His home here is an unpretentious one and so is his office in the Mellon National Bank. He does not own a yacht, nor a private railroad car or a racing stable. And aside from a pair of gold cuff links, he does not wear any jewelry."

Folliard told readers of Mellon's concept for a great national gallery in Washington for which the government would provide only the land and funds for operation. Congress was not to appropriate funds for art. Mellon believed that the private sector would join him in donating works to the nation. To this end he insisted that the museum not bear the Mellon name. While Mellon did not live to see the fulfillment of his vision, his son Paul Mellon saw his dream to fruition, and in the decades after its dedication the National Gallery received important collections from such donors as dime-store magnate Samuel H. Kress, Sears Roebuck & Co. heir Lessing Rosenwald, Wall Street investment tycoon Chester Dale, and the Widener family of financiers and industrialists.

Folliard covered the historic 1941 Gallery opening for the *Post* and witnessed President Roosevelt as he spoke to the nation amidst the splendor of seven centuries of Old World masterpieces. As World War II raged in Europe, Roosevelt asserted America's intention that the "freedom of human spirit" that created objects of beauty would never be destroyed. "I yearned for the day when great art from foreign museums would be shown in our National Gallery," Folliard said. "This became almost an obsession with me and in 1948—I wrote my friend Henri Bonnet, the French ambassador, to ask if we could borrow the Mona Lisa."

Although Ambassador Bonnet was diplomatic, he told Folliard firmly that the Mona Lisa could never leave the Louvre. Fourteen years later Folliard was still trying.

This time when he asked the Mona Lisa question, Malraux did not dismiss the idea. "He did give me encouragement," Folliard said of the visiting French minister, "a lot of it."

On the afternoon of May 11, as Malraux delivered his lecture in front of the Overseas writers, Jackie confirmed the logistics for the Malraux state dinner with White House chief usher J. B. West. "She had a total mastery of detail—endless, endless detail—and she was highly organized," West recalled. Jackie triple-checked every item reviewing her famous memos on long sheets of yellow legal-ruled paper.

The drab green State Dining Room had been repainted in shades of pastel white, and the awkward horseshoe table was replaced with round tables for eight or ten. Jackie requested the handsome chairs she had seen in Paris—small gold faux-bamboo seats—to replace the old cut-velvet eyesores. Most important, she improved the lighting, replacing the bright light of the old chandeliers with a soft glow. "Wrinkles take on wrinkles under this cruel light," she told Tish Baldridge.

Jackie coordinated the menu with White House chef René Verdon to ensure it was the very best. Plans for the meal included a light cold soup garnished with *crème fraîche* and caviar followed by *Homard en Bellevue*, a chilled lobster salad—a delectable creation once served by French courtesan Madame de Pompadour to Louis XV. An elegant French seafood dish made of fresh sea bass and spinach, *Bar Farci Polignac*, was selected as the main course. For dessert, Jackie planned to serve *La Croquembouche aux Noisettes*, a delicate pastry made of tiny cream puffs glazed with carmelized sugar and adorned with marzipan flowers. (The delicate *croquembouche* would entail one full day of labor by pastry chef Ferdinand Louvat.) To complete the meal, Jackie specifically selected fine French wines and champagne, including a 1959 Carton Charlemagne, a 1955 Chateau Gruaud-Larose, and a 1952 Dom Perignon. She insisted that the number of courses be limited to four, although in previous administrations state dinners typically offered six or more. Her streamlined menu included only seasonal items that fused "spring fare with French flair."

As the highlight of the evening, Jackie wanted a concert performed in the East Room by a gifted American artist who would represent the finest in American life. She repeatedly telephoned violinist Isaac Stern, widely known as the "Prince of Carnegie Hall," and asked him to come to Washington. Stern supported the administration's promotion of the arts, and shortly after the inauguration he wrote the First Lady: "It would be so difficult to tell you how refreshing, how heartening it is to find such serious attention and respect for the arts in the White House. To many of us it is one of the most exciting developments on the present American cultural scene." After a few well-timed telephone calls, all of the details were finalized, and the renowned violinist was scheduled to perform in the restored East Room on the new crimson velvet–upholstered stage designed by Lincoln Kirsten.

The First Lady tackled every aspect of protocol and insisted on presenting her guest with a memorable welcoming gift. To that end, she cajoled her stepfather, Hugh Auchincloss, into giving her two rare books from his private library. Inside one volume of nineteenth-century political caricatures she wrote for Malraux,

"How strange to give a book to someone whose books—and words—have given so much to me."

The guest list was also of great concern. When a proposed list had been typed and submitted for her review, Jackie asked for additional names of guests who spoke French. "List very good but ask [Ambassador] Alphand—and see if we can add a few people who speak French. Alphand might know some—you think too—send me back list soon so can OK it if we have time to add—if we get lots of refusals. Try and get authors whose plays or works have been performed or translated with success in France; Ask Alphand whom he suggests [and] send him proposed list."

It mattered to her deeply what Malraux thought, and she worked to ensure that the visit "confirmed his estimate of her intellect and taste." At one point she confided to Ambassador Alphand that she feared Malraux would become bored during his Washington visit. Alphand wrote in his memoirs that he told Jackie to invite the kind of American artists that Malraux would like to meet. When she worried if she should invite only French-speaking guests, Alphand discouraged her. "All she needed to do was fill the White House with luminaries, and Malraux would be thrilled."

Invitations were mailed to more than 175 distinguished cultural figures, and the guest list grew so large that the White House dinner had to be hosted in two rooms. President Kennedy would host twelve tables in the State Dining Room and Jackie would play hostess to five smaller tables in the Blue Room. In a break from tradition, husbands and wives were seated at different tables so that guests were forced to meet and interact with new people. The seating chart prepared by Sanford Fox, chief of the social entertainments office, underwent multiple versions with a pair of scissors as Jackie juggled the names to create the perfect arrangement. Pierre

Salinger recalled that Jackie spread the seating charts on the floor and planned exactly who should be seated next to whom. "I worked carefully on the guest list," she said, "wanting to include artists admired abroad, not only the traditional, established ones."

She found them. Mark Rothko and Franz Kline, noted abstract expressionists, were there along with oft-described "painter of the people" Andrew Wyeth. From the field of letters were Pulitzer Prize–winning writers Arthur Miller and Thornton Wilder, and future Nobel Prize winner Saul Bellow. Dramatist Paddy Chayefsky came, as did producer Elia Kazan, playwright S. N. Behrman, and choreographer George Balanchine. Tennessee Williams first balked at the invitation, saying it was "too far to go to dinner," but a phone call from Jackie persuaded him to come to Washington.

"I hoped [Malraux's] visit would call attention to the importance of the arts," Jackie said. She made sure the leadership of the nation's premier museums and libraries were also invited, including David E. Finley, the first director of the National Gallery and chair of the U.S. Commission of Fine Arts; National Gallery Director John Walker; Metropolitan Museum of Art Director James J. Rorimer, Museum of Modern Art Director René d'Harnoncourt; Leonard Carmichael, Secretary of the Smithsonian Institution; Frederick B. Adams, Jr., Director of the Pierpont Morgan Library; and Archibald MacLeish, poet and former Librarian of Congress.

President Kennedy wanted the reclusive Charles Lindbergh and his wife Anne to be invited as well because they were "Great Americans." Jackie told Tish Baldridge that she was an admirer of Anne Lindbergh's writing. To the surprise of many, the couple accepted the invitation and agreed to stay overnight at the White House. Jackie saw to it that Lindbergh was seated at the President's table, along with artist Andrew Wyeth, author Irwin Shaw, actress

Geraldine Page, and Nicole Alphand. "Even among these illustrious people," Baldridge later wrote, "the attendance of the Lindberghs caused a sensation."

For her formal gown, Jackie chose a strapless duponi shantung in a warm shade of pink designed by Guy Douvier for Christian Dior. The design of the gown assured that she would be eye-catching from any direction. The back was fitted at the top with a series of bows that flared from the waist in a cascade of fabric creating a slight train. She wore white gloves that reached the elbow and diamond earrings. In her upswept hair she fastened a jeweled ornament like a tiara. (The eighteenth-century sapphire and diamond starburst pin was one of Jackie's favorite pieces. She had found the brooch at Wartski's, the London jeweler, and traded in several significant pieces she already owned so that she could purchase it.)

For table decorations Jackie selected lilies-of-the-valley, baby's breath, red and white tulips, blue iris, gerbera daisies, lavender and pink sweet peas, violas, and leucocoryne. She preferred informal "Flemish" floral designs for the White House table settings and insisted the arrangements at the center of the table be placed below the sight line so that guests could see one another and engage in easy conversation. "The total sensual appeal of sight, fragrance, taste, and sound," noted scholar Elizabeth J. Natalle, made Jackie's White House gala a "communication extravagance that boosted everyone's ethos."

To ensure that the cultural minister received a proper toast of welcome, one that seamlessly fused the history of France with that of the United States, she turned again to Arthur Schlesinger for assistance. The White House aide had sent Jackie a copy of the recent *New York Times* profile of the celebrated Frenchman. "Could you write a toast for Jack to make to Malraux," Jackie asked, "along the lines of this article you sent me, which I adore. Then, would you send your proposed toast, plus the article, over to Jack so he can read it himself."

With less than twenty-four hours before the grand affair, Jackie wanted to read the feature a second time to be totally prepared for her guest. "Would you give strict instructions to Mrs. Lincoln to return the article on Malraux to me when Jack is through with it," she asked.

Finally, the much anticipated moment arrived. President and Mrs. Kennedy left the second-floor residence and descended the executive mansion's Grand Staircase. (Under Jackie's direction the red carpet along the stairs had been changed into a deeper crimson, less garish shade of red.) At the bottom of the stairs, the couple posed with André and Marie Madeleine Malraux as White House photographer Abbie Rowe captured the glamour and importance of the occasion.

Jackie was the "center of attention," recalled Letitia Baldridge, dressed in the daring strapless pink gown. Attired in a finely tailored tuxedo and black tie, President Kennedy had tucked a small pink rose in his left lapel. Madame Malraux wore a white floor-length gown embroidered with pearls along the neckline, and in her dark brown hair she had affixed a small diamond and pearl pin in the shape of a bow.

With the guests assembled in the State Dining Room, President Kennedy raised his glass in a toast to honor the distinguished French visitor. "I suppose all of us wish to participate in all the experiences of life," President Kennedy said of Malraux, "but he has left us all behind."

"This will be the first speech about relations between France and the United States that does not include a tribute to General Lafayette," he said. "It seems that every Frenchman who comes to the United States feels that Lafayette was a rather confused sort of intellectual, elderly figure, hovering over French politics, and is astonished to find that we regard him as a golden, young romantic figure, next to George Washington our most distinguished citizen.

"Therefore he will not be mentioned, but I will mention a predecessor of mine, John Adams, who was our first President to live in the White House and whose prayer on occupancy is written here." President Kennedy gestured to the words of John Adams carved on the nearby marble mantelpiece, including the phrase "May none but honest and wise men ever rule under this roof." Then Kennedy said, "John Adams asked that on his gravestone be written 'He kept the peace with France!'" The room burst into applause, laughter, and cheers as waiters scurried across the polished floors and prepared to serve the evening's first course.

Following the superb French meal prepared by Chef Verdon, guests were escorted into the East Room, with its enormous crystal chandeliers and flickering candelabra, where they were entertained by the virtuoso performance of violinist Issac Stern, cellist Leonard Rose, and pianist Eugene Istomin as they performed the full forty-five-minute Schubert Trio in B-flat. (The gilt-bronze candelabra purchased by President Monroe in 1817 had been stored away unseen until Jackie found them and displayed them once again.)

Photographs taken during the concert show Jackie seated close to Malraux, smiling with her right shoulder nearly tucked under his arm. Baldridge recalled that the musical performance among the giants of the arts made an enormous impression. Later that evening Mrs. Kennedy told her, "You know, these are the moments of history I will really remember the rest of my life."

The gathering of the most accomplished men and women of the American cultural scene not only underscored the Kennedys' support for the arts, but also demonstrated how adept Jackie was at employing the arts in order to add prestige to Jack's presidency. "Malraux himself understood just how profoundly she had been transformed by her trip to Paris," said biographer Barbara Leaming, "and how much an evening such as this owed to that experience." As the candlelit party came to a close, Malraux felt compelled to share his delight with Jackie. He leaned near Mrs. Kennedy's right ear. In a moment caught on film, Malraux whispered a promise that he would send her France's cultural treasure—the Mona Lisa—as a loan to her and President Kennedy. "*Je vais vous envoyer La Joconde*," he said softly.

3

An Unexpected Request

Minister Malraux may have promised Jacqueline Kennedy that he would send her the Mona Lisa, but it was unlikely that French officials would sanction the exhibition. As one historian later observed, "It did not seem appropriate to send one of the most treasured symbols of European culture to America, then regarded as a country with hardly any culture at all."

Deep tensions between both nations had resurfaced when de Gaulle returned to power in 1958. The imperious Frenchman had exasperated Allied officials during World War II with his grandstanding as leader of the French Resistance movement and unconcealed mistrust of his allies. Winston Churchill and Franklin Roosevelt considered de Gaulle unreliable, banning him from planning for the Normandy invasion and declining to invite him to the important Yalta Conference of Allied leaders in 1945.

The rift between de Gaulle and Roosevelt was kept mostly under wraps in pursuit of unity, but leaders could be more blunt in private. After only one month as president, an exasperated Harry Truman described de Gaulle as an "SOB." De Gaulle's style played better at home, where his snappish disregard for the interests of the powerful United States and its fixation on fighting communism around the world were well received by many of his countrymen. His was a nationalist message, and he took advantage of France's status in the Western alliance to torment and bully his ostensible ally.

What appeared to many of his overseas allies as bad manners was perhaps more accurately a reflection of de Gaulle's view of the world and his love of France. In his memoirs of World War II he wrote, "All of my life I have thought of France in a certain way. France cannot be France without greatness." But de Gaulle's sentiment went beyond national pride to a chauvinism that made compromise intolerable. Under "Gaullism," France would be unified and stable under strong leadership. To the outside world, France "must be a cultural and political beacon that influenced the destiny of all mankind."

So, why would the French president who loved to hate the Americans now agree to loan the Mona Lisa to President and Mrs. Kennedy? Perhaps de Gaulle's quest for international stature during the Cold War years would sway him.

Malraux's comments had already made headlines in Washington the morning after his response to Edward Folliard at the Overseas Writers luncheon. On Saturday, May 12, the words "Mona Lisa, Other Louvre Works May Be Shown At National Gallery" were splashed across the front page of the *Washington Post*.

Although de Gaulle thought Malraux was overly impressed with the Kennedys, he was willing to indulge his cultural minister's desire to reach out diplomatically at a moment of acute tension. Perhaps the loan might soothe American resentments toward France and influence U.S. leaders to give ground to France in international affairs. Later de Gaulle would call the Mona Lisa's journey "a considerable operation and altogether beneficial," while retaining his characteristic bite. "When it gets to New York," he said, "for God's sake don't let the United Nations cash in on it."

Meanwhile, Malraux continued his packed schedule of official meetings and less formal occasions in Washington, D.C. After a day of diplomatic maneuvering at the State Department, he was ready to relax. At 8:00 P.M. he was escorted to the private residence of Attorney General Robert Kennedy at Hickory Hill, twenty minutes outside Washington. Malraux was greeted at the door by a group of boisterous children and enormous dogs. As was her custom, Ethel Kennedy said grace before dinner, but she did so in French in honor of her European guest. The following morning, Malraux attended a stag luncheon at Blair House hosted by prominent journalist Edward R. Murrow, Director of the United States Information Agency.

On Sunday, Malraux and his wife joined President and Mrs. Kennedy, this time at Glen Ora, a handsome four-hundred-acre estate in Middleburg, Virginia, for a champagne brunch. The estate, located in the heart of fox-hunting country, featured a French-style villa, stables, and an Olympic-sized swimming pool. (It had been leased by the Kennedys, who used it as a weekend retreat.) Jackie presented an impressive meal for Malraux and a handful of invited guests who relaxed amid the panoramic views of the rolling Virginia pastures.

Then in New York City on May 15, Malraux delivered an exultant address for the fiftieth anniversary of the French Institute. The event was so important to Jackie that she had previously written to Vice President Lyndon Johnson to urge him in her unique manner to act as the administration's representative at the affair:

> It is such an important occasion and you are the only person who could properly respond to Malraux . . . his visit here is such an important one—for all the cultural side of our Country.
>
> His speech in New York will be a major one—and it is so vital that the most important and the most eloquent person—you—be there. I know how busy you are—and I wouldn't write if I didn't think that he and his visit are so significant.

That evening Johnson delivered a rousing speech entitled "Defiance of Man's Fate," purportedly written by Arthur Schlesinger. In welcoming Malraux, Johnson declared: "Many men have been artists, and many have been men of ideas, and many have been men of action. Our guest's triumph has been to fuse all these things into a single life. His example brings home a basic truth of our age: that, in our time, the world of 'culture' and the world of 'politics' are no longer separate and apart."

In his address Malraux lectured eloquently on the crucial role of culture in the long fight for the freedom of man. "Culture is the free world's most powerful guardian against the demons of its dreams, its most powerful ally in leading humanity to a dream worthy of man—because it is the heritage of the world's nobility," he declared. In concluding his remarks, Malraux paid generous tribute to the host nation of America: "I offer a toast to the only nation that has waged war but not worshipped it, that has won the greatest power in the world but not sought it, that has wrought the greatest weapon of death but not wished to wield it; and may it inspire men with dreams worthy of its action."

After returning home to Paris following his seven-day visit to the United States, Malraux had barely resumed work at the culture ministry when on June 3, 1962, a chartered Air France jet crashed shortly after takeoff at the Orly Paris Airport. The fiery blast killed more than 120 American tourists, and many of the victims were members of the Atlanta Arts Association who had made a month-long pilgrimage to Europe to see the world's great artistic treasures. The highlight of the art lovers' trip had been a visit to the Louvre to view Whistler's Mother, painted by American-born artist James McNeill Whistler. At the time, the crash was history's worst single airplane disaster, and as the city struggled with the human loss, the tragedy became known as "the day Atlanta died."

Shortly after news of the catastrophe reached André Malraux, the minister wrote a note of sympathy to Mrs. Kennedy. In the letter he promised that as a tribute to the deceased he would send the Whistler portrait to America. "Just as one places on a tomb the flowers that the dead would have liked," wrote Malraux, "France wishes to place in the Atlanta Museum, for whatever period it may suggest, the work that it would perhaps choose among all others."

Within days of the tragedy, French officials began preparations to loan the painting for exhibition to the fine arts museum in Atlanta. In Washington, John Walker heard rumblings about the proposed loan, but as it did not concern the National Gallery, he paid little attention. He did not know it at the time, but the crash of the airliner at Orly and the French gesture to commemorate the victims through the exhibition of Whistler's Mother set in motion a chain of events that guaranteed the arrival of Leonardo da Vinci's masterpiece.

Walker was relieved when there were no further comments in the press about the possibility of a Mona Lisa exhibition. The treatment and care of Old Master paintings was Walker's specialty, and he believed extremely fragile works of art should never move needlessly from continent to continent. The Mona Lisa was no exception.

Fortunately for Walker, the decision on whether to allow the Mona Lisa to leave Paris was not one that Minister Malraux could make alone. It would require the sanction of President de Gaulle, the French cabinet, and the council of ministers. Securing unanimous agreement from such divergent figures appeared virtually impossible.

The Mona Lisa topic, however, was of keen interest to Walker's board of trustees and in particular Gallery benefactor Chester Dale, the Wall Street titan who could be mistaken for a middleweight boxer. Walker was caught off guard when Dale quizzed him about Malraux's pledge concerning a possible loan of the Mona Lisa.

Walker felt that his primary duty as director of the National Gallery was to serve the museum's board, but he was hard-pressed to satisfy the demands of the smart and hard-nosed Chester Dale. A longtime Gallery trustee, Dale's temperament was as "fiery as his red hair." The wealthy stockbroker and avid art collector frequently called Walker on the telephone and barked autocratic orders. Walker confided to Jackie how difficult it was to cope with the opinionated Dale, telling her that when he heard the words "Chester Dale is on the phone!" he would gird himself for the worst. Dale's wife Mary and his close friends and colleagues always strung the collector's two names together and he was known as CHESTERDALE.

Chesterdale called Walker with daily demands, and the museum official claimed that the tense, drawn-out conversations afflicted him with acute bursitis. Walker was rarely obsequious with Dale, and the aging art connoisseur liked it that way. Yet Dale constantly terrorized Walker with the threat that he might recall his loaned art collection from the Gallery at any moment. Chesterdale's coveted collection was unparalleled, including some of the Gallery's most famous works such as Mary Cassatt's *Boating Party*, Renoir's *Girl With a Watering Can*, and Gauguin's self-portrait (not to mention master works by Toulouse-Lautrec, Monet, Delacroix, Morisot, and Pissaro).

When Chesterdale got wind of Malraux's intentions for the Mona Lisa, he insisted that Walker drop everything and immediately write Malraux in Paris, informing him that the Gallery would be delighted to accept the Mona Lisa for exhibition in Washington. In an effort to keep the peace, Walker wrote the cultural minister on June 4: "Mr. Chester Dale, the president of our board of trustees, and the other members of our acquisitions committee, which decide upon all works of art exhibited at the Gallery, were naturally delighted by the opportunity such a loan would provide to show the American people one of the greatest masterpieces in existence.

"Everyone in this country would appreciate such a gesture from the Louvre," Walker added. "I am writing you now to say that the National Gallery of Art is ready at any time to work out such a loan with the appropriate officials. Naturally the greatest precautions for the security of this marvelous treasure would have to be decided upon."

Walker's missive to Paris appeared sincere but Walker revealed later that he was adamantly opposed to the proposal. He also had little fear that the exhibition would come to fruition because he thought officials from the Louvre would never approve of a plan that posed such a great risk to an important masterpiece. French authorities would never permit the painting to leave Paris.

So Walker was understandably unsettled when reporters from the *Washington Post* caught wind of his letter to the French cultural minister and quoted lines from it in the newspaper. In comments to the press, Walker was careful to stress that his message only represented a "very preliminary step" toward discussions concerning the remote possibility.

"Before the art loan could be arranged," he said, "many complex problems would have to be solved." Should the exhibition become a reality, security for the artifact would be the primary challenge. Providing total security for the Mona Lisa, he cautioned, could never be guaranteed.

Two weeks later Walker was stunned to learn that an elderly man had thrown a bottle of black ink at an important drawing by Leonardo da Vinci at London's National Gallery. Museum guards had been stationed nearby but were unable to stop the attack. British officials were still analyzing the work to assess the damage. The incident intensified Walker's raw fear over the dangers that might be unleashed through Mona Lisa's Washington exhibition.

In the history of the National Gallery, not a single painting had been vandalized or stolen. Walker intended to keep it that way and had instituted elaborate security precautions, including nighttime patrolling museum guards, use of a trained police dog, and pioneering electronic surveillance. One night, however, there had been an attempted theft. After the public had been cleared out of the building and the great bronze doors were closed, Walker wrote in his memoirs, a man was found in a telephone booth. The visitor was slumped to the floor and claimed he had had a heart attack. The guards rushed for a wheelchair and commandeered a taxi. As the man climbed into the car, his coat fell open, revealing a pistol. When he was searched, guards found tools for cutting wire and glass. The amount of harm that could have been done to the nation's precious artworks was incalculable. "These were some of my worries," Walker said of the unknown threats at his museum in an "age of vandalism."

On June 10, Jackie surprised Walker by telephoning investment banker André Meyer and telling him how much she had enjoyed the exhibition of his collection of paintings on display at the National Gallery. (This was the second collection compiled by Meyer and his wife, who had begun to collect paintings in Paris in the early 1920s. The first collection had been lost during the war.) The extraordinary paintings by Monet, Chagall, and Picasso received special treatment by Walker's staff and, following their removal from the Meyers' New York apartment, they came to Washington in a National Gallery convoy with a special police escort.

"You are the kindest, nicest, most thoughtful person in the world," Walker told Jackie. "André Meyer told me you had taken the trouble to telephone him and to describe your visit to the Gallery and your impression of his pictures. Needless to say, nothing could have pleased him more and nothing could have been more helpful to the Gallery. I am more grateful than I can say."

On the 13th of June, Walker sailed to Europe to spend the summer with his wife and children at his home outside London, and days slipped past with no contact from André Malraux following his widely covered Washington visit. News of the possible exhibition, however, had spread throughout the eastern seaboard. Mrs. Albert D. Lasker, wife of the advertising mogul and one of eight women enlisted for Jackie's White House Fine Arts Committee, wrote Walker on June 21 to say that she was anxious to borrow the

Mona Lisa to display in the French Pavilion at the World's Fair to be held at Flushing Meadows in Spring 1964. "I am sure curators of the French museums will fight against its coming," she wrote. "Have you any magic powers or ingenious ideas on how we could overcome this?"

Walker managed to pass the next six weeks without any further Mona Lisa headaches, but on July 28 he received a handwritten note from Nicole Alphand, wife of the French ambassador. Known for combining social pleasures with politics, Nicole was a key player in Paris and Washington society. She fashioned the French Embassy into the center of Washington *haut monde* and was closely associated with both André Malraux and Jackie.

Following Nicole Alphand's lighthearted account of her summer escapades, the note included an important message relayed from Minister Malraux that a loan of the Mona Lisa would not be possible after all: "I spoke to André Malraux, who wanted very much to see you at any time you wish," she wrote Walker. "For *la Joconde*, as you thought it seemed more or less impossible to take the risk of having it travel, by boat or plane—but as you suggested it would be easier to send the 'Mother' of Whistler.

"We wrote to Mrs. Kennedy about it," she added. She went on to explain that Malraux would be grateful if Jackie could present Whistler's Mother to the National Gallery and to the museum in Atlanta as a tribute following the Orly plane disaster.

Walker was undoubtedly relieved. The exhibition of the Mona Lisa had been nipped in the bud. In her place would arrive the brooding icon of motherhood owned by the Musée d'Orsay that had already safely toured the United States in the 1930s. (The picture of the white-capped Victorian woman had become a familiar symbol for family values, and the U.S. Post Office had used a stylized version of the image on a stamp issued in 1934.) It was one of the best-known paintings in the world, and it would come to America with little fanfare and none of the headaches required for the security of the Mona Lisa.

John and Margaret Walker had been happily married for more than twenty-five years. "A wife in any career is important—in a museum career she is vital," Walker acknowledged. The National Gallery's growth was dependent on gifts, and for this reason a museum director must know how to entertain with a certain sophistication and charm. "If his wife is inexperienced in these matters, though he may have scholarly ability, skill as an administrator, remarkable connoisseurship, the result can be, as I have seen with many of my colleagues, disastrous."

The couple had wed on February 3, 1937, in Rome at a ceremony attended by throngs of diplomats and members of British, Italian, and American society. The young bride wore a white satin gown and veil of Earl Brussels lace held in place by a wreath of orange blossoms. After the wedding, the couple knelt for prayers at the Tomb of the Prince of the Apostles at Saint Peter's.

At the time of the nuptials, Margaret's father, Sir Eric Drummond, was the British Ambassador to Italy. Margaret had grown up in the rarified world of foreign service, and after many years of her family's association with the British embassy, she had developed sophisticated skills in the social arts. "Margaret's many years of embassy training were invaluable," Walker said. "She could handle people with self-confidence and ease."

Walker embraced life in the city of Rome, where he taught and studied fine art at the American Academy. At the age of thirty-one,

Walker thought he and Margaret would spend the rest of their lives in the Eternal City. His years as a pupil at Bernard Berenson's Villa I Tatti had been a "sojourn in paradise," and after he had moved on to the American Academy in Rome, Walker kept in close touch with the renowned art authority. (After the war, Walker visited "B. B." every summer until Berenson's death in 1959.)

When Walker was offered the position of Chief Curator at the National Gallery in Washington, Margaret insisted that he take the job. She felt he was too young to become an expatriate, and Margaret saw the offer as a momentous opportunity. "How much I owe her," Walker later recalled. He was appointed the museum's chief curator in 1938 and arrived when the new building designed by John Russell Pope was still under contruction. It was also the same time that the great art collection of Samuel H. Kress was to be gifted to the National Gallery. Under Walker's guidance, the Kress collection came to include works by many of the greatest European artists, such as Giotto, Sandro Botticelli, Fra Angelico, Filippo Lippa, Raphael, Titian, Giovanni Battista Tiepolo, Francesco Guardi, and Canaletto.

The best of these were destined for the National Gallery, and the dime-store tycoon would be the first of the American moguls to answer Andrew Mellon's call to augment his gift with outstanding pictures worthy of a truly national museum. The Kress experts worked closely with the Gallery's first director, David Finley, as well as with Walker to further the Kress goal, which was "to create the most complete collection of Italian art existing in the world." In March 1941 when President Franklin D. Roosevelt dedicated the National Gallery of Art, accepting the magnificent building on behalf of the nation, the public stepped through the doors and found a breathtaking display of paintings from the Samuel H. Kress Collection.

At the nascent institution, Walker's finely honed traits of "charm, sophistication and savoir-faire" were essential to realizing his major objective—to snare the great collections of America's wealthiest citizens. For the next eighteen years, Walker would hunt down the best art in America and its best collectors. During his quest he said he came to learn the foibles, eccentricities, and egotisms of the wealthy donors who were his targets. "Their wealth, inherited or accumulated, made possible my career," he said candidly.

Walker's most "nefarious activity" as director of the National Gallery had been in connection with the eight masterpieces painted by Paul Cézanne, and the story of their ownership illustrated the ruthless nature of Walker's desire to obtain the finest objects for the Gallery. "I still feel ashamed," Walker confessed later, "but museum directors on the whole are heartless [when it comes to] benefiting their institutions."

The mystery started to unravel shortly after John Kennedy's inauguration. Jackie had telephoned Walker at his office and said that she and the President had received a memo from Dean Rusk stating that, under the will of Charles A. Loeser, eight works by Paul Cézanne had been left to the White House. Jackie said she had seen and admired some of the pictures displayed at the National Gallery without knowing that they belonged (at least temporarily) to her.

"What do you have to say?" she asked sternly. Walker wanted to tell her that Rusk should have been concentrating on the war in Vietnam and not concerning himself with the Cézannes, but instead he proceeded to explain the long and twisted tale about how he obtained the precious pictures.

Loeser had purchased a dozen works by Cézanne for only a few thousand francs each, but by the time of his death the paintings were enormously valuable (some were worth as much as $2 million each). Under the terms of Loeser's will, his daughter Matilda had a life estate in all twelve paintings, but following Matilda's death, eight of the pictures would pass to the White House or the American Embassy in Paris.

On one of his perennial trips to woo donors, Walker had visited the sister of Lessing Rosenwald, who had a small collection of impressionist and postimpressionist canvasses of outstanding quality. To Walker's astonishment, on the wall of her dining room was a still life painted by Paul Cézanne. He recognized it immediately as one of the twelve pictures once owned by Charles Loeser. Rosenwald's sister explained to Walker that she had recently purchased the picture. "Isn't it marvelous?" she asked.

He nodded in agreement and told her it was a major work, one of the finest landscapes ever painted by Cézanne. Walker was stunned that Loeser's daughter would part with one of her father's prized pictures and sell it at auction.

Walker had known Matilda Loeser since the days when Walker resided with Bernard Berenson at the Villa I Tatti. When he visited Florence, Walker called on Matilda and joined her for tea. An empty hook was visible where the picture had once hung. Walker spoke with Matilda for quite some time and discussed the details of her father's will. He told her that he hoped the eight Cézannes promised to the White House were properly insured. He pointed out the responsibility of serving as custodian of government property and expounded on how much he feared that something might happen to one of his artworks at the museum and he might someday be accused of negligence and end up in Leavenworth Prison.

Matilda finally grew so frightened that she said that she would permanently renounce her life interest in the valuable paintings. Walker was invited to take the Cézannes any time he wished—"the sooner the better."

Walker told her that she had made a wise decision. "I behaved abominably and frightened a dear friend nearly to death," he recalled.

The eight Loeser Cézanne's were packed and eventually sent to the American Embassy in Paris. Walker then returned to Washington and managed to obtain a letter signed by President Truman stating that the pictures were unsuitable for the White House. Walker then set out to convince U.S. Ambassador David Bruce, a longtime friend once married to Ailsa Mellon, the only daughter of Andrew Mellon, to send the valuable pictures to the museum. If the pictures could be shipped to Washington, Walker told Bruce, he would see to it that they were restored to perfect condition and preserved for the ages. "All this would cost the embassy nothing," Walker said. "We were only too happy to help."

Bruce agreed and the paintings were shipped to the National Gallery. "Our eight Cézannes were an essential part of our representation of French 19th Century painting," he said. "I was proud of them and though they bore the label 'Gift of Charles Loeser, property of the United States,' a wording unlike the ascriptions on our other labels, I came to look on them as belonging to our permanent collection."

Walker told Jackie that he regretted his insolent intrusion into the life of Matilda Loeser, but he claimed he did what had to be done to safeguard the eight master works. Upon hearing the full story of his "devious machinations," Jackie agreed to be merciful.

Walker saw the pictures on the walls of the White House for the first time in May 1961. As he stood inside the formal Green

Room staring at the Cézannes, a strange sense of self-satisfaction overcame him. The sublime pictures that once hung on the walls of Loeser's Florentine villa now belonged to Jackie.

When Walker returned to Washington in September, he resumed his duties attending to matters connected with the National Gallery. The weather had cooled and, with the start of fall, it was business as usual at the museum. As the director boarded an airplane bound for New York on Gallery business, he was summoned back to the gate by an urgent telephone call from the White House. Walker picked up the telephone and immediately recognized Jackie's voice, "breathless with the news" that Minister André Malraux had agreed to send the Mona Lisa to Washington after all.

Walker was stunned. Jackie informed him that the exhibition of the picture was now possible because it would be sent as a personal loan to her and President Kennedy. The promise of May 11 whispered in the First Lady's ear by Minister Malraux at the state dinner in his honor would now come to fruition. President de Gaulle had approved of the plan and the painting would arrive in Washington before Christmas.

Because the Mona Lisa would be sent to America as a personal loan to the Kennedys, the French leader could make all the necessary arrangements without the restraints posed by most museum-to-museum exhibitions. In this manner, de Gaulle could set the exhibition in motion without the sanction of officials from the Louvre.

Caught off guard, Walker attempted to make it clear that he would not support the plan. He was absolutely against the loan of fragile art objects, and favored museum stipulations that forbid certain artworks to be loaned. Even a layperson had to acknowledge that a four-hundred-fifty-year-old picture painted on wood could not travel well thousands of miles across the Atlantic Ocean at the height of winter.

Walker was unflappable on this point: great works of art were to be preserved for the ages. There was always a risk involved in the shipment of art objects, and to take any unnecessary risk with such fragile material was unthinkable.

On October 10, Jackie asked Walker to meet with her at the White House. When Walker arrived she told him that she had received the official letter from Minister Malraux indicating that he was sending the Mona Lisa to America for exhibition with the stipulation that it was a personal loan to the President and First Lady.

"Then the blow fell," Walker remembered. "Mrs. Kennedy said she had discussed Minister Malraux's proposal with the President, and they had decided that as the loan, to their amazement, was being made to them, they would have to find someone to be responsible for the safety of the picture from the time it arrived in America until it was returned to the Louvre."

"I was the obvious choice," he said.

The First Lady then handed Walker a neatly typed letter signed by John F. Kennedy spelling out his "ghastly responsibilities." Walker tried to contemplate exactly what she was trying to tell him.

The request to safeguard the Mona Lisa unnerved Walker, to say the least. He was certain that the plan would damage the revered cultural symbol, thereby embarrassing the nation and breaking Jackie's heart. He feared the exhibition would end in disaster and finish his career; he would be tarred with the shame of orchestrating an exhibition based on the political whims of the Kennedy administration. If the President insisted that the plan for the exhibition proceed, Walker felt he would have no choice but to relinquish his post as Director of the National Gallery.

"Looking back I know I should have resigned rather than cooperate," he said later, "and I shall always harbor a sense of guilt."

It was the first test of their decades-old friendship, and soon the Mona Lisa issue became an emotional clash of wills as Walker repeated his appeal to change Jackie's mind. He emphasized the danger inherent in the venture. To Walker, the idea of moving a fragile masterpiece thousands of miles across the Atlantic Ocean tempted fates that should never be tested. The whole scheme reeked of American arrogance, and he urged Jackie to abandon the plan. To Walker's surprise, instead of reacting with apprehension, Jackie responded with mild amusement. The risk to the painting was real, she said, but exaggerated. To prove the point, she reminded Walker that Malraux had determined that the painting was in good enough shape to travel and the trip had been approved and sanctioned by French officials—including President Charles de Gaulle.

The exhibition of the Mona Lisa was the perfect expression of Jackie's interest in intermingling art with politics; she had somehow constructed the ideal union of culture and diplomacy. As First Lady she saw the loan of the masterpiece as a source of pride for both her and the nation, a loan that would lift the image of America abroad and elevate the interest in the cultural arts at home. In her mind the exhibition was the "ultimate cultural statement" about the power of the United States and her allies. It further bolstered the President's Cold War efforts to portray America as the epitome of a free society that advocated widespread support of the fine arts. "The United States will be judged—and its place in history ultimately assessed—not alone by its military or economic power, but by the quality of its civilization," observed Kennedy arts consultant August Heckscher. Jackie believed deeply that a public connection to the arts elevated America's international posture and served to enhance the well-being, happiness, and fulfillment of its democratic citizens.

Also important to Jackie, the exhibition of the Mona Lisa was a generous gesture of amity by André Malraux, the leading cultural figure in France and an intellect she deeply admired. A national policy that supported international exchange in the arts strengthened international alliances and played a critical cultural role in fighting the Cold War.

In the world of John Walker, however, objects of art never had a role in the gritty world of politics. If the painting arrived safely, it would be a defining moment for the administration and all Americans, but if the painting was damaged it would cause an irreparable rift with the French people and destroy one of history's great artifacts. Walker wanted no part of it.

Bombshell in the Louvre

On Sunday, October 14, 1962, an American U-2 reconnaissance aircraft detected what might be SS-4 nuclear missiles situated in Cuba and returned with pictures that were about to shake the world. Working through the night, analysts confirmed the existence of Soviet mobile missiles with nuclear warheads with a range of 2,500 miles that could destroy Washington, New York, and other eastern cities. By Tuesday, "a secret, self-dubbed think tank of a dozen men was hard at work, modeling the counterthrust that would shock the opaque Kremlin," reported *Look* magazine.

Half the world away, officials at the Louvre were summoned to a meeting conducted by Cultural Minister André Malraux, who announced his plan to send the Mona Lisa to the United States. The shocking news "fell upon the Louvre like a bomb," reported Madame Madeleine Hours, head of the Louvre's prestigious museum laboratory.

"The Minister of Culture considered this important enough to come and explain the project to the curators, during a special meeting," Hours recalled. Since her first days at the Louvre, she had practically lived with the masterpiece, constantly checking the small picture like a mother hen. One of the first women to achieve high-ranking status at the venerated Louvre, Hours had dedicated her career to the care and protection of great works of art. Armed with the tools of her scientific laboratory, she penetrated the inherent mystery found in every work of art. "Pictures, like people, lead two lives: one face is public and formal, the other is private and more secret," she said.

Leonardo da Vinci had painted the image of the young wife of a Florentine businessman on a single plank of poplar wood coated with arsenic and linseed oil. Because wood is a hygroscopic material, it easily absorbs moisture and careful consideration had to be given to the picture's atmosphere. Madame Hours felt that the idea of shipping the painting to America was extremely foolish. "I had had many opportunities to see how fragile and how sensitive to differences in temperature the painting was," she said.

The flimsy poplar panel was already warped, and there was a split in the upper part of the picture. Small death-watch beetles had burrowed thousands of tiny holes into the back of the painting two to three millimetres long and the masterpiece had undergone a series of other assaults and mishaps. In 1911, when the painting was stolen from the Louvre, the Mona Lisa had been hidden in a cupboard in a small Parisian hotel. The picture was returned to the Louvre on New Year's Eve 1913, where a special commission of experts had convened to examine the picture. Four scratches to the varnish had been detected: one on the landscape near the lady's neck, one on the subject's hair, and two on her shoulders. After much debate, the picture was gently cleaned without solvents and put back on display.

One year later, the Mona Lisa was moved again when she was hurriedly packed and taken to a secret hiding place as General

Alexander Von Kluck's German army marched on Paris in August 1914. Millions of dollars worth of art were secretly hidden in the back of a wine dealer's cart and taken in the middle of the night to the city of Toulouse in southern France. Some of the treasures were returned to the Louvre in poor condition, including a number of paintings that had grown moldy from sitting in wooden cases inside a damp church basement.

The picture was removed from the Louvre yet again for safekeeping during the onset of World War II, but this time it was strictly monitored. On its return, light damage to the picture was observed, including a slight "lifting and swelling apparent on the right side" in addition to "vertical and horizontal curling," according to laboratory records.

In 1952, another commission of experts convened to investigate the status of the work and what, if any, action should be undertaken to preserve the painting. Officials approved a procedure in which four cross pieces of wood covered in felt were put in place behind the picture to impede any further buckling of the panel. Some minor touch-ups to patches of varnish were executed in the upper portion of the painting's sky, and at the same time, experts at the museum's laboratory took numerous direct-light photographs and X-rays and compared them to images that had been taken in 1933 during a routine inspection.

The Mona Lisa rested safely on the walls of the Louvre until December 30, 1956, when a delusional man hurled a rock at the picture, breaking the glass and damaging the portrait near the elbow. The strike of the blow and the breaking glass lifted "both the paint layer and ground layer" at the point of impact. These were "reaffixed using a putty of glue and whitening," and painted in with tempera. Museum records show that a double layer of burnt umber was delicately painted in tiny strokes on the putty and isolated with retouch varnish, followed by a layer of ivory black mixed with cobalt and cadmium green. Around the spot where the rock had hit the wood, there was a halo where the paint surface was "deeply disturbed as if it had been heavily abraded." This was also gently repaired with a coat of light tempera, then a thin layer of retouch varnish was spread evenly over only the restored areas.

In her scientific analysis Madame Hours and a team of experts evaluated the Mona Lisa's current condition and reviewed a number of critical issues including "the tendency of the panel to absorb moisture, its reactivity to any atmospheric variations, its considerable warping, the crack toward the panel's top and the associated butterfly-shaped brace, and the upturned edge of the paint layer."

The picture was deemed "relatively healthy," but also very fragile. Under all circumstances it had to be kept in a stable atmosphere, where it was subject only to slow and minor fluctuations in temperature. The Louvre itself was not air-conditioned, but its giant cavernous-like interior provided the perfect stable conditions for the Mona Lisa and the museum's other works of art. "Any contraction and relaxation of the panel resulting from over-sudden atmospheric variations could prove fatal," Madame Hours told colleagues.

With the museum's curators assembled in the laboratory's State Room, the painting was delicately removed from its frame and placed horizontally on trestles. The team examined its front and back and attempted to show Minister Malraux the crack on the upper part of the panel that had been visible since the eighteenth century. "I made quite an accurate summary of the possible hazards,"

Madame Hours explained. Minister Malraux listened to her analysis, then asked her to describe the findings in a written report.

The rarefied world of fine art had played a central role in Madeleine Hours's life since childhood. Born in 1913 in the Fourth Arrondissement, a central district of Paris that includes Notre Dame Cathedral and other medieval landmarks, she grew up in a family home that dated to the early seventeenth century. Her father, Lucien Miedan, supported the family as a civil servant after squandering his considerable inheritance during France's jubilant *belle époque* in the decades around 1900.

"Life seemed narrow to me in a financially ruined, melancholy family, where there was a longing for former days, and where a love of the past and an interest in history were instilled in me," she recalled in her memoirs. As a child she was taken once a week to the Tuileries, where she and her mother would visit the Louvre. She was particularly fascinated by the mysterious and ancient artifacts found in the Department of Egyptian Antiquities. Madeleine never got over her first encounter with a pair of winged bulls that guarded one entrance, and, even years later when she headed the department, she "could never see them without emotion."

At her local high school named for French activist hero Victor Hugo, however, she was a distracted student who frustrated her teachers and ended up getting expelled. "Take your daughter back," the directoress said in an imperial tone to Madeleine's mother. "She's just about good enough to become a seamstress."

Fortunately her mother, Suzanne, ignored the advice and put Madeleine in private classes. On a fateful day in 1933, a heated discussion on the merits of Rembrandt and the characteristics of Dutch master works left her feeling so ignorant that she decided to study painting and finished her education at the I'Ecole du Louvre and Paris's famous university, La Sorbonne.

In 1937, she was hired as a laboratory assistant by the Louvre, where she rose through the ranks of museum connoisseurship in a fiercely competitive male-dominated environment. In 1946, she was named head of the Research Laboratory of French Museums (later known as the Centre de Recherche et de Restauration des Musées de France or C2RMF). By 1962, Madeleine was the mother of three boys and divorced from Jacques Hours. She had a soft side, but at the Louvre, where her work consumed her full attention, she was known for her emotionless style based on reason and logic. Her work ethic was unmatched, and she spent so much time at the museum that her coworkers referred to her as "Madam Hours of the Louvre."

She was meticulous about her appearance and wore a crisp, white laboratory coat over her stylish street clothes. Of medium height and build, she had piercing brown eyes offset by wavy brown hair and a tinge of grey along the temple. She wore sensible shoes and worked long hours without complaint. Conducting her meticulous work inside the Louvre's laboratory, she "shook off the dust of centuries" through her probing scientific examinations of the world's great works of art.

Her scrupulous analysis of the Mona Lisa's condition anticipated the worst possible harm that could come to the masterpiece were it allowed to travel. She felt certain that her alarming conclusions would discourage the authorities, but her report accomplished the exact opposite. Malraux dismissed the concerns as exaggerated and announced his decision that the exhibition would proceed as planned.

Malraux's unusually close bond with de Gaulle was vital to the plan going forward. This Jupiter-meets-Prometheus alliance was stronger than ever, and if Malraux wanted the Mona Lisa to visit America, he would get his wish. President de Gaulle desired a gesture of solidarity to the Americans that didn't require alterations to his independent nuclear weapon program, and the Mona Lisa, the ultimate icon of French cultural superiority, could serve as the roving ambassador of French goodwill.

To Madame Hours' horror, once the final decision had been made, Minister Malraux assigned her the agonizing task of organizing the packing and transport of the fragile masterpiece. "Our tactics had backfired," she recalled. Filled with apprehension, she was forced to undertake the difficult job of figuring out how the painting could be shipped safely to Washington across the Atlantic Ocean during the freezing winter months.

On Tuesday morning, October 16, Press Secretary Pierre Salinger entered President Kennedy's office and found him in a "black mood." The President was seated at his desk, "drumming his teeth impatiently with his fingertips." The night before, the CIA had examined aerial photographs that confirmed that Soviet nuclear missile installations under construction in Cuba, when completed and armed with warheads, would be capable of targeting cities throughout the southeastern United States. "By the President's own definition, the offensiveness of the weapons was undeniable," noted one scholar. "And Kennedy had pledged to take action if such a situation arose."

During the next few days, Salinger kept a tally of the senior government officials who met with the President in secret sessions, including Vice President Johnson, Secretary of State Dean Rusk, UN Ambassador Adlai Stevenson, Defense Secretary Robert S. McNamara, Attorney General Robert Kennedy, Treasury Secretary Douglas C. Dillon, CIA Director John A. McCone, former USSR Ambassador to Moscow Llewellyn Thompson, State Department

Soviet Specialist Chip Bohlen, and General Maxwell Taylor, the new chairman of the Joint Chiefs of Staff. This group of close advisers became known as "EXCOM," or the Executive Committee of the National Security Council. Over the next few weeks the chilling deliberations of this extraordinary group would grip the nation's attention.

At his town home on N Street in Georgetown, John Walker struggled with his decision whether to accept Jackie's request to protect the Mona Lisa. It was a deeply painful conflict that could end his career. Unable to make a final decision, he called Jackie at 3:15 P.M. on Wednesday October 17, in the hope of dissuading her from moving forward with the exhibition. The details of their conversation remain unknown.

On Thursday, President Kennedy met with Soviet Foreign Minister Andrei Gromyko and advised him that the United States would not tolerate Soviet missiles on the island of Cuba.

That same day, Walker sat alone in his office. His mind went one direction then another, and after writing several drafts, he dictated his final letter to President Kennedy. In his letter of acceptance, the words Mona Lisa and Whistler's Mother were never mentioned:

My Dear Mr. President:

I am very honored to act as your personal representative in connection with the loan to you and Mrs. Kennedy by President de Gaulle and The Minister of Cultural Affairs for France, André Malraux, of two paintings for exhibition in certain American museums.

I have been in touch with Ambassador Alphand and plans for the shipment of the pictures are progressing. I am sure the exhibition of these two masterpieces will be deeply appreciated by the thousands of people who will see them.

Very sincerely yours,
John Walker

At 2:45 P.M., after the letter had been posted, he telephoned Jackie at the White House to inform her of his change of heart and to apprise her that he had already sent the letter to the President.

Walker never disclosed why he changed his mind, but he always maintained that the exhibition should never have taken place. "My only excuse," Walker later said, was that the initiative was that of the lender, and to have refused to accept the loan would have "deprived the American people of the opportunity" to see the masterpiece.

By any measure, it was an awesome responsibility. The exhibition of this single artwork would consume Walker's full attention for the next five months. Unlike any other museum show, this one would be watched by all the world.

On October 20, from his desk at the *Washington Post*, Edward Folliard telephoned Press Secretary Pierre Salinger at 10:08 P.M. and informed him that columnist Walter Lippmann had just told *New York Post* editor Al Friendly that the nation was on the brink of war. Salinger immediately called the President, who reacted with anger. "This town is a sieve," he said.

On October 22, Salinger requested that the three television networks prepare for a presidential address of the "highest national security." From the National Gallery, John Walker placed telephone calls to Jackie at the White House at both 9:20 A.M. and 2:00 P.M. During one call, Jackie cancelled her planned visit to the National Gallery dinner and preview connected with the exhibition of the old master drawings from the Devonshire collection. Although Walker's opening-night dinner at the Sulgrave Club for the Duke and Duchess of Devonshire took place as planned, there were many empty chairs as the crisis escalated.

That evening Kennedy informed the nation that nineteen Soviet ships with bombers, nuclear warheads, and missile parts were steaming toward Cuba. He announced that he was ordering a blockade of the Soviet ships and was in negotiation with Soviet Premier Nikita Khrushchev. If the ships did not turn back, he would order an attack. For the next thirteen days, the world teetered on the brink of an unknowable nuclear engagement.

Walker waited nervously as the nation's leaders met in frantic all-night sessions. He was overwhelmed by the security needs at the museum, directing his staff to prepare to move the institution's most important pieces into a specially contructed windowless bunker known as "Vault X" should the need arise. In the event the unthinkable occurred, America's most important artistic treasures would endure.

Walker and his staff remained glued to radio and television news reports during the unfolding crisis. The museum remained open, but it was by no means business as usual. Like many Americans,

Walker was deeply moved as he watched television reports showing Jackie as she remained in the White House. The President "wanted her and the children to be there when he was making these awful decisions," recalled family confidante and British Ambassador David Ormsby-Gore. Jackie did her best to keep up a sense of normality on the home front and not add to her husband's concerns, even though John Jr. was sick with a fever.

B-52 bombers were kept aloft in continuous shifts with instructions to bomb specific targets if the order was given. Civil Defense agencies across the country swung into action, with officials admitting that there was no possibility of surviving a direct nuclear hit and only some possibility of escaping radioactive fallout in adjacent areas. Citizens made confused evacuation plans and stormed markets for bomb shelter supplies.

On October 25, with the crisis still dire, Jackie stuck to her prepared social schedule, including a morning visit with the Maharajah of Jaipur and his wife. In the afternoon, Scottish aristocrat Robin Douglas-Home was an invited guest who kept Jackie company as she was being filmed by NBC for a television program on the planned National Cultural Center, which would later be renamed the John F. Kennedy Center for the Performing Arts. After the filming, Caroline showed up carrying a large hollowed-out pumpkin and asked Douglas-Home to carve a Halloween face on it.

Meanwhile, the world waited in suspense and terror over the prospect of a nuclear conflagration. In tense top-level negotiations, Kennedy agreed to pull U.S. missiles out of Turkey if the Soviets would stand down in Cuba.

On Sunday, October 28, Kruschchev broadcast a message to Kennedy on Radio Moscow, thanking Kennedy for his "sense of proportion" and promising to turn the cargo ships around and dismantle Cuban missile launching sites. Kennedy's steady, statesmanlike performance under extreme pressure is widely regarded as one of the high-water marks of his presidency yet remains the subject of protracted scrutiny and fierce debate.

At the same time, back in Paris, Madame Madeleine Hours was conducting numerous scientific tests to determine how best to protect the Mona Lisa. Plans for the picture's transport provided the laboratory expert with a complex set of problems. She started with a study of the current exhibition conditions in the Louvre and determined that if a similar temperature and humidity level could be maintained in Washington, the painting might successfully make the trip. The most difficult matter would be planning the best method of transportation with the best possible conditions. "We had to create a new type of packing case," she noted in her report, "which could minimize as far as possible any vibration which would render fragile the preparatory layer of paint." The case also had to be designed so that the painting would never come into contact with another surface.

To increase security, Hours decided that the case had to be small enough to easily be carried by two men, but impossible to be carried by only one. Moreover, the travelling apparatus had to be unsinkable in the event the painting had to be thrown overboard into the sea.

A firm specializing in the construction of packing cases manufactured a prototype that pleased her. According to museum records, the container, which was double-wrapped, was made of a sandwich of aluminium panels with a core of expanded polyvinyl chloride (also known as Klegecell). The picture was held inside with a core of polyvinyl chloride plates. Measuring four feet three inches high and three feet three inches wide, the container without the painting weighed 160 pounds.

"I knew that if the liner *France* were to catch fire or to sink," Madame Hours added, the packing case would have to be tossed over the side. "So I had the French flag painted on it, to show that it was French property." Hours worried that without the markings, maritime law concerning the salvage rights of property retrieved outside territorial waters might allow the painting to be wrenched from the possession of France.

Hours and her team carefully tested the experimental case with a real work of art. "With a go-ahead from the Painting Department, we placed inside the packing case a painting on wood dating from the sixteenth century and a thermo-hygrometer. Once the case had been shut it was subjected to variations in temperatures from –5°C (23°F) on the balcony of the entry of the Laboratory and 25°C (77°F) next to our radiators."

To her surprise, the thermo-hygrometer showed no variations in humidity and extremely minor differences in temperature. The results were positive for the picture, and Hours observed neither "condensation nor any foxing of the varnish."

The tests of her "guinea pig" were satisfactory, and Hours came to the conclusion that the Mona Lisa could attempt the journey in relative security. Of course she could not guarantee how the painting would fare under real-life conditions, and she continued to voice her concerns to Minister Malraux and other museum officials. With the winter approaching, the atmospheric conditions of its temporary home in Washington were still to be determined.

Minister Malraux asked Monsieur J. Jaujard to visit Washington and examine conditions at the National Gallery. (Jaujard had successfully organized the evacuation of the Louvre just prior to World War II, and now served as General Director of Arts and Letters.) At the last minute a decision was made that Madame Hours would accompany Jaujard in order to make a precise assessment of all of the technical conditions.

The two art officials arrived in Washington on November 28. "We hardly had time to put our suitcases down," she recalled, before the team's scientific experiments were coordinated. The duo first visited the French Embassy at 2221 Kalorama Road to meet with Ambassador Alphand to discuss plans for the exhibition. "I was most concerned with finding the ideal placing for the painting," Hours recalled, which would enable the public to move freely but still provide the utmost security.

In early meetings with John Walker and his staff at the National Gallery, Madame Hours provided a laundry list of concerns and security measures she wanted put in place. She insisted on a bank vault with an independent air-conditioning system, ready at all times, in case of "any blackout, strike or any other difficulty."

Walker stared at her in disbelief. He had managed the exhibition of many master works during his long career, and even the display of the ancient treasures from the tomb of King Tutankhamen loaned from the Cairo Museum didn't require such conditions. Walker had placed the artifacts in a series of glass cases in the museum's rotunda and, despite the crowds, the ancient objects at the conclusion of the exhibition were in perfect shape.

He threw up his arms when he heard Madame Hours's demand that in the case of a labor strike or loss of electricity, she would need to be connected to an emergency hospital or the Pentagon. By the end of the afternoon, she had succeeded in so completely terrifying Walker with her extensive details about the painting's delicate condition that he felt deeply uneasy. She further explained that the entire museum staff at the Louvre was horrified over the idea and were angry at Minister Malraux for forcing them to send so fragile a picture across the Atlantic.

She also confided to Walker that a few years earlier, when "the maniac" had attacked the picture, she had taken it to her laboratory office to see whether any damage had been done. And, indeed, because of the change in relative humidity, within just a few hours the panel had curved so badly it nearly broke.

Walker wondered if she was exaggerating the facts to alarm him, but his stomach pains worsened when Hours made him look at the X-rays she had brought with her from Paris. When held up to the light, the grainy black and white sheets clearly showed there was "an incipient split in the panel" that, if extended, would run "right through the celebrated smile."

"After listening to her," Walker wrote in his memoir, "my horror far exceeded that of the officials of the Louvre." Despite his outwardly cool demeanor, over the years Walker had suffered from chronic anxiety and endured frequent migraine headaches as well as neck and back aches. His medical problems, he explained later, were the direct result of the enormous pressures attached to running a major art institution. The added responsibility of safeguarding the Mona Lisa in addition to his normal duties as director of the National Gallery could only raise his blood pressure and exacerbate his condition.

Despite his high anxiety, Walker tried to keep his French visitor happy while keeping Jackie fully informed. On November 29, he spent a few quiet moments with her following the White House tea for her Fine Arts Committee, and they spoke again about the exhibition in a telephone call placed the following day. To help ease the tension, Jackie sent Walker one of her breezy personal notes laced with humor. She had developed a keen understanding of the power of interpersonal relationships and how best to maneuver them to her full advantage. As scholar Elizabeth J. Natalle observed, Jackie utilized rhetorical strategies to achieve her personal goals for the arts and culture, and one of these was her widespread use of handwritten letters and notes. Her humorous birthday card, written to Walker on November 29, referenced understandings between the two of them and was a perfect example of the power of her technique.

Dear Mr. Walker,

I forgot your birthday this year—and so to make up for that—I am sending you under separate cover—TWO Cézannes—sorry it couldn't be more,

Affectionately,
Jackie

Walker laughed out loud when he read the note. His birthday, as she well knew, was December 24. Unlike previous leisure-filled celebrations, however, this Christmas Eve would be consumed with the task of ensuring the safety and security of Jackie's enigmatic visitor from Paris. He well might have preferred two Cézannes.

Part Two

"La Joconde Must Not Leave!"

On December 3, John Walker sent a three-page letter to Jackie detailing the extensive French stipulations for transportation of the Mona Lisa. French officials demanded that the painting travel in a customized isothermal aluminum packing case in which the temperature would be set at precisely sixty-three degrees. In the event of an excessive atmospheric variation during the voyage or a breakdown of the cooling system within the crate, the picture would be seized by French authorities and returned to the Louvre.

Walker was informed in one French communiqué that the Mona Lisa would be "the object of special surveillance," but precisely what that meant, he wasn't sure.

The painting was to be consigned to the President of the United States and would arrive in New York on the SS *France* on December 19, 1962. The French specifically requested *grandes manifestations* to coincide with the painting's arrival. "This means they hope the *France* will come up the harbor escorted by United States Naval vessels," Walker told her. "There will be television and press, but all they'll see will be the box. Perhaps a Marine Guard of Honor would be attractive."

A special convoy would then transport the painting to the National Gallery in Washington, D.C. "I suggest one or more FBI agents, some Marines, and some National Gallery guards," Walker added. A motorcycle escort would accompany the group of vehicles. "At the Gallery," he said, "I would like two Marines on guard while the picture is on view to the public, and some FBI representation 24 hours a day."

French officials insisted that at least one delegate from the Louvre be in constant attendance while the painting was in Washington. Upon its arrival, the crate would be moved to the vault of the National Gallery where the air-conditioning would be set at the precise temperature of that inside the traveling crate. (The same temperature and humidity levels as those recorded by Madame Hours inside the *Grande Galerie* at the time of departure.) Next, museum officials would remove the picture from the crate and place it on a special easel inside the vault.

The French communiqué was insistent on both proper ceremony and proper temperature: "On the eve of the day set aside for the inaugural ceremony to be led by the President of the United States and Mrs. John Kennedy—January 8, 1963—the picture will be transported to the Gallery called the West Hall, main floor, opening on the Great Rotunda, where it would remain during the entire period of exhibition.

"The air conditioning of the Hall and of the contiguous rooms will have been so regulated as to assure conditions of temperature and hygrometry as close as possible to those of the vault.

"For the duration of the exhibition all technical measures will be taken to maintain the stability of the atmosphere and the humidity. In the event of an excessive atmospheric variation in the gallery or a stoppage of the air-conditioning system, the picture would be immediately transported to the vault of arrival where the air conditioning can be effected by an installation functioning independently of the general air-conditioning system of the museum."

Above all else, it was essential for the temperature to remain constant. As for the painting's physical security, the French listed their additional requirements: "For the duration of the exhibition exceptional measures would be taken to reinforce the exterior, interior, diurnal and nocturnal surveillance of the building, particularly of the area where the picture will be exhibited. Members of the police force will be added to the museum guards. During the hours the museum is open to the public, two armed policemen will constantly be surrounding the picture. Police officers will be in attendance in the adjoining galleries and along the way of access leading from the entrance of the museum to the exhibition gallery. At night, an observation post with police surveillance will be installed in the exhibition gallery. Visitors will be absolutely forbidden to enter the museum bearing packages."

"At the end of the exhibition," officials added, "the picture will be put back into the isothermal crate in which it arrived. The same security measures which were taken for the arriving voyage would be put in effect for the return from Washington to New York."

Of particular concern was the glare of flashing camera lights that might harm the painting, something that had worried Madame Hours and the other curators at the Louvre: "In no instance would the public be allowed to photograph the picture. Photographers from the press, motion pictures, television, will be able to photograph only with the authorization of the Director of the National Gallery of Art, providing that the picture was at its place of exhibition, framed and shown under its protective glass, and that the photographers were kept at a distance from the work of art so as not to cause over-heating of the panel." Any unnecessary filming of the Mona Lisa would be prohibited. Furthermore, officials added, "admission to the exhibition of '*la Joconde*' at the National Gallery will be free."

The French surprised Walker by suggesting that the Mona Lisa might be sent to New York for a brief visit, but only if the French deemed the conditions satisfactory. The Metropolitan Museum was at that moment installing an enormous air-conditioning system, and officials couldn't yet know if the system would be completed in time. "The possibility of exhibiting '*la Joconde*' for a month in New York might be considered," French officials advised Walker, "if the air-conditioning system which is being installed at the Metropolitan Museum permits it, and if the picture's reaction to its sojourn in Washington causes no concern." Until the cooling system was operational and working properly, though, Mona Lisa's extended visit to New York was placed on hold.

Walker advised Jackie that on the evening of the Mona Lisa's debut, Nicole and Hervé Alphand would host a formal dinner party at the French Embassy for eighty VIPs. Invited guests would then drive to the National Gallery where the unveiling ceremony would take place in the West Sculpture Hall at 10:00 P.M.

"The French hope that the President and Minister Malraux will say a few words in front of the picture," he told her. "If the speeches are ready in advance it would be helpful to have them printed and distributed to the guests. This would avoid the necessity of a translator for Minister Malraux and also provide a souvenir for the guests."

Walker recognized that the details connected with the guest list were fraught with problems, and the final list would be of keen interest to Jackie. "Admission would be by invitation only," he said. He went on to state: "We would invite all the Congress, the Supreme Court, the cabinet, the trustees of the National Gallery of

Art, and of the Metropolitan Museum, and the representatives of the Society of Art of Atlanta. To this we would add any other government officials you might suggest and any friends you wish. I think the number should run about 1,500. The French will suggest the wording of an invitation. They have promised that I would have this wording by Dec. 10th. I can show it to you and get your approval when I come to dinner that night. I hope the invitation will be printed and sent out by the White House, so that the President and yourself would be host and hostess at the Gallery. This will make the ceremony more impressive, and I am sure will please the French immensely."

For reasons of security, the announcement of the exhibition dates would be made only after the painting departed France. Statements to the world press were to indicate that the French government had chosen the date of January 8 for the unveiling to concur with the opening of the American Congress and the visit of Minister Malraux to Washington. The picture would remain for four weeks at the National Gallery and then, if satisfactory "*climatisation*" could be provided, it would travel to the Metropolitan Museum of Art, where it would be exhibited for several weeks.

"I need a little help from you," Walker told Jackie. "Would you tell the President's Naval aide that I will come to see him about Naval vessels to escort the *France* and also about a Marine guard. Please also let me know whether the[se] arrangements are satisfactory to you and to the President."

After reviewing Walker's list, Jackie replied that it sounded fine, except any matters pertaining to *grandes manifestations* must be checked first with the President. She instructed her secretary to make arrangements to schedule an appointment between Walker and Tazwell Shepard, the U.S. Navy captain and security advisor, making sure that "all be cleared with JFK."

Back in Paris the proposal to ship the fragile wood panel across the Atlantic Ocean had sparked angry nationalist outbursts in the streets. French newspapers published impassioned editorials denouncing the American exhibition. Art experts and commentators protested the insane scheme—*aliéné* they raged—of Culture Minister André Malraux, who had the nerve to even think of allowing the Mona Lisa to leave the Louvre.

Though strictly speaking, the Mona Lisa was an Italian masterpiece, the French public had long claimed it as theirs and its popularity reigned supreme. No other artifact, not even the *Winged Victory of Samothrace*, considered the Louvre's crown jewel, received such attention and adulation. Each day multitudes of determined visitors flocked to the museum to view the Mona Lisa inside the *Grande Galerie*. The Florentine lady with the inscrutable smile was the uncontested mistress of the palace.

Over the years, the history of the Mona Lisa and the Louvre had been so intertwined that when the painting was stolen in 1911, French citizens were outraged. French officials closed the borders in the hopes of finding the masterpiece, and when it was not recovered the entire nation entered a state of public mourning. One disgraced government official tried to commit suicide. When it was revealed that a former museum worker had walked out of the Louvre with the picture tucked under his coat, citizens were shocked. Investigations were demanded among cries for heightened security.

Italian-born housepainter Vincenzo Perugia was arrested for the theft in 1914. "I thought of taking a Raphael, a Titian, a Correggio and several other masterpieces," he told police, but the Mona Lisa had much more appeal.

The picture was returned to Paris by train amid widespread jubilation under heavy guard aboard the Milan-Paris Express. Perugia was placed on trial in Florence, where surprisingly he gained popularity as a patriot who returned the artifact to its original homeland. Louvre officials instituted new security measures, including electric alarm wiring and steel rods to lock paintings to the walls. Secret chambers where unseen guards could keep watch were constructed and police dogs were stationed every fifty feet to keep visitors from getting too close. French citizens had grown fiercely protective of the masterpiece, and any plan to allow her to leave the Louvre seemed unthinkable.

"The unbelievable news item seems true," blasted the French newspaper *Le Figaro* on December 3. "We are about to pack the Mona Lisa and send it to America for a traveling exhibition. During the 400 years this masterpiece has been in France, it has never crossed our borders except when a thief took it to Italy in 1911. Five years ago, a maniac stoned the Mona Lisa and damaged part of the panel. A third aggression is now planned."

Irate Frenchmen expressed their fears that the long ocean journey would destroy the fragile portrait. Some went so far as to claim that American gangsters might kidnap her and hold the Mona Lisa for ransom. On December 7, the morning edition of *Le Figaro* printed a passionate appeal to all Americans to refuse the loan of the Mona Lisa in order to spare "endangering the world's most famous painting."

The fiery protests reached such a crescendo that even *The New Yorker* felt compelled to chime in on some of the reasons to stop the exhibition. "Indignant letters against the proposed journey of this invaluable, fragile *chef-d'oeuvre* have been pouring into the offices of *Le Figaro*, leader of the vociferous campaign," noted the magazine. "She is not considered lucky despite her immortal smile."

Adding to the fire, a committee of the curators of France's fine art museums sent a written appeal to Malraux demanding that the painting remain in Paris based on a long list of concerns over security and preservation. Malraux found himself pummeled by attacks from officials at the Louvre, who, like nearly every art authority around the world, raised passionate objections against the exhibition.

French intellectuals also protested the Mona Lisa's trip to America on cultural and political grounds. Critics accused the culture minister of succumbing to the charms of the American First Lady, claiming it was more advisable to hurt the feelings of Mrs. Kennedy than risk the utter ruin of the Mona Lisa. Minister Malraux simply ignored the taunts and maintained his typical *joie de vivre*, making only limited statements to the press. He kept up his normal pace of activities and planned to leave for Washington as scheduled.

Le Figaro, however, continued its campaign, publishing an interview with Louis Hautecoeur, the man who was said to know more about the Mona Lisa than anyone else in the world. Following the painting's recovery after the theft of 1911, Hautecoeur had been asked to determine if the painting was genuine. He had examined the picture inch by inch with a microscope and reported that its wood panels were now "curved like a warped bicycle wheel."

Hautecoeur expressed doubt that it was possible to protect the painting from sea air even with the use of the specially designed air-tight crate. "Handling," he said, risked "aggravating the curvature of the panels, provoking the scaling off of the very thin coating of the pigment."

Le Figaro also quoted the fears expressed by American expert Hubert Von Sonnenberg, head of the restoration department of New York's Metropolitan Museum: "In my opinion it is never a good idea to transfer old works of art from one continent to another. The loan of the Mona Lisa originates [solely] in political reasons."

Popular French painter Roger Chapelain-Midy reinforced the point, arguing that the idea to move her was madness. "Masterpieces should never move. It is for the public to come to them. Masterpieces are much more vital than all the important people who could look at them. We are not protesting out of chauvinism, trying to keep the Mona Lisa for us and for the Louvre Museum, but because we are custodians of this masterpiece."

The core of the opposition to Mona Lisa's American visit, however, came from the prestigious Académie des Beaux-Arts, a French cultural institution dating to the 1600s, which unanimously called for the Mona Lisa to stay home. In support of the institution, bold headlines throughout Paris cried out: "LA JOCONDE MUST NOT LEAVE THE LOUVRE."

Reports soon surfaced of widespread spontaneous rioting among French youths, and embarrassed government authorities reportedly ordered a "Mona Lisa news blackout" in an attempt to quell further outbursts. This did little to quiet the uproar, however, and the French newspaper *Libération* added fuel to the fire when it angrily declared that the Mona Lisa must remain in Paris. "After all," the paper implored, "one does not ask a pretty woman to come to one's home. One goes to her."

Indeed, the French commitment to preserving the country's great works of art for future generations had been amply demonstrated during the world wars, and Madame Hours was among the many who had protected the treasures of the Louvre as a Nazi invasion loomed in the late 1930s. Melancholy over the recent death of her first child, an infant daughter, Hours threw herself into efforts to prepare the museum for a possible takeover by the enemy. She helped store her laboratory machines, files, and radiographic photographs in the basement and then joined volunteers packing up the art. Many of them were clerks from nearby department stores. Madame Hours remembered working in "this surreal army," wrapping dozens of fourteenth- and fifteenth-century objects, including works by Girolamo di Benvenuto and Domenico Ghirlandajo.

On the day France declared war on Germany in 1939, orders came to remove all important works from the museum by nightfall, and they were spirited away in convoys of trucks to be hidden throughout France. Among them was the Mona Lisa, believed to be on a list of masterpieces the Nazis planned to take to Germany. Fearing its seizure, museum officials moved the Mona Lisa half a dozen times.

During the occupation, Hours gave birth to her first son, Antoine, and she and her family huddled under a blanket inside a windowless bathroom listening to English radio broadcasts. "We listened with passion to those voices full of hope and their strange poetic messages," she recalled. One of the communiqués was particularly moving: "The Mona Lisa is smiling." Several years after the liberation of France, Madame Hours learned for the first time that the statement was sent to furtively alert officials that the great masterworks of the Louvre had been saved and were safe.

As protests continued to swell abroad, the Associated Press cheekily asked, "Why, then, [will] the French permit the Mona Lisa to come? Do the French know, for example, that a certain lady named Jacqueline Kennedy has an insatiable yearning for art?"

With Malraux's support, President de Gaulle's official blessing, and Jacqueline Kennedy's ingenuity, the Mona Lisa's visit to America was quickly becoming a reality. The outcry against the exhibition triggered a "tug [in] every French man's heart," one newspaper wrote, and moans of despair from international art experts, but the exhibition was essentially a *fait accompli*. Only the logistics remained to be sorted out.

Despite the *mélodrame* surrounding the well-being of the painting, the concerns were justified. It was almost impossible to fully protect the picture from fluctuations in atmospheric conditions; temperature changes could occur through the opening of a door or the rise in room temperature from the expected crowds.

The portrait's 1911 theft had damaged the wood panels and temperature changes had already caused the painting to crack. And while the damage done by the "mad Bolivian waiter" who threw the rock and shattered Mona Lisa's glass shield in 1956 had been hidden by delicate restoration, it was not known how much the enamel-hard pigment had been scarred by the concussion. X-rays showed an incipient split in the panel.

What would happen if a chunk of the pigment detached itself from the picture's surface during its journey to America? How could it be worth the risk? Curators feared that the crack visible in the upper part of the poplar panel could burst open, and the slightest vibration or change in temperature could destroy the masterpiece.

Saving the picture from the ravages of the environment was one thing, but Walker was hard-pressed to guarantee the painting's safety from thieves or terrorists in an era before global satellite positioning systems, cell phones, or sophisticated video surveillance. French officials considered travel by airplane too risky (the possibility of a catastrophic crash or an explosion during flight was cited) and insisted instead on transportation via ocean liner, but the five days and nights required to cross the Atlantic would make the Mona Lisa a sitting duck for terrorists, thrill seekers, and criminals. Walker could not fully grasp why transporting the painting by air had been rejected by French officials.

Another thorny issue with the French was the matter of insurance. Walker recognized it was impossible to insure the exhibition. No insurer would dare underwrite the risk. False reports surfaced in the media that the painting might be insured by one unnamed source for $100 million. Jean-Claude Winckler of the French Embassy tried to end the speculation by saying that the masterpiece would carry no insurance because the painting was "priceless." Emphatically he told reporters that the only insurance for the Mona Lisa would be the painting's "elaborate care and protection."

In Walker's view, transporting the picture via airliner was the safest option. It would not subject the painting to the ravages of the salty sea air or the hazards of a long, rolling ocean ride. Positioned inside its special traveling case, the picture could easily be placed onboard any commercial aircraft. Alternatively, the painting could be transported to Washington aboard the President's official airplane already known as "Air Force One." The presidential aircraft—with its state-of-the-art navigation and communications equipment, its interior configuration, and stylish furnishings—was the perfect cocoon to safeguard the Mona Lisa during her trip to America.

Walker watched with interest as arrangements were made to bring Michelangelo's enormous statue known as the *Pietà* to the United States for exhibition at the 1964 World's Fair. Pope John XXIII had agreed to the loan in April, and, like his French counterparts, the Pope considered travel by air too risky for the extremely heavy marble statue. Officials at the Vatican had selected a different option, and plans were underway for the masterpiece to travel to America via nuclear submarine.

With the Pope's blessing, an underwater journey was selected for the 4,000-mile trip from St. Peter's Basilica to the World's Fair "as offering the safest, smoothest and most shock free trip for the priceless 463-year-old statue of the dead Christ and the Virgin." The U.S. Navy had accepted the responsibility for the "delicate task," and Pentagon officials were finalizing the details of the operation. Walker had snorted out loud in amusement when he learned about plans for the 8,000-pound Virgin to travel from Europe to America underwater in a U.S. nuclear sub. The Mona Lisa, on the other hand, would glide across the pond inside her spacious first-class cabin aboard one of the world's biggest passenger ships.

The time of departure was a closely guarded secret. In fact, four different itineraries were prepared, and one was chosen at the very last moment. French authorities insisted that no public announcement about the Mona Lisa's departure be made until after the painting had been taken from the Louvre and was safely aboard the ocean liner bound for America. But on Saturday, December 8, the French Embassy in Washington leaked word that the Mona Lisa would soon arrive in the United States. "The principle seems accepted that the Mona Lisa will come," the embassy spokesman said, adding that it had no specific information as to when.

To Walker's chagrin, a dispatch published by the *London Observer* released later that day announced that the painting would be placed aboard the superliner SS *France* on Friday, December 14, on its five-day journey to New York. At the National Gallery, Walker received dozens of calls from the international press, but he declined to make any comment, referring all inquiries to the French Embassy.

Walker continued to receive telephone calls from colleagues who urged him to consider canceling the exhibition. Why risk a sad ending to Leonardo's masterpiece—one of the most fragile paintings in existence? Why expose her to such terrible dangers?

"Is it possible," noted the *Parisien Libéré*, "that the American people thank Monsieur Malraux for his generous intentions but deny responsibility for endangering the most famous painting in the world?"

Criticism kept coming from all corners as Walker kept his focus on preparing for the picture's arrival. Undoubtedly, he must have smiled when he learned of one more stinging rebuke from the French over the Mona Lisa's impending trip to Washington: "Knowing the Americans, they'll probably have her parading down Fifth Avenue in the bitter cold in an open car under tons of confetti."

On the morning of December 10, Letitia Baldridge typed a short memo for Mrs. Kennedy that described the immediate decisions still required to be made regarding the exhibition. Walker was expected at the White House later that evening, and Miss Baldridge facilitated the quick briefing concerning the "Mona Lisa Project" in anticipation of his visit.

"Taze [U.S. Navy captain Tazwell Shepard, Jr.] probably hasn't had a chance to tell the President yet," Baldridge wrote Mrs. Kennedy, "but Admiral Anderson says it would be most improper to bring the U.S. Navy into the welcoming ceremonies of the French liner bearing the painting. It will have to be Mayor Wagner and the City of New York that go all out with tug boats, etc. Anyway, that's a Navy matter that I shouldn't be telling you—let Taze tell the President!

"Also," she added, "the President said to not break precedent by having the invitations to the Gallery sent from the White House—so they will go out either under the National Galley's heading or the French Embassy—but with it made quite clear that you and the President will be present and opening the exhibition."

Concerning the extensive VIP guest list, Baldridge continued, "We are helping Johnny with his list of officialdom." Jackie promptly responded that she agreed: "France wants all the pomp they can get at this—it is really a big headache and responsibility for us . . . [I] agree completely—no navy [and] no White House invitations."

On December 12, President Kennedy spoke briefly with Walker on the telephone concerning the proper protocol for the invitations. He approved use of the phrase "on behalf of the President of the United States" in connection with the trustee's invitation, and within hours the invitations were rushed to the printer with the new wording. Time was running out. The Mona Lisa would arrive in America in less than seven days.

6

A Chat with the Mona Lisa

On the weekend of December 8, White House Press Secretary Pierre Salinger confirmed that Jacqueline Kennedy was indeed the impetus behind the historic exhibition. In a low-key briefing, Salinger told reporters that the First Lady had helped persuade the French to lend the Mona Lisa for exhibition in America. Salinger didn't elaborate further, and the item was slipped into a collection of footnotes to the week's news called "Post Scripts" printed in the *Washington Post*.

On Monday, December 10, a flurry of phone calls transpired between Mrs. Kennedy and John Walker, working out the details of the painting's imminent departure. Walker first telephoned the White House shortly after 10:00 A.M., and he and Mrs. Kennedy spoke two more times later that afternoon.

Walker informed Mrs. Kennedy of new reports broadcast in the media that another committee of experts had warned the Ministry of Cultural Affairs not to allow the painting to leave France. But for the first time, Walker pointed out, the newspaper *Le Figaro* printed opinions of experts who supported the American exhibition, a promising sign that perhaps the tide had turned.

The next morning, *Washington Post* reporter Waverly Root, stationed in Paris, told readers that the question of whether the painting would stay or go was still undecided. His front-page dispatch appeared under the rather intriguing headline: "While First Lady Beckons, Sea Trip Risks May Keep Mona Lisa at Home."

"The controversy about entrusting the world's most famous painting to the chances of travel has put Minister of Cultural Affairs André Malraux on the spot," he wrote. "It is understood here that he virtually promised Jacqueline Kennedy to send the Mona Lisa. But he now discovers that in authorizing shipment of the painting he may incur formidable responsibility. The question with which he must wrestle is whether it is more inadvisable to risk hurting the Mona Lisa or Mrs. Kennedy."

As word spread about the Mona Lisa's pending journey, the telephones at the National Gallery rang nonstop. Walker firmly referred all inquiries to French authorities. "All answers must come from the French Embassy," he said. Jean-Claude Winckler, first counselor of the French Embassy in Washington, told reporters with a stern poker face, "the final word must come from Paris."

On the freezing morning of December 12, 1962, President Kennedy convened his forty-fifth press conference with newsmen. The President wore a blue pinstripe suit and a "cheery look" as he strode to the microphone. Before the questions were to begin, the President had several important announcements to make. The most unexpected of these concerned the travels of the Mona Lisa: "On behalf of the American people, I wish to express my gratitude to the French government for its decision to lend the Mona Lisa of

Leonardo da Vinci for exhibition in the United States. This incomparable masterpiece, the work of one of the greatest figures of the greatest western age of creativity, is to come to this country, as a reminder of the friendship that exists between France and the United States. It will come also as a reminder of the universal nature of art."

He added that the painting would be exhibited at the National Gallery in Washington beginning January 8, with the special care that a great work of art merits. "Mrs. Kennedy and I particularly want to thank President Charles de Gaulle for his generous gesture in making possible this historic loan, and Mr. André Malraux, the distinguished French Minister of Cultural Affairs, for his good offices in the matter."

According to *Time* magazine, the one hundred-plus reporters gathered inside the State Department Auditorium seemed uninterested in the announcement concerning the Mona Lisa, doodling on their notepads in boredom. Not a single question was asked of the President concerning the exhibition. The news was quickly buried by an avalanche of spirited queries concerning a "flap" over Adlai Stevenson and the Cuban missile crisis, nuclear propulsion into space, communications with the Kremlin, severe inflation in Brazil, and a nasty dispute involving the American Athletic Union.

The following morning, Walker telephoned the First Lady at 9:46 A.M. with additional updates concerning the preparations for the Mona Lisa's departure. They spoke twice more that day, with the last call at 2:22 P.M. Walker gave her a detailed account as the plan unfolded. It was up to French officials to protect the painting from the moment it left the Louvre until it reached New York Harbor. Then, the responsibility would be handed to the Americans. The painting was scheduled to leave Paris in twenty-four hours.

The last museum visitor at the Louvre to see the Mona Lisa was a young Parisienne woman named Josette Venouil who arrived just before the Louvre closed. "I wanted to see it one last time," she told reporters. "For me it is the most beautiful painting in the world."

Shortly after dawn on Saturday, December 14, under heavy guard, the painting was gently lifted from the wall of the *Grande Galerie*. Her absence left a large vacant spot on the wall, and suddenly the giant portrait of King Francis I by the great Venetian painter Titian looked lonely. "For centuries his companion, hanging just to the right of him in the Louvre's Grand Gallery, has been the Mona Lisa," wrote Edward Folliard from Paris. "But this evening Leonardo da Vinci's portrait of the Florentine beauty has been crated and made ready for the trip to Washington."

Dispatched by the *Washington Post* to Paris so as to cover Mona Lisa's journey to America, over the next few weeks the normally serious political reporter would file some of the most amazing and fanciful copy to ever cross his editor's desk. Edward Folliard and *Washington Post* colleague Waverly Root were both present as the Mona Lisa was inserted inside her special high-tech traveling case and placed in a large wooden crate. Museum workers dressed in matching overalls slowly loaded the box inside the back of a medium-sized steel fortified truck used by the Louvre to transport delicate objects. Inside the vehicle the crate was mounted on cushioned springs specifically designed to guard against vibrations that might shake bits of pigment from the picture's surface.

Escorted by two police cars "running interference in the front" and another following closely behind, the truck departed the museum garage. A squadron of six motorcycle police formed a protective square around the convoy and accompanied the painting along its 160-mile journey to the Paris-Le Havre dock.

As soon as the box left the museum, Madame Hours telephoned John Walker at the National Gallery in Washington to give him the exact temperature and humidity levels at the Louvre at the moment of departure. Walker took note of the readings and handed them to Gallery engineers, who started adjustments to the Gallery's ventilation system.

Officials at the Louvre and police escorts were unusually anxious that day because noxious icy fog—the worst seen in Paris in more than ten years—had descended on the city. The streets were slick and visibility was poor. Less than eighteen hours earlier along the icy Lille-Arras Parkway, a skid caused by one car had triggered a colossal accident in which 500 automobiles collided into one another. No deaths from the accident were reported, but the parkway was still closed as crews attempted to clean up the mangled mess of steel.

During the lengthy trip, Edward Folliard followed behind the convoy in a separate car with a driver hired by the *Washington Post*. The motorcade traveled along the Seine River, moving through the town of Vernon—where American soldiers had crossed the river in their march toward Paris in 1944. As the convoy traveled through scenic Mantes, Folliard snapped a few pictures with his Kodak camera. No one in the group, including the American journalist, was able to draw a deep breath and relax until the convoy safely reached its destination.

Under secret surveillance, the wooden crate housing the special metal box was reverentially loaded onto the ocean liner SS *France*, where it was then bolted to the floor of Cabin M-79 and covered with a thick dark gray wool blanket. Monsieur Jean Chatelain, Director of the French Museums, ensconced himself in the adjacent Cabin M-77. Maurice Serullaz, the chief curator of the Old

Master Drawing Department, occupied Cabin M-81 on the opposite side of the narrow hallway. And reporter Edward Folliard occupied a less expensive lower-class cabin at M-120, quite a distance from the illustrious traveler, but "as near as he could get."

As the Mona Lisa sat inside her cabin waiting to depart, *Le Figaro* tempered its campaign against the loan, and the newspaper "took its defeat philosophically," noting President Kennedy's news conference in which he thanked President de Gaulle for the historic loan and reminding readers that the French Ministry of Cultural Affairs had fully approved the journey. "Thus, the risk is being run in spite of the warnings of the top authorities on the conservation of art works," noted the editors of *Le Figaro*. "May the Mona Lisa successfully brave all the perils!"

After six months of tedious negotiations between Washington and Paris, the Mona Lisa was at last aboard the SS *France* bound for America. Nine French guards, two officials from the Louvre, and American newsman Edward Folliard all accompanied her. At 3:15 P.M. on December 14, the regal SS *France* slowly departed Paris. After leaving Le Havre, she crossed the English Channel and stopped briefly at Southampton, where 120 additional passengers embarked.

Steaming west into the North Atlantic, the SS *France* finally set out for its five-day journey to America. Onboard were many prominent passengers, including a handful of political figures, musicians, and artists, as well as two American bishops. The ship's roster listed prominent American business figures, including the president and director of the Ford Motor Company of France and the president of the Bissell Corporation. None of the passengers was aware when they booked passage that they would become part of history, traveling with the Mona Lisa during her first voyage to the New World. The Mona Lisa was dressed for the occasion, nestled in her custom strongbox.

In Washington at the National Gallery, Walker was informed that the Mona Lisa had left Paris and that newsman Edward Folliard was aboard the SS *France*. The men were already closely acquainted. The two had first met when Walker was a young curator and Folliard was covering the construction and opening of the National Gallery in a series of high-profile features written for the *Washington Post*.

Walker took a moment to write Folliard a short personal letter anticipating his own arrival in New York to greet the ship at Pier 88 and take custody of the Mona Lisa on behalf of President and Mrs. Kennedy:

> *I wanted to write you a note to tell you how much I know the American people will appreciate the visit to the National Gallery of Art of the Mona Lisa, which we owe to your question to Monsieur Malraux and to your interest in this project over many years.*
>
> *I read in the paper this morning that you were to accompany this great masterpiece across the ocean, and by the time you have received this letter I shall probably have greeted you in New York. I did, however, want to write you a personal note in any case. With all best wishes for a happy Christmas.*

The French superliner with its slender hull, gracious appointments, and sweeping enclosed decks made her an ideal temporary home. The 66,000-ton ship featured twenty-two elevators, eleven decks, and six dining rooms. Its wealthy passengers traveled in much the same luxurious style as the passengers of the *Titanic*, observing the formalities of the captain's table and the elite camaraderie of the salons.

According to one account, when several passengers were refused entrance to an area of the first-class passageway and noticed unusual activity, their suspicions were aroused. When further reports of extensive security and strange military-like activity started circulating among the ship's passengers, some feared that the ship was carrying a secret device—possibly nuclear—of the Cold War.

Against the express wishes of Mona Lisa's French escorts, the ship's captain was forced to reveal the truth: the passengers were not traveling with a secret Cold War weapon but with the illustrious Mona Lisa. Once the cat was out of the bag, the lady's first visit to America was toasted by the ship's captain, who broke out the fine wine and champagne. Apprehension quickly turned into celebration as passengers engaged in Mona Lisa costume parties and drinking games. The superliner's butchers, pastry makers, and table cooks prepared delicacies of *Roast Beef Leonardo*, *Salade Mona Lisa*, and *Parfait La Gioconda* to celebrate the painting's transatlantic travel. Passengers feasted under a fifty-two-foot, star-studded dome in the first-class dining room and danced until dawn, oblivious to the elaborate security precautions discreetly exercised amidship. One night, a mischievous passenger even managed to slip past the heavy security to place a pair of women's shoes outside Mona Lisa's well-guarded cabin.

With the masterpiece safely situated in her air-conditioned crate, Edward Folliard, who had been given the assignment to cover the ocean voyage, found himself a newspaper reporter with nothing to report. His editors at the *Post* expected him to file a story daily as the ship steamed across the Atlantic Ocean, but Eddie could not see the picture and wracked his brain for ideas. He remembered the old song "I'll See You in My Dreams," which gave him the inspiration to write about a midnight rendezvous with his special French paramour. In his first dispatch, Folliard told a tale of sleepwalking inside Mona Lisa's cabin, where he engaged in intimate conversation with the traveling ambassador. The reporter's fantasy went something like this:

> "Shall I call you Signora or Madame?" I asked her.
>
> She gave me her smile, which so many have described as enigmatic, and replied: "In the beginning, when Leonardo da Vinci painted me in Florence, you would have addressed me as Signora. But, as you know, I have spent the last 446 years in France, therefore, I suppose you would address me as Madame. But why don't you just call me Lisa?"
>
> "Merci, Lisa. Now for some questions. What do you think about all this fuss in Paris? I mean the uproar started by *Le Figaro* about your leaving the Louvre for a three weeks' visit to the National Gallery in Washington?"
>
> "I think the trip is very exciting."
>
> "Yes, but one commentator in Paris had this to say—You don't ask a beautiful woman to come to you—you go to see her."
>
> "Well, not everybody would agree that I am beautiful. Valentin said that my face was a very commonplace one. But Vasari said that, at least as Leonardo painted me, I was very beautiful. What do you think?"
>
> "Well, as we say in the States, I think you are a lot of woman."
>
> "*Merci.* To get back to the matter of this trip. Why shouldn't I go? Over the years millions of Americans have come to see me. There was your Benjamin Franklin. He was a dear and they used to say that he had an eye for the girls.

"And then there was Thomas Jefferson. What a brilliant man, a genius. I am sure he and Leonardo would have got along well.

"And then besides the hordes of tourists who came to see me, there were your brave soldiers. They were first called Doughboys in the First World War and GIs in the second one.

"And so I say why should I not go to Washington now? It seems to be the polite thing to do. I owe the Americans a visit."

I told her that I knew very little about art, that I was just a White House reporter who also wrote about politics.

Lisa said she ought to know something about art, having sat for Leonardo for three or four years and having met many of his artist friends, but that politics and foreign policy were out of her line.

"But," Lisa said, "I do know that the United States and France are very good and very old friends. Is that not another reason why I should go to Washington?"

Here for the first time Lisa showed a trace of apprehension. Was it true, she asked, that Jacqueline Kennedy, Madame Alphand, Lady Ormsby-Gore and all the Kennedy girls, including Ethel Kennedy, wife of the Attorney General—was it true that they all were very fashionable?

"What will they think of my clothes?" she asked plaintively. "As you can see, they are not very distinguished and are very much out of style."

"Oh," I said, "I wouldn't worry about that. You might even start a new vogue, a return to Florentine fashions of 450 years ago."

Lisa found this hard to believe but her smile returned. I then went on to tell her about what would happen at the National Gallery on January 8. How President Kennedy would unveil her in the presence of Congress and other dignitaries.

I also told her that Mr. Kennedy had a genius for saying the right thing at the right time and that she could expect that he would make her feel at ease and leave no doubt about her good looks.

Lisa seemed pleased. "*Voilà*," she said, rehearsing for her American visit.

The tender story of the reporter's dreamy chat with the Mona Lisa was printed above the fold on the front page of the *Washington Post* and read by nearly everyone in Washington, including the White House staff and the President and First Lady. The only American journalist invited by French officials to travel with the painting, the hard-boiled newsman and self-described romantic covered the voyage with his daily encounters with the Mona Lisa, helping to build the sensation the exhibition would unleash. Copies of Folliard's fanciful musings were found in the various White House files connected with the exhibition and had seemingly been widely distributed and enjoyed.

Folliard's imaginary conversations with the Florentine beauty were sent by telegram from the ship's pursor's office and were then edited and printed in the *Post*. A delight to read, they were also of grave concern to the Secret Service for fear his reports might trigger the interest of criminals, art thieves, or terrorists. Folliard's dreamy interludes and descriptive passages of the iconic masterpiece, they feared, might serve as the perfect temptation for the criminal mind.

During the week in which the Mona Lisa left Paris and was traveling across the Atlantic, John Walker telephoned the White House more than six times, apprising Jackie of the changing situation. As French officials kept a twenty-four-hour vigil over the great treasure, every conceivable detail was provided for her safety and comfort. Such noble precautions, however, couldn't safeguard the Mona Lisa from the threats of Mother Nature. Only two days into her voyage, the eleven-deck luxury liner encountered rough seas as the ship entered an unexpected storm with fierce winds.

In Paris, the winds "whipped, whined and whistled through the streets of the Capital as it never does except when there is a [great] storm on the Atlantic," wrote Waverly Root in the *Post*. "With the tempest which arose in the night over all Northern Europe, producing winds of 60 to 80 miles per hour in France, many minds turned to the ocean, where the liner *France* was carrying the world's most famous painting towards the United States."

As the storm intensified and the ship was hit by turbulent and choppy seas, dishes crashed to the deck and passengers were knocked to the ground. Many aboard ship stayed inside their cabins waiting for the worst to pass. Broken glasses and wine bottles were strewn about the floor.

On the evening of December 16, conditions worsened as the ship encountered gales of near hurricane force. Passengers lurched into each other's arms as forty-five-foot waves and winds of sixty miles per hour struck her abaft and broadside. By daybreak, all of France learned of the threat and feared for the Mona Lisa's safety.

For a brief period communication with the ship was lost. One headline summed up the peril facing the masterpiece: "PARIS FEARS FOR MONA LISA'S SAFETY IN STORM AT SEA." Straps securing the painting's crate were tightened, while woozy guards kept vigil outside the Mona Lisa's cabin as the massive ship heaved from side to side.

It took Captain Georges Croiselle nearly six hours to maneuver the giant ship completely out of harm's way. Apprehension in Washington was eased only after Radio Station Europe No. 1 managed to contact the ship and learned from Captain Croiselle that the *France* was now beyond the storm area, and the Mona Lisa was "perfectly secured."

French officials alerted Walker that the crisis had passed. He in turn relayed the good news to the President and Jackie. The positive reports only added to the Christmas spirit in both Washington and Paris. As Walker busily prepared for the Mona Lisa's imminent arrival, the longstanding traditions of the holiday season commenced.

In a nationally televised ceremony on December 17, President Kennedy lit the national Christmas Tree, a splendid seventy-two-foot cut blue spruce shipped from Colorado. The tree lacked the dancing lights of 1961, but was decorated with 5,000 multicolored bulbs and 4,000 ornaments. The U.S. Marine Band and the Tuskeegee Institute Choir from Alabama provided musical Christmas tidings. In his prepared speech, Kennedy expressed his hope for peace "after a year when the peace has been sorely tried."

Jackie continued the tradition she had initiated the previous year of selecting a theme for the White House indoor Christmas tree. This year her children's themed tree sported brightly wrapped packages, candy canes, gingerbread cookies, and straw ornaments.

For the official Christmas card, Jackie broke away from use of the presidential seal and instead selected an enchanting black-and-white photograph of herself with Caroline and her friends enjoying a sleigh ride on the white snow covering the south lawn. The photo had been taken the previous February when a heavy snow had fallen on Washington. Jackie had asked that a sleigh be brought to the White House along with Caroline's pony, Macaroni. She then took the children on a sleigh ride across the White House lawn in a scene right out of Currier and Ives.

"Could there be a more convincing emblem of true friendship and mutual trust than the gracious loan of the Mona Lisa to the United States?" asked one correspondent. The loan of the masterpiece was a well-chosen gesture of amity, shrewdly maximized by President de Gaulle and Minister Malraux to promote French national pride.

Nor did Americans miss the political and diplomatic significance of the loan of the Mona Lisa. The Kennedy administration would utilize the exhibition as a tool to shape, influence, and manipulate public opinion. The exhibition of France's revered cultural prize would be carefully engineered to amplify the domestic and international popularity of America's engaging, articulate, and media-savvy president, and the timing coincided with the introduction of television into the political mix.

The spectacle of the Mona Lisa's unveiling would be telecast to a huge American audience so as to make an indelible impression. Always attuned to the deep power of symbols, Jackie played a critical role in her husband's understanding that the new media of television, as author David Halberstam observed, conflated theater with politics. Behind the scenes, Jackie was responsible for much of this coordinated activity, and her papers contain notes of instruction to White House aides, speech writers, and advisors for the Mona Lisa's arrival and unveiling. She carefully planned media coverage of the museum exhibition through her close alliance with John Walker.

It was the first time an exhibition of art had been an official duty for the White House, and it was the first time that a painting would serve as the icon of the free world. "Never before had a work of art directly and expressly been lent to a president and his wife, never before had the organization of an exhibition ever been an official matter for the White House, never before and never again did a president of the United States personally inaugurate an art exhibition, much less give an inaugural speech for it," wrote scholar Frank Zöllner.

"Nobody suspected back then, not even the President," observed fashion designer and friend Oleg Cassini, "that Jackie was to become his best public relations tool." The First Lady may not have been fully aware of all of the forces at play, but the record demonstrates that she was the principal catalyst in the enormous undertaking, all the while employing the full force of her influence to see that the plan succeeded. She knew exactly what she wanted, and through a smile, a handwritten note, a timely telephone call, or a memo of instruction, she achieved her objectives for the unprecedented exhibition.

When the loan of the Mona Lisa had been jeopardized by a lack of funding for the extensive security required to protect the painting, $50 million in private funds to finance the exhibition was secured. Letters written by August Heckscher and John Walker state that funding for the exhibition was provided through the generous donation of an anonymous private donor in addition to federal funds. Walker never made public the name of the mysterious benefactor, and it is not known if Walker himself knew the donor's identity. Although records no longer exist fully documenting the source, enough evidence exists to surmise that the funds for the exhibition may have been provided by Paul Mellon, the only son of Andrew W. Mellon, who had made the National Gallery of Art his gift to America in 1941. Mrs. Kennedy's close association with Paul Mellon's wife, Bunny, may well have facilitated the extraordinary gesture. It was one of many unanswered questions connected with the Mona Lisa's unlikely expedition.

7 The Queenly Voyage

When the SS *France* departed Le Havre, Walker was nervously concluding a weeklong trial in conditioning the air of the National Gallery to the precise range of humidity and temperature of that found in the Louvre. Although the Louvre was not air-conditioned, its huge open spaces assured little change in the temperature and humidity. This relatively dry environment was the condition that the Mona Lisa was accustomed to and any slight change might bring disaster.

Under Walker's specific directions, engineers at the National Gallery delicately adjusted the controls of the ventilation system so that the atmosphere of the Mona Lisa's temporary home simulated the air she had "breathed" in Paris. Every few hours engineers at the Gallery checked the readings of the hygrothermograph (a self-contained instrument that measures and records ambient temperature and relative humidity), which provided atmospheric data on the museum's interior conditions.

In anticipation of the painting's arrival, Walker had instructed workers to temporarily move some of the Gallery's prized sculptures, including a sixteenth century bronze, *Bacchus and a Faun*, to make room for the Mona Lisa. Walker meticulously designed the setting in which the painting would be displayed—against a background of burgundy velvet and mounted on a special wall erected along the Gallery's West Corridor west of the Great Rotunda. The new partition would close off the view of the rest of the west wing. Visitors would first glimpse the portrait as they walked down the long, marble corridor. All of the other artworks would be removed, and no other paintings would be visible.

Walker selected a deeply hued wine velvet for the dramatic baffle to hang behind the painting, and he decided to add a new fireproof material to the hundreds of yards of drapery affectionately nicknamed "Mona's Kimono" by the museum staff. He hired the best drapery installers in the business, who hung a stupendous three-part sweeping curtain from the ceiling.

As the arrival of the painting drew near, Walker found himself running from one urgent problem to the next. A soothing telephone call from Jackie helped calm his nerves, but Walker continued to suffer from severe migraine headaches and sleeplessness. He tried to keep his anxiety under wraps, but the depth of his torment was obvious to those who knew him best.

On the morning of December 17, the French Embassy announced that, following the picture's exhibition in Washington at the National Gallery, the Mona Lisa would be placed on display at the Metropolitan Museum from February 7 until March 4. French officials had apparently deemed the newly installed air-conditioning system and resulting "*climatisation*" at the Metropolitan Museum satisfactory. The *New York Times* immediately printed a feature announcing the forthcoming exhibition, which triggered worldwide interest.

The responsibility of a second exhibition was surely the last thing Walker wanted, but it was exactly what he got. Forced to leave behind his ongoing preparations at the National Gallery, he traveled to New York for meetings with Metropolitan Museum of Art Director James J. Rorimer to coordinate the complex arrangements. No records exist documenting the conversations between the two renowned museum authorities, but they were undoubtedly filled with tension. It was widely known that Walker intensely disliked Rorimer and, on occasion, seriously questioned his judgment.

While in New York, Walker was surprised to receive a telephone call from Evelyn Lincoln, President Kennedy's personal secretary. The topic of conversation, however, did not involve the Mona Lisa. When President Kennedy came on the line, he told Walker that several friends had mentioned to him that there was a watercolor drawing by Constantin Guys at Wildenstein & Company, a major art gallery in New York City, that they thought Mrs. Kennedy would like as a Christmas present. The President asked Walker to examine the drawing and tell him what he thought. Kennedy also asked him to keep it a secret.

Walker immediately ventured to Wildenstein's, saw the drawing, and decided that it was not of outstanding quality, but he arranged to bring it back to Washington along with several better works by the same artist. When Walker showed them to the President, he recalled, "At a glance, he recognized that the drawing he had been told about was inferior." The President, however, didn't like any of the others.

Kennedy asked whether Walker could arrange for someone from the gallery to meet him at the Carlyle Hotel in New York and bring some additional selections. Walker contacted Wildenstein & Company and, on the following morning, Daniel Wildenstein visited the Carlyle Hotel. The President looked at a number of pictures that Wildenstein thought might be a suitable gift for Mrs. Kennedy. Following the President's return to Washington, he asked Walker to come to the White House to look at what he had selected. Walker later recalled that: "He was very diffident about his taste and said that he thought I would probably think he had made a foolish choice. I was surprised and pleased when he showed me an exquisite small painting by Maurice Prendergast which he had chosen himself.

"It is one of the best works by Prendergast I have seen, and it is a picture I would be only too delighted to include in the collection of the National Gallery of Art."

Walker anticipated that Jackie would fall in love with the Prendergast handpicked by her husband. It was a role Walker relished—museum curator advising and guiding an eager pupil. Walker could hardly wait for Jackie to open it on Christmas morning.

Ernest R. Feidler, the Gallery's administrator, had started to work out the specific details for the Mona Lisa's convoy once it arrived safely in New York, and it was decided that the Gallery's longtime driver, Hillary Brown, would drive the Gallery's panel truck with the masterpiece. There would be seven cars in the motorcade in addition to the Gallery van, including two passenger cars, one station wagon, one security vehicle, and two cars for the press (one with Edward Folliard and Jean White of the *Post*, and the other with three French reporters and one writer from *Life* magazine).

Feidler notified the commissioners and superintendents of each police force within Mona Lisa's route from New York to Washington in order to alert them to the sensitive situation. Feidler wrote Commissioner Michael J. Murphy of the New York City Police Department:

> On December 19, 1962, a motor convoy carrying an extremely valuable work of art having implications of international political amity will move from New York to Washington.
>
> We would like to have an escort for this convoy by the various jurisdictions through which it will pass. We should be grateful if you could provide such service from the French Line Pier, North River, to the Lincoln Tunnel.

The Mona Lisa would pass through the jurisdictions of New York, New Jersey, Delaware, Maryland, and Washington, D.C. To ensure her safe passage, the Lincoln Tunnel and the Baltimore Harbor Tunnel would need to be closed. All traffic would have to be rerouted and blocked from entering the normally bustling Baltimore-Washington Parkway.

Back in Washington inside the director's office, Walker fretted over the mushrooming VIP guest list for the exhibition's opening night. When he read Jackie's near-final list for the Embassy dinner preceding the unveiling ceremony, he noticed that an important collector had not been invited. Always attuned to moments when a potential donor could be coddled, Walker acted to correct the mistake by immediately contacting Nicole Alphand.

"Everything seems to be progressing well," he told her. "You can imagine my eagerness and excitement. I don't know whether your dinner party is too large, but if you find you have room for Bobby Lehman it might be a good idea to invite him. He gave an interview to the press in support of the loan, and as you know, he lent all his collection to Paris several years ago." A quick fix was made to Nicole's guest list. (Six years later, the Robert Lehman Collection, considered "one of the most extraordinary private art collections ever assembled," would be donated to the Metropolitan Museum following the collector's death.)

Lloyd D. Hayes, the Gallery's assistant administrator, was suffering from his own Mona Lisa problems. Hayes was responsible for installing a hygrothermograph recorder in Vault X in order to measure the room's temperature and humidity. The bomb shelter–like room with reinforced steel doors looked like a large prison cell with a catwalk and glaring lights. As the vault was not normally air-conditioned, Hayes activated the vault's two special air-conditioning units so that proper readings could be made once the space cooled. To his knowledge, the vault had never been air-conditioned in the Gallery's history, and he could not guarantee what would happen.

In conducting experiments inside the West Hall to get the temperature and humidity levels as demanded by French officials, Hayes found he was getting readings in other galleries that exceeded acceptable limits. In nervous conversations with chief curator Perry B. Cott and restorer Francis Sullivan, they determined that the humidity levels in Gallery 8 were too high and posed a serious threat to the other paintings.

After frantic debate, Hayes tried raising the humidity levels in the West Hall through the use of one or more room-type humidifiers. The machines, which could be hidden near the temporary partition so that they were not visible, were supposed to alleviate the problem, making the temperature readings in the nearby galleries safe for the museum's regular collection and at the same time approximating the conditions found in the Louvre. According to Madame Hours, at the moment of Mona Lisa's departure the temperature was 17°C, and the humidity was 45 percent. It remained to be seen whether Hayes could replicate these conditions. Madame Hours was expected to arrive in Washington on December 28 to measure the museum's atmospheric conditions and inform French officials of her findings. "I hope all will go well," she wrote John Walker from Paris.

As the celebrated lady's voyage aboard the SS *France* continued, Edward Folliard's imaginary encounters expanded. In his second installment for the *Post*, he imagined that Lisa had escaped from her crate and stood leaning against the starboard wall as she told the reporter her life story. When she was 24 years old, she suffered the loss of her only child. A year later her husband, a merchant named Giocondo, commissioned Leonardo da Vinci to paint her portrait.

> "What's new?" Lisa asked the reporter.
>
> Folliard hesitated but decided to tell her about a story that recently appeared in a newspaper saying that Leonardo's model for the Mona Lisa was not a young woman but a young man.
>
> "*Oh là là*," exclaimed Lisa. "That, as you have taught me to say, is one for the birds. And you, Edouard, do you believe it?"
>
> "Heavens above, no," he replied. "I think you are the most utterly feminine creature I have ever known—that is, except for some ladies at my home and some associated with the *Washington Post* and the White House."
>
> "That is nice, but I perceive, *cher ami*, that you are *très discret*."

On the next evening of the voyage, Edward Folliard dreamed that he sleepwalked into Mona Lisa's luxurious cabin. This interlude, he told his readers, had been brought on by the evening's rich dinner entrée, "*Quartier d' Agneau de Grave Roti Périgourdine*," which when he was a boy was known as "rack of lamb." The mysterious encounter with the inscrutable lady went something like this:

> "Edouard," Lisa told him, "tell me about this National Gallery of Art in Washington where they are taking me. It is very large, I suppose?"
>
> "No not nearly as large as your home in the Louvre. But it is very beautiful, especially in the rain, when its Tennessee marble turns pink. There is a very nice story behind the Gallery."
>
> "Oh tell me about it, please."
>
> "Well, back in the 1880s, two young Americans who were determined to become giants in the industrial and financial world made a grand tour of Europe. They were Henry Clay Frick and Andrew Mellon.
>
> "In their travels they visited the galleries in London, Rome, Florence and Paris. They developed an interest in art that became a passion with them. You may have had something to do with this, Lisa, because it is almost certain that they saw you."
>
> "You think so? How nice."
>
> "In time both Frick and Mellon acquired great collections of their own. But they disposed of them in different ways.
>
> "Frick provided in his will that his Fifth Avenue mansion in New York be converted into a museum for the public and that it house his collection of masterpieces. It is now called the Frick Gallery and always will be, I suppose.
>
> "Mellon, who was known as the Pittsburgh Croesus and who was Secretary of the Treasury under Presidents Harding, Coolidge and Hoover—well he had a different idea. He decided to establish a gallery in Washington. He gave $15 million for its construction along with his collection valued at $50 million.
>
> "The big difference was this Mellon wrote a letter to President Franklin D. Roosevelt offering the gallery and his collec-

tion to the nation—that is to all the people. He asked that it be called the National Gallery of Art, and was very emphatic in saying that it should not be called the Mellon Gallery.

"His hope was that owners of other great collections would add theirs to his. He could hardly expect them to do so if it were called the Mellon Gallery. Why should they thus add luster to his name?

"Now Lisa, we come to the best part. What Mellon hoped for came true. Other great collections have been turned over to the Gallery, those of Samuel H. Kress and Rush H. Kress, Joseph E. Widener, Chester Dale and many others.

"Well that's the story, Lisa."

"Monsieur Mellon," she said, "was very generous and very magnanimous, eh?"

"Yes, but I think he is more appreciated now than when he was alive." Folliard's Lisa sighed and remarked that life is often like that. Then she giggled. She said she was wondering what her husband of 450 years ago, Francesco del Giocondo would think if he knew what was happening to his Mona Lisa now.

The hours ticked by in rapid succession, and only minutes before he was to leave for New York to be present when the SS *France* docked at New York Harbor, Walker received gut-wrenching news: Longtime Gallery benefactor Chester Dale had died.

The New Yorker once wrote that Dale was the only man in the world who had had his portrait painted, seriatim, by the likes of Jean Lurçat, Diego Rivera, and Salvador Dali. He had displayed his works of art with total "gusto," amassing a collection of historic size and value.

"As long as Chester was alive, the Chester Dale collection was never committed to any institution," Walker recalled. "But as hope springs eternal in museum breasts, there were several directors who felt at one time or another that they were destined to be the 'Proud Possessors.' They too thought, as did Chester himself occasionally, that 'permanent loan' meant 'irrevocable gift.'"

The great collector who had tormented Walker for so many years was gone. Walker could hardly believe it. Outwardly aggressive and hard-hitting, CHESTERDALE was inwardly sensitive and emotional. "When I think of him I have so many blocks I need a psychiatrist," Walker said.

For the moment, the delicate issues of what would become of Dale's great collection, so coveted by the Gallery, were put on hold, and Walker walled away his emotions for the passing of his difficult friend. The care of the Mona Lisa required his full attention now.

8

The Director's Inspection

On the brisk clear morning of December 19, 1962, a flotilla of small ships bestowed a bellowing welcome as fireboats sprayed columns of seawater high in the air and the SS *France* entered New York Harbor. The U.S. Coast Guard cutter *Campbell*, once called the "fightin'est ship ever seen," and dozens of tugboats sounded their horns as the world's longest ocean liner steamed into view. The $80 million French superliner was a breathtaking sight, with her sleek design and huge red and black canted stacks. Despite the early-morning hour, many of the ship's passengers lined the decks, waving scarves and tiny flags announcing their arrival.

The enormous luxury liner docked safely in New York Harbor at Pier 88. The illustrious passenger hidden inside her $2,000 first-class suite had completed her sea trial and now received a queen's welcome.

"She is Here!" declared Edward Folliard to the world on the front page of the *Washington Post*. The fragile treasure of the Old World had finally arrived in the New. "Washington will receive the

Mona Lisa with all the care due a lady of her high station and fragile beauty."

Four uniformed French line crew members carried her from her first-class stateroom into the luxury liner's Grand Salon as the ship's public address system played the "stirring strains" of Modest Mussorgsky's "Pictures at an Exhibition," adding a spiritual dimension to the ambiance.

During a forty-five-minute ceremony, press photographers swarmed the heavy metal container snapping thousands of pictures "as if it were [Swedish sex symbol] Anita Ekberg in the flesh," one newspaper reported.

"How does it look from the back?" one photographer yelled as his colleagues jostled one another to get a better shot.

"It looked exactly like the back of a 52 × 40 × 20 inch metal case," noted the *Washington Post*.

As bulbs flashed in rapid-fire succession, Jean Chatelain, director-general of the museums of France, ceremoniously handed safekeeping of the Mona Lisa to National Gallery Director John Walker, who accepted the painting on behalf of President Kennedy. The President was in Nassau, Bahamas, meeting with British Prime Minister Harold Macmillan for discussions concerning the multilateral force and the Skybolt missile program.

In remarks barely audible over the din of cranking cameras, Chatelain said it was both a great responsibility and a joy to accompany the masterpiece on her first visit to the United States. In perfect English tinged with a hint of a French accent, France's leading museum official called the portrait a symbol between two great nations. After the men grasped hands in a warm handshake of good relations, Walker declared that the visit would "leave a deep imprint on the cultural history of the United States."

Walker and Chatelain patiently posed for photographs. Immaculately dressed in a finely tailored, double-breasted wool suit with a narrow gold and black striped tie, Walker looked dashingly handsome. Despite his extreme anxiety, he managed a large toothy grin, turning his face one direction and then another as photographers shouted his name.

The ship's pastry cook had baked a sugar and butter cream cake in the image of the Mona Lisa, and the "culinary masterwork" was placed atop the real lady's traveling case. It was the only image of the Mona Lisa reporters would get to see that day, and pictures of Walker posing awkwardly near the funny cake were printed in newspapers around the world.

When it came time for Walker's formal remarks, he did not disappoint the crowd tightly packed in the ship's Grand Salon. He had worked for weeks on his welcoming speech and delivered the text completely from memory. The noisy din of the room became quiet as Walker put the moment into eloquent historic perspective:

> The most important single work of art ever to cross the ocean, the Mona Lisa by Leonardo da Vinci, has come to America through the generosity of the French Republic. I would like to express the gratitude of the American people for this gesture of solidarity and friendship.
>
> His Excellency the Minister of Cultural affairs, André Malraux, on a recent visit to Washington, said very truly that the supreme achievements of genius belong to all humanity. Instinctively we feel that such masterpieces are the real justification of our precarious life on this planet.
>
> But though in one sense the Mona Lisa belongs to all humanity, in another it is an important part of the artistic patrimony of France. For it was one of the pictures Leonardo took with him across the Alps when he made his final journey, at the invitation of the French King, Francis I, to his newly adopted country where he stayed the remaining years of his life.
>
> Thus the travels of this great work of art are woven into the history of France. Its present journey, its longest voyage, will leave a deep imprint on the cultural history of the United States. An ambassador of good will between the two republics,

> this most inscrutable of ladies, will I am sure, perform her mission of friendship with unparalleled success, and when she leaves America she will take back to France the affection and gratitude of us all for the honor of her visit.

With the handoff to the Americans complete, Mona Lisa was whisked through customs without the need to open her traveling case. Her most famous American escort, reporter Edward Folliard, also passed quickly through customs without the ordinary protocol.

"I've nothing to declare except a hangover," he told customs officials. Folliard had taken full advantage of the ship's fine wine list during the ocean voyage, and during the trip with the Lady of his fantasies, he had happily indulged in such offerings as Château Beychevelle Saint-Julien and Chambertin Clos de Bèze. "What could I do?" he said with a shrug.

A special gangplank had been built to protect the painting from the winter chill as she disembarked from the enormous ship. The custom-built passageway was sheathed in clear plastic and fully heated by three giant blowers that provided constant air flow at precisely sixty-two degrees.

Thousands of New Yorkers had descended on the harbor to witness the arrival, and at Pier 88, hordes of people pushed up against the circle of New York police that formed a protective barrier against the crowd, creating a security nightmare. At moments the situation grew tense and Walker closed his eyes, but order was immediately restored by uniformed New York City police who stood guard surrounding the National Gallery's dark black truck.

The painting was reverently loaded into the Gallery's air-conditioned vehicle for the 250-mile trip to Washington. The interior of the truck had been lined in thick, soft foam rubber, and the painting's metal box was "nestled in a special cradle and covered with a padded comforter."

First Lady Jacqueline Kennedy touring the museum with National Gallery of Art Director John Walker, April 11, 1961.
National Gallery of Art, Washington, D.C., Gallery Archives

Harvard-educated National Gallery of Art Director John Walker. The First Lady made him responsible for the painting's safety once it reached America. *National Gallery of Art, Washington, D.C., Gallery Archives*

French Minister of Culture André Malraux, Jacqueline Kennedy, John Walker, and Madeleine Malraux tour the National Gallery on the morning of May 11, 1962. *National Gallery of Art, Washington, D.C., Gallery Archives*

All eyes turned toward the First Lady prior to the White House dinner in honor of Cultural Minister André Malraux, on the evening of May 11, 1962. Seen here are Malraux, Madame Malraux, Mrs. Kennedy, President Kennedy, and Vice President Lyndon Johnson (*in the background*). *Abbie Rowe, White House/John F. Kennedy Presidential Library and Museum, Boston*

The First Lady provided the finest entertainment for her distinguished French visitor. *Robert Knudsen, White House/John F. Kennedy Presidential Library and Museum, Boston*

Jacqueline Kennedy with André Malraux. As the evening came to a close, Malraux whispered a promise that he would loan the Mona Lisa to President and Mrs. Kennedy. *Abbie Rowe, White House/John F. Kennedy Presidential Library and Museum, Boston*

The special container with the Mona Lisa is loaded aboard the French liner SS *France* on December 14, 1962. Transporting the painting by air was considered too dangerous and French officials insisted that the painting travel by ocean liner. *Bettman/Corbis*

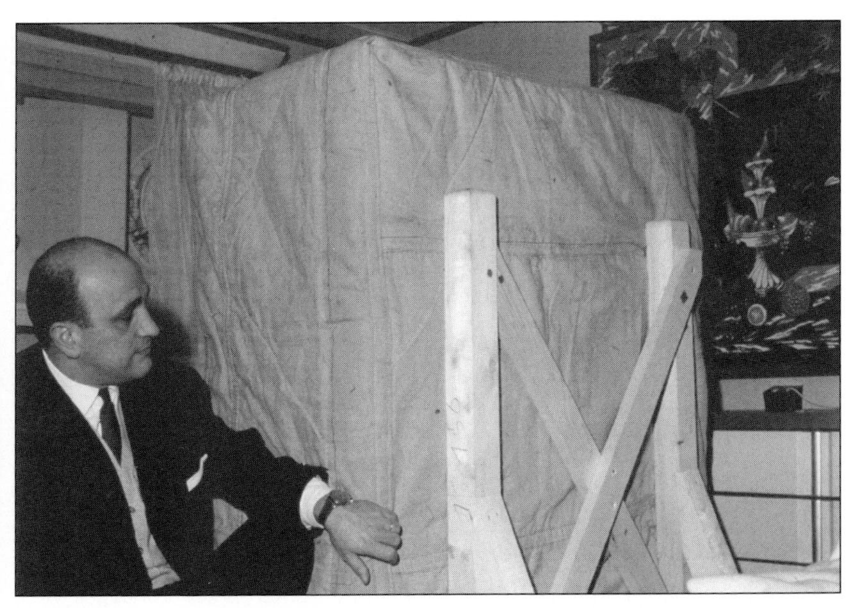

As the Mona Lisa crossed the Atlantic, French officials guarded the painting inside her luxury cabin. To protect the painting from choppy seas, the traveling crate was bolted to the floor and secured by wood braces. *Robert Sisson*/National Geographic *Image Collection*

National Gallery Director John Walker (*left*) takes custody of the painting from Jean Chatelain (*right center*), Director of French Museums. A cake of the Mona Lisa, created by the ship's baker in honor of the occasion, sits atop the painting's custom climate controlled traveling case. *Robert Sisson*/National Geographic *Image Collection*

The Secret Service escorts the Mona Lisa along a red carpet as the painting disembarks from the SS *France* at New York Harbor on the morning of December 19, 1962. *Robert Sisson*/National Geographic *Image Collection*

Washington Post newsman Edward Folliard and Secret Service Agent John Campion pause for lunch as the convoy transporting the painting stops for gas. "France asked us to treat Lisa like a sovereign, and we are," said Folliard. *Robert Sisson*/National Geographic *Image Collection*

This is William Spaar's conception of what may happen this morning when Edward T. Folliard of The Washington Post and the Mona Lisa disenbark from the S. S. France.

Pulitzer Prize–winning reporter Folliard was the only American journalist invited to travel with the masterpiece. His romantic dispatches during the ocean voyage prompted widespread interest and parodies. The veteran newspaperman claimed it was his dream to see the Mona Lisa visit America. *Courtesy of the* Washington Post

The Mona Lisa is uncrated at the National Gallery, where she will rest inside an air-conditioned vault until her American debut in the Gallery on January 8, 1963. *Bettman/Corbis*

John Walker and Jean Chatelain, Director of the Museums of France, in front of the painting at the National Gallery, January 1963. *National Gallery of Art, Washington, D.C., Gallery Archives*

A National Gallery guard keeps vigil over its prize locked behind the steel reinforced doors of a windowless air-conditioned bunker known as "Vault X." *Robert Sisson*/National Geographic *Image Collection*

President Kennedy and Mrs. Kennedy arrive at the National Gallery on January 8, 1963, for the painting's unveiling. Madame Madeleine Hours of the Louvre can be seen standing next to the Marine guard. *Robert Knudsen/White House/John F. Kennedy Presidential Library and Museum, Boston*

President John F. Kennedy and Madame Hours following the President's speech, which highlighted the historic ties between France and the United States and elevated the Mona Lisa to her status as a powerful tool in the Cold War. *Courtesy of the Louvre Museum*

The First Lady poses with Nicole Alphand, wife of the French Ambassador. To her left are Hervé Alphand and Madame Malraux. Mrs. Kennedy is wearing a full-length Empire-styled gown of mauve silk chiffon designed by Oleg Cassini. *Robert Knudsen/White House/John F. Kennedy Presidential Library and Museum, Boston*

President Kennedy, Madame Malraux, André Malraux, Mrs. Kennedy, and Vice President Lyndon Johnson following the ceremony honoring the American debut of the Mona Lisa. *National Gallery of Art, Washington, D.C., Gallery Archives.*

The Mona Lisa in all her glory displayed in the West Sculpture Hall at the National Gallery. *Cecil Stoughton, White House/John F. Kennedy Presidential Library and Museum, Boston*

White-capped U.S. Marine Guards with bayonets keep watch in the National Gallery. The hygrothermograph, the instrument used to record climate conditions inside the museum, is visible behind the flower pots. *Courtesy of National Archives*

A long line of visitors queue up outside the National Gallery on January 13, 1963, despite the cold rainy weather. More than half a million people came to the National Gallery to see the masterpiece by Leonardo da Vinci, painted in the sixteenth century. *Bettman/Corbis*

School children encounter the Mona Lisa. *AP/Wide World Photos*

A line stretches down Fifth Avenue as visitors wait for admittance to the exhibit at New York's Metropolitan Museum of Art.

Viewers gaze at the painting inside the Medieval Sculpture Hall at the Met. *The Metropolitan Museum of Art images © The Metropolitan Museum of Art*

Crowds line up on a rainy February morning outside the Metropolitan. More than one million New Yorkers came to see the painting as "Mona Mania" swept the nation. *Bettman/Corbis*

Jacqueline Kennedy relaxes with Jack Kerouac's popular novel about the Beat Generation, *On the Road*, while aboard the *Caroline*, Kennedy's private plane. *Estate of Jacques Lowe*

Under direct orders from President Kennedy, Secret Service agent John E. Campion was locked inside the back of the van with the painting. Campion was heavily armed under his loose-fitting, dark gray wool overcoat. New York City police cleared traffic from the city's tunnels along the route before the van carrying the masterpiece passed through. According to one report, several sharpshooters were stationed on rooftops in a few strategic locations, but the details of the security operations in place were kept strictly secret.

With sirens screaming and red lights flashing, the eight-car convoy made up of police, Secret Service, and Treasury agents proceeded to the Lincoln Tunnel. The motorcade was escorted by state troopers in New Jersey, Delaware, and Maryland. As the procession crossed each state line, motorcycle officers roared into view and joined the convoy, taking turns as her official escort. During the entire route, the Mona Lisa's entourage never stopped for a single red light.

"I've traveled with kings, queens, and presidents during my newspaper days," Folliard said. "I'll be darned if I've ever seen anything like this."

When the truck carrying the picture was down to less than one gallon of gas, the caravan was forced to stop. One National Gallery car in the entourage "limped" into the gas station on a flattening tire. Once the procession fully stopped, the doors to the Gallery truck were unlocked and Campion leaped into the fresh air.

Folliard dashed inside the gas station where he promptly purchased two cups of coffee and a hot dog.

Campion stood near the van, drinking coffee with Folliard and keeping a close eye on the precious cargo. Despite the sensitive nature of the assignment, Campion could not help smiling as Folliard downed the dog and shared colorful details about the painting's historic voyage across the Atlantic. Campion lit a cigarette and held it discreetly to his side as he listened to the reporter's remarkable tale.

"France asked us to treat Lisa like a sovereign," Folliard told Campion at Mona Lisa's rest stop, "and we are."

The Secret Service had served similar guard duty in the past. In 1941, the service had provided security for the transport of the Constitution and the Declaration of Independence from the Library of Congress to Fort Knox, Kentucky, as the United States had entered World War II.

Campion had sheltered the Kennedy family from danger since the inauguration, and the President had specifically asked that he head the Mona Lisa detail. In his early forties, Campion boasted soft fleshy features and salt-and-pepper hair that disguised his capabilities. His code name, known only to other agents of the service, was "Dragon." (Jackie Kennedy's Secret Service code name was "Lace," while the President was known as "Lancer.")

As the motorcade neared the outskirts of Washington, Mona Lisa's escorts grew somber when the skies turned cloudy. Icy wind whistled through the streets and temperatures fell below 20°F. The small fleet slowed to a crawl as the streets became dangerously icy, and Walker grew increasingly worried as the outdoor temperature plummeted into single digits.

At last, the convoy entered the streets of downtown Washington, and the black van with the words "National Gallery of Art" painted in gold leaf on the driver's door was forced to drive less than five miles per hour. The skies grew dark and visibility became poor as the van's tires crunched against the icy asphalt and the motorcade inched its way toward Constitution Avenue.

After what must have seemed like an eternity for Mona Lisa's nervous escorts, by mid-afternoon the painting arrived at the loading dock of the National Gallery. Several heavily armed guards stood nearby as Gallery workers gingerly moved the crate to its temporary home in the Gallery's basement.

Once the Mona Lisa was inside, museum curators locked the steel doors to Vault X, and Gallery guards and a small bevy of Secret Service agents kept vigil over the masterpiece via a closed-circuit television system that consisted of a single camera and two grainy black-and-white monitors. By morning the world would want to know the condition of the famous face. Walker feared that it might not be a madman or terrorist who would destroy Leonardo da Vinci's great artwork, but the icy conditions of a Washington winter. Alone inside the vault, exhausted from her travels, Mona Lisa rested until her grand American debut.

The following morning, John Walker nervously paced the floor waiting confirmation from Perry Cott that the painting had arrived in good condition despite the brutal weather. Walker had complete faith in Cott's professional judgment. Cott had earned his Ph.D. in fine arts at Princeton University and during the war had served as one of the "Monuments Men," rescuing priceless artifacts from Nazi theft. Cott came to the Gallery in 1949 and was appointed chief curator seven years later. Since 1956, the Gallery had acquired dozens of significant paintings, and Cott had influenced every decision. "To find a scholar and administrator of Perry Cott's knowledge and taste is never an easy task," Walker said. "But to find one who also possesses his connoisseurship [would] be difficult indeed." As chief curator, the highly trained fifty-three-year-old scholar would be one of only a handful of Americans who would come face to face with the Mona Lisa outside her bulletproof glass and gilded frame.

At Walker's direction, the picture was removed from its aluminum and polyvinyl traveling case and gently situated on a special pedestal. It was the moment of truth. Wearing gloves and a lab coat, Perry Cott fastidiously took a series of photographs of the painting from the front and back and examined the poplar wood closely with an optician's lens. His examination took over an hour. Walker stood nearby with his hands thrust deep in his coat pockets. To his considerable relief, there appeared to be no further visible buckling or warping of the aged wood. Despite the unexpected snowstorm, the Mona Lisa still smiled. Walker instructed Perry Cott to place the painting in her golden oak frame and cover it with a double layer of bulletproof glass. The temperature was held constant at sixty-two degrees. Somehow, for Jackie's sake, Walker had to keep the painting safe until its grand debut on January 8.

The First Lady left Washington for Palm Beach with John Jr. and Caroline to celebrate the Christmas holidays at the "Winter White House." Walker kept Jackie informed of the condition of the Mona Lisa through telephone messages left with her staff.

On Thursday, December 20, he penned a brief message to President Kennedy, who was still in Nassau for meetings with British Prime Minister Harold Macmillan and Ambassador Ormsby-Gore.

"You have many worries, but I can relieve your mind about one," Walker wrote President Kennedy. "The Mona Lisa arrived in perfect condition."

Referring to the secret plan to find a watercolor of quality as the perfect Christmas gift for Jackie, Walker added, "I think the Prendergast is a jewel. You have a very good eye for pictures. It is much better than anything I showed you."

At Jackie's suggestion, Walker offered a giant-sized Christmas present to the Washington press corps, when he invited reporters to get an exclusive preview of the masterpiece under what he called "very special conditions." Walker made the invitation even more memorable by including the children of the press corps as well. The private viewing inside Vault X would take place on January 9 for two hours beginning at 5:30 P.M. Admission was granted only on proffer of the printed invitation that read:

The Trustees of the National Gallery of Art
Invite you and your children to

A PRIVATE EXHIBITION

OF THE

Mona Lisa

BY

LEONARDO DA VINCI

More than seventy-five reporters and their offspring would come to witness history as the small portrait sat on its special easel deep beneath Washington's National Gallery. Despite the upbeat nature of the occasion, Walker continued to face sharp questioning about why the Mona Lisa would wait so long in the vault before she would be put on public display. Walker emphasized that the French government had specifically requested that the painting not be unveiled until "Congress and Malraux were in attendance."

"The French to whom ceremony is no trifle," noted the *Washington Post*, "apparently wanted to make their gesture of friendship to the United States in as grand a manner as possible." The

January 8 ceremony was selected to coincide with the opening of Congress the next day; the December 14 sail date had been the last voyage of the SS *France* that could get the painting to Washington in time.

At her laboratory at the Louvre, Madame Hours nervously telephoned Washington at the first possible hour. She asked her superior, Monsieur Chatelain, to call her as soon as the box had been opened and the painting had been inspected.

When Chatelain returned her telephone call, Hours recognized his voice immediately. "How is she doing?" she asked tremulously.

"She's covered with mold!" he answered. Seized with alarm, Hours could hardly catch her breath. Chatelain then laughed heartily and immediately reassured her: "She's fine, [and] she's waiting for you."

With great relief that her subject had safely made the journey to America, Madame Hours relaxed for the next few days and spent Christmas with her family. Soon she would leave for Washington, where she would join museum officials and examine the painting for herself.

As the Lady rested in her temporary home inside Vault X, more than five inches of snow—the deepest snowfall ever recorded on Christmas Day in Washington—covered the city's streets. Walker found himself constantly checking the weather reports, as if his actions would help ward off the cold from his illustrious European visitor.

Meanwhile, the President and First Lady were enjoying the warmth and sunshine of Palm Beach, Florida. On Christmas morning, the couple attended services at St. Anne's Church followed by a leisurely cruise aboard the *Honey Fitz*, the presidential yacht named for the maternal grandfather of the President. They were accompanied by Jackie's sister and brother-in-law, Princess and Prince Radziwill.

At 5:30 P.M. on Christmas evening, the Kennedys hosted a party for members of the Secret Service and White House press corps who were traveling with the President's entourage. Absent from the holiday party was Agent John Campion, who remained in Washington guarding his world-famous charge.

Consumed with every detail concerning Mona Lisa's care, comfort, and security, Walker was anxious, irritable, and short on patience. He spent the day after Christmas at his office firing off memos and dispensing orders. He had grown paranoid that harm might somehow come to the painting inside the vault—despite his verbal orders restricting access—and he sent a terse memo to staffers with written orders concerning the requisite authorization required to get near the chamber. "On instructions from the French, no one is permitted to enter Vault X except on official business. This rule must be strictly enforced.

"If anyone on the curatorial staff feels that he should see the Mona Lisa on official business, before doing so please clear this with me or, in my absence with Mr. Cott."

With the opening ceremony less than two weeks away, Walker's assistant, J. Carter Brown, ably helped with many of the pressing details, working closely with White House staffers in preparation for the official occasion. Brown took the chaos more or less in stride, offering his usual sense of humor and boundless energy. He seemed calm and cool on the exterior but, as the opening neared and the problems piled high, even Brown referred to the enormous preparations for the exhibition as "our Days of Trial."

New Year's Eve morning, President Kennedy met with reporters in the living room of his Palm Beach residence for an off-the-record interview to assess his first two years in office. That evening, President and Mrs. Kennedy attended a party at the exquisite orchid-filled estate of Mr. and Mrs. Charles Wrightsman. As noted by biographer Sara Bradford, "Nineteen sixty two closed for Jackie on the same note of fashion and pleasure that it had held throughout. Celebrating New Year's Eve in Palm Beach as usual at the Wrightsmans' were no less than six of the World's Best-dressed Women: Jackie herself and Lee, plus four others who were on her international social circuit—Jayne Wrightsman, Gloria Guinness, Marcella Agnelli and Nicole Alphand, wife of the French ambassador in Washington."

The new year promised to be filled with new beginnings, and Jackie had reasons of her own for celebration: she was pregnant. The news was met with great joy between husband and wife and remained a private piece of information, known only to a handful of intimates.

On January 2, Madame Hours left Paris aboard an Air France jet bound for Washington. She arrived in America in an optimistic frame of mind. Her first stop was a visit to the gray stone, Tudor-style French Embassy on Kalorama Road for a meeting with Ambassador Alphand, and from there she left for the National

Gallery where she met museum colleagues and Gallery Director John Walker.

She had only a few days to examine the painting and check temperature readings in order to make any adjustments she thought necessary in light of the unusually cold temperature.

Walker instructed his secretary, Mrs. Martin Foy, to telephone the White House and leave word for Jackie that Madame Hours had arrived, and, for the moment, everything seemed to be proceeding according to plan.

Walker's update to Jackie was confirmed when, the following day, Madame Hours sent word by telegram via the American Cable and Radio System to Louvre officials that "*tout va bien*" (all is well).

Only hours into the new year, Kennedy's ablest White House minds were working on the speech to be delivered by the President during the Mona Lisa ceremony. On January 4, arts advisor August Heckscher delivered to Arthur Schlesinger his rough draft for Kennedy's remarks. "This is my suggestion for the Mona Lisa text," Heckscher wrote Schlesinger on the cover sheet. "I leave it with you."

During the course of the week the speech underwent numerous revisions until it had been worked into a remarkable oration that touched on stirring themes of art, history, and international diplomacy. The speech was intended to infuse the occasion with the most pomp and circumstance possible to reflect the administration's unprecedented commitment and celebration of the arts. The text of the President's speech would be distributed prior to the unveiling so that reporters could cover the event for the morning newspapers. White House files suggest that Jackie was sent several drafts of the speech as it underwent multiple revisions.

Mrs. Kennedy drew on her innate understanding of image crafting in order to infuse the exhibition with a sense of drama, spectacle, and pageantry. Visual imagery became a central theme for Jackie, and she used it to brilliant effect in the American visit of the Mona Lisa. The detailed program Walker devised for the ceremony met Jackie's exacting standards and projected an indelible image of history, internationalism, and fanfare. Jackie understood that the relationship of the President to the American people was one of the most documented relationships in American life, and the unveiling of France's supreme national treasure in front of the assembled leadership of the nation was the ultimate political statement.

"Never before had any president sought to identify the White House with the whole range of the nation's intellectual life," wrote Arthur Schlesinger Jr. in his memoir. "He saw the arts not as a distraction in the life of a nation but as something close to the heart of a nation's purpose. Excellence was a public necessity, ugliness a national disgrace. The arts, therefore were, in his view, part of the responsibility, and he looked for opportunities to demonstrate this concern."

Schlesinger recalled that the "President's curiosity and natural taste had been stimulated" by Jackie's "informed and exquisite response" to the fine arts. "They couldn't live without them—it [was] woven into the pattern of their lives."

With the stars aligning, even Jackie could not have coordinated the one element that made the Mona Lisa exhibition truly an event of global interest. Orbiting the earth was "an astonishing piece of equipment" built by private industry and fired into space by the U.S. government.

Relay, the second U.S. communications satellite developed by the Bell Telephone Laboratories, had initiated a new era in communications. From high above earth the satellite was in perfect position to transmit the first live television pictures from the United

States to Europe. If everything went according to plan, the historic images of the unveiling of the Mona Lisa would be flashed on two continents simultaneously.

It was left to Walker to orchestrate the massive occasion for Jackie, which was more like a queen's coronation than the opening of a museum exhibition. Walker dictated to Mrs. Foy a remarkable list of categories for invitations to the private ceremony: All members of U.S. Senate, the House, the Supreme Court, and the Cabinet (State, Treasury, Defense, Justice, Post Office, Interior, Agriculture, Commerce, and Health, Education, and Welfare); all of the heads of the executive offices (Budget, CIA, CEA, NSC, NASC, and OEP); former ambassadors to France; important donors to the Gallery; directors of Washington's museums (Dumbarton Oaks, Phillips Gallery, Museum of Modern Art, Corcoran Gallery, National Collection of Fine Arts, and the Freer Gallery); the heads of the Smithsonian Institution, the National Trust for Historic Preservation, and the Cultural Center; and all former trustees of the National Gallery of Art. In addition, Walker felt the need to add the presidents of the nation's best universities; the Librarian of Congress; leaders of the World Bank and the International Monetary Fund; plus a handful of prominent publishers, reporters, and newspaper columnists.

Once Jackie had submitted her lengthy list of names (which included every member of the extended Kennedy and Auchincloss families) and various White House requests, the guest list had mushroomed to nearly 2,000. Walker was hard-pressed to conceive of how he could possibly manage so many prominent guests at one time. Dozens of frantic phone calls occurred between the White House and the Gallery as the list was refined—and refined again. Some calls placed by Carter Brown to Tish Baldridge and members of her staff were only minutes apart as the appointed hour drew near.

As for the logistics of the public exhibition of the Mona Lisa, Walker planned to remove the masterpiece from Vault X and mount the painting on the baffle on the Main Floor in the center of the West Sculpture Hall. The picture would hang rather high, so that visitors could see the painting from as far a distance as possible. Walker, who feared only seven to ten seconds would be granted to each visitor to pause in front of the painting, felt this element was crucial. The public, if all went according to plan, would march up the stairs four by four to the rotunda as they made their way toward the viewing in the West Sculpture Hall. Every element of the installation had been worked out beforehand with precise sketches and meticulous measurements. Even the quarter-inch screw (with eye open on top to receive the quarter-inch hanger rod) had been carefully considered so that when it came time to mount the picture, it would be surprisingly quick.

Next to the painting was placed a bust of Giuliano de' Medici by Verrochio, made at the same time as Leonardo's masterwork. Madame Hours had requested this juxtaposition, moved by her "romantic taste for historical coincidences." Walker loved the idea as well and was only too happy to oblige. When told of the gesture, Jackie must have been especially amused.

Some historians believed that Leonardo's small masterpiece had been painted at the request of Giuliano de' Medici, who may have been the lover of the real-life Mona Lisa. "By a strange turn of events, Giuliano and Mona Lisa, two lovers separated for 500 years," Madame Hours said proudly, "were reunited in the United States."

There was one other intriguing historical connection related to the Mona Lisa. A team of genealogists later discovered records that indicated that the Kennedys may have had distant family relations with the subject of Leonardo da Vinci's masterpiece. The genealogical link stemmed from the fact that the Fitzgeralds of Ireland (the ancestors of Rose Kennedy) can be traced to members of the Gherardini family of Tuscany, Italy, who moved to Ireland in the twelfth century. ("La Gioconda," the woman who sat for the artist, was the former Lisa Gherardini, before she married Francesco del Giocondo.) Evidence exists to suggest that President John F. Kennedy was in fact a distant relative of the Mona Lisa.

Below the painting, hidden in the flower pots, Hours had situated the hygrothermographs that monitored the temperature and humidity levels—the instruments critical in determining the picture's well-being. The French flag and the Star-Spangled Banner, both protected by white-capped Marines with bayonets, stood on opposite sides of the painting. Several feet from the wall, Walker had erected a velvet rope barrier to keep visitors at a safe distance.

Walker wasn't completely alone in feeling that the weight of the world rested on his shoulders. He at least had the companionship of Agent Campion with whom he could share the burden. Campion rarely left the museum during the Mona Lisa's visit, except for a few hours each day to get some sleep at a nearby hotel, when another agent took his place. But in reality, the real responsibility was Walker's. It may have been Jackie's exhibition, but it was Walker's museum, and at the end of the day, the buck stopped with him alone.

"There will be need for Director Walker's humor and stamina equal to his eloquence once the doors are open to the public," noted Edward Folliard in his front-page feature in the *Washington Post*. It remained to be seen if every precaution and every prayer would be enough to keep the Lady safe.

Part Three

An Evening to Remember

On the day prior to the unveiling of the Mona Lisa, Madame Hours entered Vault X to conduct her own inspection of the painting. At 11:00 A.M., she noted that the curvature in the back of the poplar panel was "very slightly more accentuated" than it was during her examination of the painting in October. She sent off a telegram to officials at the Louvre.

Hours expressed concern over the temperature to the Gallery's chief curator, Perry Cott, who immediately informed John Walker that Mona Lisa's caretaker was unhappy. The Gallery's administrator was asked to adjust immediately the interior temperature to Madame Hours' exact specifications. The Gallery engineers obliged and also increased the humidity inside Vault X and the West Hall to approximately 52 percent.

The engineers nervously watched the atmospheric readings as Walker and Carter Brown were mired in the massive details required to coordinate the safe arrival of nearly 2,000 distinguished figures. A handful of special guests, including President and Mrs.

Kennedy, Minister Malraux and his wife, and Secretary of State Dean Rusk, would arrive at the museum's Seventh Street entrance. John Walker and Lady Margaret, along with Huntington Cairns, secretary-treasurer and general counsel of the Gallery, would meet the group at the door.

The plan was for VIP guests to assemble in the Seventh Street Lobby and go immediately into the West Stair Hall. From there, President and Mrs. Kennedy would be escorted to the elevator; once at the main floor level, a protocol officer would guide the President and First Lady across the West Garden Court into Gallery 46, then into Gallery 48, and then to the speaker's platform. (Mr. Cairns and Mrs. Walker were to remain in Gallery 48.) The President would enter the West Sculpture Hall to the sounds of the Marine Band Orchestra's rendition of "Hail to the Chief." On a second platform on the opposite side of the Mona Lisa, Walker had positioned chairs for Vice President and Mrs. Johnson, Secretary of State and Mrs. Dean Rusk, and Ambassador and Madame Alphand.

Following an introduction by Secretary of State Dean Rusk, Minister Malraux would deliver his speech in French and, after he completed his remarks, the speech would be read in translation. The Secretary would then return to the lectern and introduce President Kennedy. Following the President's speech, the U.S. Marine Band was to play "*La Marseillaise*" and "The Star Spangled Banner." After the music ended, those in the President's party were to look at the Mona Lisa and then leave the same way they entered.

Walker and Carter were nervous about the crush of dignitaries to be packed inside the West Sculpture Hall. The men walked the scene with a tape measure, and Walker determined that in the rotunda, the space outside the columns could accommodate 768 people; inside the columns the room could hold 528 people; and the space between the hall's west side door and Gallery 48 could handle

576, for a total of 1,872 standing guests. Walker tabulated the numbers repeatedly to make sure there was enough square footage.

He was also concerned that the huge throng might not be able to hear adequately the speeches delivered by the dignitaries inside the museum's cavernous interior, so Walker instructed Ernest Feidler to find and install "the most perfect sound system that could be devised" for the occasion. Feidler, in turn, hired Frank H. McIntosh, the president of the same firm who had provided the museum's vanguard audio system known as "Lectour." McIntosh's previous work for the Gallery had been flawless, and Feidler had full confidence in him. Early sound tests showed that the specially installed speakers were difficult to hear in the first half of the West Sculpture Hall due to the highly reflective sound created against the limestone walls and marble floors. So McIntosh installed a total of five amplifiers and sixteen speakers to solve the problem.

Less than a handful of VIPs sent their regrets, so Walker expected a full house. One celebrity, singer Nat King Cole, known for his famous song "Mona Lisa," sent a telegram to Gallery trustees with news that sadly he could not make it to Washington. "My wife and I sincerely regret our inability to join you at a showing of that famous lady Mona Lisa. As you know she has been the heart of my career therefore it is with a great deal of sentiment that I shall continue paying her tribute in song."

Mindful of the rarity of the occasion, Walker also wanted his staff to experience an encounter with the illustrious Mona Lisa. He set aside one hour between 8:30 and 9:30 A.M. on Wednesday morning so that museum workers and staff could view the picture. No one on duty failed to take advantage of the once-in-a-lifetime occasion. In a memo to employees, Walker announced the special exhibition, but reminded the staff that all photographs were strictly prohibited.

"In Vault X of the National Gallery of Art, a celebrated lady rests," noted the Associated Press, "waiting for somebody to let her out of the box so she can turn her inscrutable smile on the Americans."

On the afternoon of January 8, Jackie returned to Washington from Palm Beach in time to have her hair done and to get dressed before her arrival at the National Gallery. She had asked Oleg Cassini to design her gown for the unveiling, and they had worked closely together on it. "We had discussed what Jackie should wear for the reception," Cassini wrote in his memoirs, "which was viewed as the cultural high point of the administration."

Cassini said he recalled Jackie's visit to Empress Josephine's home, Malmaison, in 1961, and suggested something in the empire style. It suited his client well because it showed off her shoulders and strong neckline. "The gown I created was a pink chiffon column encrusted with pearls and brilliants. It was strapless—quite a dramatic departure from our first few months in the White House, when Jackie had been so worried about wearing a one-shouldered gown!"

Very early in her pregnancy, the size 10 dress fit perfectly. Cassini remembered that Jackie looked spectacular in the full-length gown of mauve and silk chiffon that featured a "wrapped bandeau bodice with gathers of silk chiffon falling to a jeweled hem." The pink-toned strapless evening dress was patterned with hand-sewn crystal beads. "Some dresses are conspicuously successful," he said, "and this was one of our favorite gowns."

For her part, Madame Malraux had selected a floor-length black velvet and taffeta dress with a tailored bodice and full skirt, presumably designed by Chanel. She wore black satin gloves to the elbow and three long ropes of pearls. Paris may have been the paragon of fashion, but the typically stylish Madame Malraux looked positively matronly dressed all in black standing next to the lilac-hued youthful First Lady. The first couple looked tanned and rested following their holiday in sun-swept Florida, whereas the Malrauxs by contrast looked pale and exhausted.

Finally the great moment arrived. On the day of the unveiling, January 8, 1963, Mona Lisa was removed from Vault X and gently carried into the long marble corridor of the Gallery's West Hall. With Walker supervising, Perry Cott and a handful of curators mounted the painting on the specially constructed temporary wall. Once the painting was in place, workers installed the velvet backdrop. John Walker and Madame Hours lingered in front of the masterpiece scrutinizing their display. "There is the satisfaction of a beautiful installation," Walker recalled in his memoirs. "When an arrangement seemed inevitable and perfect I felt as though I were the successful director of an orchestra."

The celebration to honor the unveiling of the Mona Lisa began in the candlelit dining room at the French Embassy where Ambassador and Madame Hervé Alphand "were hosts at a dinner and a tableau that was worthy of da Vinci himself." At the main table sat President and Mrs. Kennedy, all of the President's brothers and sisters, Cultural Minister André Malraux and his wife, Vice President Lyndon Johnson and Lady Bird. Seventy-two years old and in poor health, French President Charles de Gaulle had decided not to travel to Washington for the historic occasion. "De Gaulle stayed in France," noted author Donald Sassoon, "there was room for only one star."

"Renowned in Washington not only for her looks and her style, but for her abilities as a hostess, Madame Alphand turned out a dinner that had Francophiles kissing their finger tips in joy," gushed *Time* magazine. The menu began with a delicate *foie gras* followed by *filet de boeuf Charolais sous la cendre garni renaissance*. This was accompanied by a "profound *Chateau Gruaud-Larose en magnum* 1952; an unassuming little hearts-of-lettuce salad with mimosa dressing. And for a windup, *Poires Mona Lisa*—poached pears, swaddled in hot chocolate sauce, bundled into a pastry shell—trailed by a superb Dom Perignon 1955."

A trio of effusive toasts was made by the Ambassador to President Kennedy, who in turn toasted the absent French president. Walker gave the final toast, bringing loud cheers to the room when he gallantly raised his glass in honor of the Mona Lisa.

Tucked among the specially invited guests were three couples known for their notable art collections, which later would join the galleries of the world's great museums: oilman Charles B. Wrightsman, banking heir Paul Mellon, investor and diplomat W. Averell Harriman, and their wives. Walker made sure that he paused to visit each of these extraordinary collectors who someday might make permanent gifts of their private collections to the National Gallery.

Nicole Alphand had gone full bore in preparation for the party. Parisian decorator Stéphane Boudin had hung painted wood panels from the Petit Trianon at Versailles in the dining room and added gilded ballroom chairs (identical, the *Post* noted, to those used by Mrs. Kennedy for her tables of ten). Throughout the room, modern French art objects, displayed among the "flickering shadows" of yellow and pink tapers, decorated the tables.

Dressed in a rented tuxedo, news photographer I. C. Rapoport had been dispatched by *Paris Match* to cover the embassy dinner. Rapoport recalled that Madame Alphand grabbed his arm and asked him to photograph her with the president. At the same time she also warned him that journalists were "*interdits*" (forbidden) to be present at the reception.

As Rapoport was "ushered through the crowd of celebrants," President Kennedy spotted the photographer. Nicole apologized to the President, knowing that the White House had instructed that no members of the press be admitted. "This fellow flew all the way from Paris, today, just to be here, and I could not say 'No' to him," Nicole whispered.

Rapoport snapped a photo of the wife of the French ambassador with the palm of her hand embracing the President's elbow. "Kennedy was grinning his famous grin," Rapoport recalled. President Kennedy immediately recognized the photojournalist despite the rented tuxedo, and said with a smile, "You're out of uniform, Private Rapoport!"

After Madame Hours felt she had addressed all of the pressing security problems at the National Gallery, she too joined the dinner at the French Embassy. Her hair in a semi-bouffant, she wore a light-colored, full-length gown with a tasteful plunging neckline. Over her shoulders was a stunning pink satin stole, and see-through black lace gloves covered her hands.

"It was a wonderful dinner," she recalled. "There were ten or so round tables with eight guests seated at each one. President Kennedy presided at table one, [and] I was at table number two, [next to] the Italian Ambassador in homage to the nationality of the Mona Lisa, and to its creator."

On her right side, Hours recalled, was "a stranger." In front of her was seated the President's mother, Mrs. Joseph Kennedy, who spoke perfect French. Also at her table were Robert McNamara and two others. "Madame Rose Kennedy asked a lot of questions about the Mona Lisa and I tried to answer and include the person on my left, the Italian Ambassador, in our conversation, which began to sound like a dialogue.

"Suddenly the man on my right tried to speak, and, to my amazement, Rose Kennedy cut him short with the following words: 'Quiet, Johnson!'

"It was only then I realized who the man on my right was: the Vice-President of the United States! I smiled at him and tried to interest him in our conversation, which he more or less grasped."

Madame Hours remembered that Rose Kennedy introduced her to her sons in an authoritarian manner, and she summoned Attorney General Robert Kennedy by saying, "Bobby, come here." He arrived, bowed, and his mother said simply: "He runs the Justice department."

At one point during the dinner party, President Kennedy acknowledged Madame Hours with a smile and thoughtfully called her "Mona's Lisa's younger sister." Later, Lyndon Johnson referred to the museum official as the "mother of the Mona Lisa," and Hours cringed at the thought that she was perceived as old enough to be the mother of the famed Lady in the painting. "John Kennedy was much more gallant," she recalled.

Of all the participants, possibly no one was more overcome with emotion than Mona Lisa's suitor, "Edouard" Folliard. The reporter who had been at the front lines of the Battle of the Bulge to cross the Rhine with the Ninth Army and then witnessed VE-Day in Paris was now seated with the luminaries of American and French society gathered in anticipation of the unveiling of the great painting.

Folliard had traveled with King George and Queen Elizabeth, but such encounters could not compare to the evening about to unfold, in which a lifetime ambition would be realized. At the end of the lavish dinner party at the French Embassy, as he left the dining room, President Kennedy spotted Folliard and his wife Helen seated at a table near his mother. Folliard seemed out of place dressed in a tuxedo and black tie, and Kennedy hardly recognized him.

With a wave of his hand, President Kennedy called out to the reporter, "Thanks for a nice dinner, Ed!"

As photographers caught the moment on film, the President and First Lady exited the embassy and stepped into the back of the Lincoln Continental presidential limousine. By the time they arrived at the National Gallery of Art, where they were greeted by John Walker, nearly 2,000 guests—"black-tied and be-gowned," as one newspaper described them—had jammed into the West Sculpture Hall.

As the presidential party arrived, John Walker escorted the entourage and their Secret Service guards to the elevator, which was to take them to the main floor. But the Gallery's longtime elevator operator became so nervous at the sight of the First Lady that he hit the "stop" button by mistake. When he next pushed the button to go up, nothing happened. He pushed it again. Nothing. Walker glanced at Jackie, who simply smiled.

After several anguished moments as the operator clumsily tried to get the elevator moving, the President decided that the entourage should take the stairs. Mrs. Kennedy lifted her gown and gingerly climbed the stairs holding the President's arm. Vice President Johnson, who had recently suffered a heart attack, followed closely behind. Johnson, who had been misinformed about the dress code, was wearing white tails instead of black tie.

The red-coated Marine Corps band was playing "The Star Spangled Banner" in anticipation of the President's entrance, but as the regal group unexpectedly entered the viewing area, the band abruptly shifted to "Hail to the Chief."

Elegantly coifed in her strapless pink chiffon gown embroidered with brilliants and pearls, Mrs. Kennedy instantly stole the spotlight. Diamond drop earrings designed by Harry Winston sparkled against her face as a flood of flashbulbs popped inside the great marbled hall.

"The Mona Lisa, first lady of the world among paintings and Jacqueline Kennedy, first lady of the nation, came face to face," reported the *Washington Post*. "It was a long awaited reunion," exclaimed *Life* magazine, and "both ladies were at their glowing best."

André Malraux stood to address the packed audience of politicians and diplomats, none of whom could see the Mona Lisa because of the bright television lights. The glare of the spotlights ricocheted off the shatterproof, bulletproof glass protecting the Mona Lisa, making the painting a whitewashed blur.

Standing at the podium, Malraux turned toward President Kennedy and eloquently fused the identity of Western Civilization with the nation of France through the Mona Lisa, paying homage to America's role in delivering twice the victory of civilization over upheaval: "There has been talk of the risks this painting took in leaving the Louvre. They are real, though exaggerated. But the risks taken by the boys who landed one day in Normandy—to say nothing of those who had preceded them twenty-five years before—were much more certain. To the humblest among them . . . I want to say . . . that the masterpiece to which you are paying historic homage this evening, Mr. President, is a painting which he has saved."

"Why was the Mona Lisa sent to the United States?" he asked. The answer, he declared, was that, "No other nation would have received her like the United States."

But few, if any, heard him. The microphone system had failed and the cocktail-drinking crowd was growing noisy. The Marines guarding the painting soon worried that the mob would surge forward, and Secret Service agents whisked the President's mother into another wing of the Gallery for protection.

Secretary Rusk, his voice barely audible above the tumult, attempted to soothe the crowd by proclaiming that since the early days of the frontier, "irreverence has been one of the signs of our affection." But to no avail.

Even the President himself failed to silence the chatter, and he barely disguised his irritation. While thanking the nation of France for lending the priceless "Moner Liser," as he pronounced it, he wryly recalled that once when it was displayed in Florence, an unruly crowd had broken the gallery windows. "Our own reception is more orderly," Kennedy shouted, "though perhaps as noisy."

As the president continued on, no one could hear a word; to John Walker's dismay, the loudspeaker system stopped working entirely. Walker scrambled to find the Gallery's sound engineer, but the director, unable to squeeze through the mob, was pinned into a corner. The long-awaited debut of the world's most famous face was suddenly in shambles.

Without hesitation, the President dropped the dead microphone and moved closer to the throng. With a voice trained by many political campaigns, he shouted defiantly in an attempt to get the audience to quiet down. Kennedy extemporized, told a few jokes, and struggled to save the evening. Summoning all his vocal strength, he repeated key portions of Minister Malraux's evocative speech.

Once the audience was more or less quiet, Kennedy read from his prepared address, a finely crafted tribute to the painting, its artist, and the two countries' shared aspirations and beliefs, written with great care by August Heckscher and Arthur Schlesinger:

> The life of this painting here before us tonight spans the entire life of the New World. We citizens of nations unborn at the time of its creation are among the inheritors and protectors of the ideal which gave it birth. For this painting is not only one of the towering achievements of the skill and vision of art, but its creator embodied the central purpose of our civilization.
>
> Leonardo da Vinci was not only an artist and a sculptor, an architect and a scientist, and a military engineer, an occupation which he pursued, he tells us, in order to preserve the chief gift of nature, which is liberty. In this belief he expresses the most profound premises of our own two nations.
>
> We here tonight, among them many of the men entrusted with the destiny of this Republic, also come to pay homage to this great creation of the civilization which we share, the beliefs which we protect, and the aspirations toward which we together strive.

The unveiling coincided with the opening of the Eighty-eighth Congress, and because nearly everyone in both chambers was present, the speech was infused with poignant political underpinnings. The President astutely utilized the Mona Lisa to rise above issues of difference and to stress the profound historical and political ties between France and the United States. His speech highlighted the ways in which both nations had fought side by side in four wars and how their respective revolutions had come to define the very notions of modern democracy and liberty.

It was an oration that shrewdly transformed the Mona Lisa into a symbol of the Cold War, representing Western progress in contrast to the repressive regime of the communist block. His closing would become the single most quoted line by the world press: "Politics and art, the life of action and the life of thought, the world of events and the world of imagination are one." The Mona Lisa had instantly become America's claim to the "guardianship of Western Civilization."

In the days to follow, the president's speech appeared on the front pages of newspapers around the world. Dramatic images from the evening had been successfully broadcast on television as planned, via Bell Lab's satellite *Relay*, delivering the first live, color, U.S.-to-Europe satellite transmission. "Television straddled the Atlantic via's America's new space communications station," noted the *Chicago Daily Tribune*, thereby flashing Mona Lisa's smile on two continents simultaneously.

In London and Paris, early-morning television viewers were able to watch Mona Lisa's unveiling live, and the broadcast was repeatedly replayed the following day. Thankfully, none of the chaos of the opening ceremony was caught on film, and a worldwide audience saw only the serene images of the President and First Lady standing majestically alongside the Mona Lisa. The audio transmission from the President's stirring speech came across perfectly, skillfully conveying his message: the French and American revolutions created the ideals of freedom and democracy, and these same ideals were ones that both France and America felt bound to uphold.

One scholar noted that Kennedy's speech had turned a political ceremony into a nearly religious service with the adoration of sacred images. "Our two revolutions helped define the meaning of democracy and freedom which are so much contested in the world today," Kennedy said. "Today, here in the Gallery, in front of this great painting, we are renewing our commitment to those ideals which have proved such a strong link through so many hazards." It didn't take much to recognize the President's references to war and the threat to freedom as a "cultural declaration of war" on communism. Indeed, the Mona Lisa had been elevated into a powerful tool of propaganda in the Cold War.

"I was exhausted and my face showed my anxiety," Madame Hours recalled of the moments following the unveiling. "The minute he had finished his speech, President Kennedy came towards me. 'You look worried, Madame Hours? Is it about the Mona Lisa?' he asked.

"Indeed, *Monsieur le Président*, I am worried, for if anything happens, I not only would lose face, but also my job!"

"If anything happens, I too will have problems," the President said, smiling. Then he asked several questions in English to which Madame Hours answered clumsily and begged his pardon.

"I speak English like a Spanish cow!" she said. He laughed and told her in precise French: "You can talk to me in French, Madame Hours."

Madame Hours wrote: "I was so happy, I took him by the arm." Then she asked, "How is it, *Monsieur le Président*, that you speak French?"

"I do not," Kennedy told her. Then in French he added: "The President of the United States only speaks English." At that instant, a photographer immortalized the encounter between the President and Mona Lisa's devoted guardian. A cherished souvenir of the historic evening, the photograph with President Kennedy was later proudly displayed in Madame Hours' laboratory office at the Louvre.

Once the evening ended, Walker escorted the President and First Lady to their car and waved goodbye as the limousine sped away to return to the White House. Walker later recalled the night as the worst moment of his professional life. As Lady Bird Johnson was leaving, she took Walker's arm and drew him aside to comfort him. She told him she knew how he felt.

"I feel worse!" she added. "I did not look at the invitation which read 'black tie,' and I told Lyndon to wear white tie." Vice President Johnson was the only person at the entire affair in full evening dress.

"After that night, so far as I know," Walker wrote later, "he never wore a white tie again, and when he became President tails were never to be seen at the White House."

Lady Bird's words of consolation helped soothe Walker's jangled nerves. "Mrs. Johnson's few words that night, however, restored my will to live," Walker said, "and I have been grateful to her ever since."

The last to leave the Gallery that night, Madame Hours returned to the French Embassy to rest. "I was exhausted but the first contact between America and the Mona Lisa had gone off extremely well," she said—in spite of the breakdown of the audio system and the unruly crowd.

When she arrived, Minister Malraux and Ambassador Alphand were seated in the embassy's Grand Salon drinking and talking. As she entered the room, the men stood to greet her. "Well then, how is she doing?" Malraux asked.

"Splendidly," she replied. "The conditions are stable." Malraux asked if Hours would return to the Gallery the following day and judge the public reaction so that he could describe the atmosphere for President de Gaulle.

"Of course, Monsieur le Ministre," she replied.

The next day, Madame Hours awoke with satisfaction, confident that the worst was over. An important lunch honoring French poet Saint-John Perse, winner of the Nobel Prize for literature, was planned at the Embassy, so Hours quickly dressed and raced to the National Gallery so that she could return in time for the luncheon. Hours arrived before the museum doors opened and verified the climatic conditions inside the West Hall as acceptable. She then waited for the throngs of visitors that had been queuing since dawn to "spend a few seconds face to face with our star."

"Women were carrying babies," Hours recalled. "One of them burst into tears on seeing the Mona Lisa to my amazement. I thought that our campaign had been well done since the visitors were clearly emotional and thrilled. For them, it was like meeting the effigy of European civilization."

Hours stood in the back of the West Hall for over an hour watching the thousands of museum visitors pass the painting one by one. Near 11:00 A.M., she suddenly felt the temperature in the room shoot dramatically upward.

At first she thought she was just tired and had become overheated, but her face became flushed from the heat caused by so many bodies in the room. Slipping between the visitors, she rushed toward the potted plants below the painting to examine the readings of the hygrothermographs.

She stepped over the red velvet rope, momentarily forgetting the security rule that she herself had established. At that moment the white-capped Marine guarding the Mona Lisa lashed out with his bayonet and hit her on the shoulder. The bayonet broke the strap of her brassiere and stopped her cold. The Secret Service agents, recognizing her immediately, shouted to the Marine not to harm her.

Yet one agent instinctively executed a "Japanese technique"—a blow given to the throat by the flat of the hand that takes the victim's breath away, and Hours fainted and collapsed to the ground.

She came to her senses in a museum office surrounded by two nurses proffering cold compresses. "What on earth happened?" she asked.

"The shock had been so violent that I remained unconscious for an hour," she remembered. "The moment I came somewhat to my senses, I thought about the time and how long I had been unconscious." After she regained her composure, she expressed her apologies to the museum's staff (in her haste she had forgotten to warn anybody that she was about to step over the rope and examine the hygrothermographs). When Walker learned of the incident, he was aghast.

Later that morning, a Gallery car took her to the Embassy where she changed her clothes and refreshed her hair and makeup. The luncheon guests were already seated in the Embassy's Grand Salon. When she walked into the room, Ambassador Alphand said dryly, "We've been waiting for you for the last quarter of an hour!"

Shaken from her ordeal, Hours was seated across from André Malraux and poet Saint-John Perse. The two literary giants talked amiably about the Mona Lisa and why she was so popular. "By transfiguring a profane face, Leonardo da Vinci gave to the soul of woman the idealization that Ancient Greece had previously given to her features," Malraux told the group. Saint-John Perse nodded in response.

Malraux then turned toward the tardy luncheon guest and asked Madame Hours for her opinion. "A portrait is always a projection of its creator, just as much as a reproduction of the model," she explained. "For me, she is the very image of the initiated, she is the one who knows, which is why she both intrigues and subjugates."

Noting that Madame Hours looked unusually pale, Malraux finally asked why she was late and what had happened.

"It was then that I told him about my misfortunes," she said, "the blow from the bayonet, the Japanese martial technique and my fainting."

"If you had been lying dead in front of the Mona Lisa," Alphand told her, "we would have had the front page of every newspaper in America."

Everyone at the table laughed. Some time later, following lunch, Hours asked permission to leave and lie down in her room. That night, the Ambassador's wife organized a luxurious tray loaded with lobster and champagne to be brought to her in bed, and she slept until morning.

Interestingly, there was an alternate version of the bayonet story that spread like wildfire among the museum staff. In this account, Madame Hours rushed up to Malraux and proceeded to tell him about the Marine who nearly stabbed her. Malraux looked her in the eye and reportedly told her, "Madame, had you been killed, I would have seen to it that you had a hero's burial."

John Walker read the morning newspapers with trepidation. Headlines declared that the affair planned with such high hopes had resulted in a chaotic disaster. One newspaper described the historic evening, "attended by the entire listing of the Green book," as a debacle. "But seldom, if ever, had the ruling class of the nation assembled in such full force." The press noted with amusement that no visiting head of state had ever been treated with as much care.

"Everything went wrong that night. And the papers picked up everything," recalled one longtime museum employee. It was no secret that Walker was in a state of despair at the newspaper reports filled with bad publicity concerning the National Gallery.

Minister Malraux may have quietly fumed over the disrespectful reception, but he never said so publicly. He seemed to go out of his way to add a patina of sophistication to the evening, and in one speech after the opening, Malraux again dismissed his French critics. Partially repeating his thoughts from the unveiling, he said that "the world's most powerful nation [paid] the most brilliant homage a work of art has ever received." Malraux also praised Mrs. Kennedy as one who is "always present when art, the United States and my country are linked."

Despite the political sensitivities, Walker was grateful that the French cultural minister seemed unaffected by the rude reception he had received. He was so bowled over by Malraux's character and good manners that Walker felt moved to write Malraux with his appreciation:

> *I want to thank you for all you have done to make possible the loan of the most famous painting in the world. Your speech last night was, in my experience, the most moving ever delivered about a work of art. I was deeply touched; as I know my compatriots will be when they read it in the newspapers and hear it on radio and television. With my warm appreciation of a gesture of friendship for the U.S. which will long be remembered.*

On the evening of January 10, White House advisor Arthur Schlesinger and his wife joined President and Mrs. Kennedy for dinner. The other guests included columnist Joseph Alsop and his socialite wife Susan Mary Alsop, and Jackie's sister, Lee Radziwill. In his diary, published by his sons in 2007, Schlesinger recalled that the President and Jackie were both in great form that night. The assembled guests—except possibly for her sister, Lee—were unaware of Jackie's pregnancy.

The conversation, Schlesinger recalled, ranged widely. "JFK discussed his conversation the night before with [André] Malraux. He said that he had tried to say to Malraux that all the talk about European nuclear deterrents, multilateral forces, etc., was unimportant and irrelevant, since it was all based on the expectation of a Soviet attack on Europe," which was highly unlikely.

The President dismissed the notion that nuclear weapons were necessary for prestige in the global community. What matters, he said, was the strength of the currency. "It is this, and not its nuclear weapons, which makes France a factor." The real danger for the future, he argued, was the potential for Chinese nuclear capability.

When Schlesinger asked how Malraux had responded, the President said that Malraux had not displayed any clear reaction. President Kennedy then mused to Schlesinger on the subject of the candor of political wives. "Whenever a wife says something, everyone in this town assumes that she is saying what her husband really thinks," he said. "Last night I suddenly heard Jackie telling Malraux that she thought [Konrad] Adenauer (the embattled West German Chancellor) was 'un peu gaga' [a little gaga]. I am sure that this has already been reported to Paris as my opinion."

Three days after the reception, Walker summoned the nerve to write Jackie a note of gratitude and regret. The note was laced with humor, but it could not conceal his deep embarrassment. It was the rare occasion in which Walker, known for his dry official correspondence, penned a note with any exclamation marks. Undoubtedly, the note made Jackie smile:

Dear Jackie,

I want to write you to ask you to thank the President for all he did Tuesday to save our opening from complete and absolute disaster! His humor, the heroic way he managed to make his voice a Public Address System in itself, his kindness to me in my darkest hour, all this I shall never forget. I simply cannot express my gratitude to him and to you. (I am sending you the other six Cézannes under separate cover !!!)

With affectionate best wishes from Margaret (who kept all sharp instruments away from me when we got home Tuesday night!) and from your devoted friend,

As ever,
John Walker

Later that evening, feeling the pressures of the past two weeks, Mrs. Kennedy wrote a memo to her new social secretary, Mary Gallagher, announcing that she planned to withdraw from many of her official duties and focus fully on her children. "I am taking the veil," she wrote. "I've had it with being First Lady all the time and now I'm going to give more attention to my children. I want you to cut off all outside activity—whether it's a glass of sherry with a poet or coffee with a king."

The botched evening at the Gallery may have had more of an impact than she let others know. By any measure, it was a disappointment. "No more art gallery dedications," she added, "no nothing unless absolutely necessary."

On January 13, André Malraux said his goodbyes and left Washington as thousands of museum goers waited in line to see the Mona Lisa. Walker expected large crowds, but even he was shocked by the steady stream of visitors who came to see the picture. Never in the history of the National Gallery had a single painting drawn so many in so few days. Museum visitors stood ten abreast in long, snaking lines that stretched for nearly a third of a mile. The amount of foot traffic was so voluminous that Gallery guards who normally recorded the number of visitors on a handheld device were unable to keep up. The last occasion when the Gallery had seen such crowds was in 1948 at the exhibition of art treasures from the German salt mines that had been brought to the National Gallery for safekeeping. Attendance during the forty-day exhibit was considered a world record for any museum in a comparable period.

Now a new phenomenon known as "Mona Mania" swept through the nation's capital, and no one could ignore it. Walker and his staff expected more than 1,000,000 Americans would come to the Gallery over the course of the next few weeks. For the first time in its history, Walker expanded the museum's visiting hours to accommodate the crowds. On weekdays, the Gallery would open at 10:00 A.M. and close its doors at 9:00 P.M., on Saturdays the Gallery would stay open an extra hour and close to the public at 10:00 P.M.

Despite the enthusiasm the exhibition unleashed, Walker could not shake his disappointment over the chaotic unveiling. "Crushed by the fiasco of what had been planned as a scintillating yet dignified evening," wrote Mary Van Rensselaer Thayer, Walker wrote "a sad letter of apology" to President Kennedy.

It was up to Jackie, however, to answer for the President, and she did so on the morning of January 15. The letter from the White House was hand delivered to the Gallery's executive offices, and Mrs. Foy rushed inside the director's office. She excused herself and shut Walker's door. Inside was a neatly typed note from the First Lady written on White House stationery:

Dear John,

What a sweet note you wrote. The president feels you have given him too much credit, and that it was a wonderful occasion. Please do not feel badly. That is the only thing that would really upset me.

You have been so wonderful and made so many undreamed of things possible. I could never tell you how much we both appreciate all that. You mustn't brood and make it worse in your mind. It was a fantastic evening. It is, as Malraux said, part of the magic of the Mona Lisa, almost an evil spell. She made it worthwhile and continues to do so every day—and Malraux adores you.

If you think a microphone going off was bad—wait until you see what happens when they see the Blue Room white!

So please don't ever have a backward thought again, and just think how beautifully you have hung the picture, and how happy it makes everyone to have it there with you watching over it.

Affectionately,
Jackie

The painting's American debut coincided with President Kennedy's escalating international and domestic prestige. Superbly utilized by the administration on the heels of the Cuban Missile Crisis, the exhibition helped solidify the President's image. The succeeding weeks were an exhilarating time, described by Arthur Schlesinger as a golden interlude in which Washington engaged in a collective effort to make itself brighter, gayer, and more intellectual. The First Lady was at the center of this new feeling.

"The most powerful nation in the world was represented by the most stunning couple imaginable," observed Jackie's friend, designer Oleg Cassini. "There was nobody who could touch Jackie in using style as a political tool."

"The things people had once held against her—the unconventional beauty, the un-American elegance, her taste for French clothes and French food—were suddenly no longer liabilities but assets," observed Arthur Schlesinger. He went on to state that "She represented all at once not a negation of her country but a possible fulfillment of it, a suggestion that America was not to be trapped forever in the bourgeois ideal, [but instead achieve] a dream of civilization and beauty.

"She had dreaded coming to the White House, fearing the end of family and privacy. But life for herself and her husband and children was never more intense and more complete. It turned out to be the time of the greatest happiness."

10

"Let Them See a Little Rembrandt, Too"

Despite his gracious note to Jackie, Walker was consumed with anger over the chaotic opening ceremony; he simply could not shake the disgrace of the night. The widespread news coverage of the affair only added to his irritation, and the very poor press proved an acute embarrassment. He told one close friend he could not help but recall the historic night at the Gallery in 1941, when the public address system worked so well for five times as many people.

"Unfortunately, Ernie Feidler had great confidence in a man called McIntosh who had installed our Lectour system," Walker told a friend. "He seems to have proved himself incompetent, and I am afraid the derogatory remarks about the Gallery were for the most part justified. It was very sad because we had planned everything with great care, and I am only now recovering from the state of shock I was in most of the evening."

A postmortem of the ceremony showed that much of the undesirable acoustics was caused by the din of the noisy crowd. Following the remarks made by Secretary of State Dean Rusk, the audience was quiet, but once Cultural Minister Malraux was introduced and he spoke in French, the crowd, not understanding his remarks, grew noisy, and the chatter increased until it was many times louder than the optimum loudspeaker level. This enormous sound was further amplified by the marble and became one hundred times the level of a single voice. Once the sound was picked up by the microphones, it overpowered the room.

Whatever the cause, Walker had disappointed Jackie and President Kennedy at the most important cultural function of the administration. Walker fired off terse letters to the professionals who had provided the malfunctioning sound system, wrote memos about immediate changes that he planned to institute at the National Gallery once the exhibition ended, and fielded unhappy phone calls from museum trustees. Employees and friends felt sorry for him, and family members worried about his health. The fiasco was, as the British liked to say, a "Dog's Breakfast."

Edward Folliard weighed in on the disastrous fête, which he had witnessed firsthand, but he took a longer view, waxing on the Gallery's important history and the impact on ordinary citizens: "The late Andrew W. Mellon would have enjoyed the official unveiling, which was by invitation only. He would have enjoyed it even though the arrangements went haywire and Mrs. Joseph P. Kennedy, Cabinet officers and other big shots of the New Frontier were blocked off by an overflow crowd and never even saw the ceremony.

"But what would have interested Mr. Mellon most of all were the remarks that came the next day when the general public was admitted. For the Pittsburgh Croesus, it should be remembered, made his princely gift of the National Gallery of Art, together with his own collection as a 'nucleolus' to the American people. Naturally, therefore, he would have listened keenly to the judgments of

Joe Blow, Mrs. Blow and all the little Blows as they gazed at the Mona Lisa."

Once the doors opened, the real purpose for the Lady's visit—a chance for everyday Americans to see one of the most beautiful works of art in human history—was put into motion. Shivering visitors stood in the freezing cold as the line stretched down the sidewalks of both Constitution Avenue and Madison Drive all the way to Sixth Street.

The first visitor to arrive was Ruth Amanuel of Langley Park. "I'm frozen stiff," she told reporters with frosty breath and lips turned blue. "I've been here since 7:30 A.M., but I think it will be worth it." After she glimpsed the painting, Ruth was overcome. "Oh, her smile! Everything they said about her was true."

The Gallery guards managed the traffic flow with skill. Once the line of ten abreast entered the museum, guards thinned the line to three or four inside the Great Rotunda, and by the time viewers neared the painting, the line was reduced to two abreast. As viewers approached they could see the Lady from a distance suspended against the sweeping wine-colored baffle.

"It is not a knock-out at first glance," noted *Post* reporter Jean White. "But no one, it seems, views the Mona Lisa without comment."

During the first hour it was on view, nearly 3,000 people filed past the painting. Walker calculated that by the end of the day, more than 12,000 people would pass in front of the picture. On day two, more than 28,000 people endured the bone-chilling cold to come and see it. Many visitors brought their children. Walker noticed that in particular, many poor families from the surrounding neighborhoods had bundled their children in hats and scarves and brought them to the museum to see Leonardo's masterpiece. According to news reports it was the largest number of people to ever visit the National Gallery of Art in a single day.

Even André Malraux was moved by the extensive outpouring of humanity for the Mona Lisa. "In Washington, poor women came with their children and approached the Mona Lisa with their eyes lowered, raised them to see it, then went into the crowd and came back again, as if seeing icons," he said later.

In the exhibition's first four days, nearly 80,000 people saw the painting. By comparison, average weekly museum attendance numbered approximately 3,000. Walker now predicted that the exhibition would be the largest in the Gallery's history, surpassing the attendance of any exhibition in America.

Walker showed little emotion publicly, but he was so anxious that he was never able to relax and fully join in the "Lisa Fever" sweeping the capitol. As he watched the crowds stream through the museum, Walker later wrote, he wondered about the significance of those endless lines of people who waited for hours for a glimpse of Leonardo's painting. At the height of the exhibition he heard one visitor call out to a guard, "Say officer, what do they use this place for when the Mona Lisa isn't here?" Walker was stunned by the question, and it haunted him for several days.

Finally, he later confessed, he decided that—despite his earlier protestations—he had been given a gift by becoming temporary custodian of France's precious relic. Never before at the National Gallery had a single painting drawn so many visitors in so few days.

There were many amusing and touching occurrences along the way. One young boy opened his coat and let his puppy peek out for a quick glimpse of the picture before guards could stop him.

Thirty-six art lovers from North Carolina chartered a plane to fly to Washington and painted a likeness of the Mona Lisa on the fuselage. Visitors came from Memphis, Myrtle Beach, New Orleans and New London, Connecticut, *Time* magazine reported, for their chance to experience the treasure from the Louvre. As the exhibition gained unprecedented attention, Walker directed guards to route visitors through other galleries so they would be forced to view more art objects before they exited the museum.

"This is delightful," Walker said. "She's attracting people who have never been here before, and we route them through other rooms on their way out—let them see a little Rembrandt, too."

The international pageantry connected with Mona Lisa's visit to America failed to sustain U.S.-Franco goodwill for long. On January 14, President de Gaulle hosted a rare press conference at the Elysée Palace in front of 700 newsmen in which he rejected Kennedy's offer of Polaris missiles and rejected Great Britain's entry into the European Common Market. "The American interest is not always the French interest," he declared. De Gaulle preferred to pursue an independent nuclear arms program known as the Force de frappe outside the U.S.-dominated NATO. "We cannot accept Polaris missiles and, at the same time, pursue our national effort . . . We have the A-bomb. We will have the H-bomb. And, eventually, we will have three-stage missiles," he announced waving his hands vigorously amid the haze of television lights and flashbulbs.

Near the Mona Lisa exhibition, however, these serious disagreements were ignored, and goodwill seemingly reigned between representatives of the two nations. President Kennedy did, however, slip in a humorous reference to the two countries' nuclear arms debate in his remarks at the opening:

> Mr. Minister, we in the United States are grateful for this loan from the leading artistic power in the world, France. In view of the recent meeting at Nassau, I must note further that this painting has been kept under careful French control, and that France has even sent along its own commander-in-chief, Minister Malraux. And I want to make it clear that, grateful as we are for this painting, we will continue to press ahead with the effort to develop an independent artistic force and power of our own.

Malraux and de Gaulle appreciated Kennedy's play on words and understood that the mocking reference to France's grand plans for its own nuclear defense system was meant to be taken lightly, but the French press responded indignantly at what they perceived as ridicule of France's ambitions. The French media fray irked de Gaulle because he fundamentally supported the deep historic ties between the two countries, even if he not-so-secretly believed France was superior.

De Gaulle complained to his cabinet members at the time, "No French newspaper has remarked that the prestige of France has risen to such a degree that the president of the United States strengthened his own position in America by showing the intimacy of his ties to de Gaulle!"

Such were the tenuous ties of diplomatic amity between America and France. "So tangled are the strains and stresses of the affair," noted the *New Republic*, that references to the relationship ought to be called "Franco-American spaghetti."

In the middle of Washington's encounter with the Mona Lisa, Jackie completed her extensive restoration of the Green Room. It was now an authentic Federal Parlor of the early nineteenth century. It had been a complicated affair to restore the odd-shaped space with its six doors, and Henry Francis du Pont and Stéphane Boudin had painstakingly considered every square inch before the room was finally finished. Several major pieces of antique furniture were acquired, including Daniel Webster's sofa and the tea urn once owned by John and Abigail Adams.

The walls were now covered in a delicate moss green watered-silk moiré fabric. The room featured matching green drapes, an Empire mantelpiece, and the early American furnishings of Sheraton, Chippendale, and Hepplewhite. Mounted prominently in the room was James McNeil Whistler's mysterious painting *Nocturne*, a gift from Kennedy friends Averell and Marie Harriman. Jackie adored the painting, and after it was displayed she wrote the Harrimans: "Think of people seeing it generations from now. It will be like seeing a Poussin given by Talleyrand—our Talleyrand!"

The two landscapes by Paul Cézanne from the National Gallery moved upstairs to the Yellow Oval Room, the semiformal drawing room in the private quarters of the executive mansion that featured picturesque views of the rolling green lawns and the city's monuments. The president found the completed Louis XVI sitting room "an inviting place for private meetings and gatherings of friends, and he referred to it as his easy room," noted two experts on the history of the Kennedy White House restoration. "The Yellow Oval Room was the most completely French room in the White House, and this alone made it one of the First Lady's favorites."

From the moment the exhibition opened on January 9, 1963 until it closed on the evening of February 3, Mona Lisa played to a full house, and the National Gallery looked like Grand Central Station. Once Walker announced that the Gallery would extend its hours and remain open until 9:00 P.M., the crowds grew even larger, and museum guards were on high alert watching for anything unusual or suspicious.

On January 14, alarming news came from the nearby Phillips Gallery that a watercolor by Swiss artist Paul Klee had been stolen. Police reports indicated that the frame and painting had been wrenched from the wall despite a new security system that had recently been installed. Officials were shocked that the burglary could take place with such apparent ease and so close in proximity to the highly watched Mona Lisa exhibition.

Theft of the Mona Lisa had been a serious concern during the voyage at sea, but the Klee burglary renewed Walker's fear that something untoward might occur inside the museum despite the presence of the Secret Service and extra guards. Walker could do little more than put his faith in John Campion and the detail of Secret Service agents who remained on vigil inside the museum twenty-four hours a day.

Americans who saw the Mona Lisa and witnessed the "most comprehensive smile in the folios of Western art" became instant art lovers. The National Gallery confirmed this in its exhibition catalogue: "The enthusiasm and adoration showered upon it have never been equaled. It is regarded by many as the most beautiful painting in the world."

When the question was posed to John Walker as to what exactly made the Mona Lisa so great, he said to ask Madame Hours. "It is a picture that takes one in completely. I cannot resist it," she replied.

From a scientific point of view, the portrait of feminine wonders was very much a mystery. Experts at the Louvre closely examined the painting with ultraviolet and infrared rays and yet still couldn't explain exactly how it was painted by the artist. "There is a quality to the brush work," Madame Hours observed, "that defies analysis."

The painting technique that produced the translucent brush strokes was known as sfumato, derived from the Italian word *fumo*, meaning smoke. Leonardo da Vinci was known for the technique, which created the delicacy and realism of the flesh tints and smoky shadows of the Mona Lisa's eyes and mouth.

"The fine and well-pumiced gesso ground is covered with a thin layer of paint transparent to X-rays," noted Walker. "The subtlety of the transitions between light and shadow is extreme but quite perceptible in photographs of details as well as in X-ray photographs . . . we may wonder with Madeleine Hours 'if this is not the ultimate of art, but of an art which is no longer painting, when the physical phenomenon dissolves in the expression.'"

Walker labored over the text for the exhibition catalogue, knowing that it would be scrutinized closely by art authorities from around the world. He felt the public was owed an accurate historical description of the painting and its importance to humanity. He sent his composition to the world's finest art authorities for corrections, and, after officials at the Louvre including Madame Hours had approved the text, Walker published the catalogue that became an instant collector's item:

PORTRAIT OF

Mona Lisa

KNOWN AS "LA GIOCONDA"

BY LEONARDO DA VINCI

CATALOGUE DESCRIPTION

Mona Lisa is seated; the semi-circular wooden chair with arm and rails is just visible. She is shown from below the waist, her arms bent and leaning a little on the left arm of the chair, her bust turned slightly toward the spectator, almost full face. Her hands are crossed, the right hand over the left wrist. Her fingers are long, her face round, her cheeks full. Her dark chestnut hair falls in ripples onto her shoulders and is covered with a dark but transparent veil. Her only faintly reddened lips suggest a smile. She wears a dark green low-cut gown pleated across the front of the bust and embroidered with a tracery of gold threads. She is wearing no jewels.

Mona Lisa's head is silhouetted against a landscape seen from a bird's-eye view and forming two distinct sections. In the lower section and as high as the model's neck, there is a reddish-brown landscape, with a bridge over a blue stream on the right, and on the left a winding road that leads the spectator into an imaginary world. In the upper section, the atmosphere shades from olive-green to greenish-blue, and the mountainous landscape, bristling with rock peaks, disappears into the mist.

WHO IS MONA LISA?

Mona Lisa, born in Florence in 1479, was the daughter of Antonio Maria di Noldo Gherardini, who lived in the via Maggio, in the San Spirito district of Florence. In 1495 she married Francesco di Bartolommeo di Zanobi del Giocondo (hence the name "La Gioconda"), a Florentine official already twice a widower. She was about twenty-four when Leonardo painted her portrait.

Some critics have claimed the model to be Isabella d'Este, an admirer of the painter and one of the most cultivated princesses of the period, whose portrait Leonardo had drawn in crayon.

Venturi has attempted to identify the painting of La Gioconda with the lost portrait of Costanza d'Avalos, Duchess of Francavilla, painted by Leonardo, according to a contemporary poem, in a mourning costume "under the lovely black veil." Charles de Tolnay accepts the identification with Lisa Gherardini del Giocondo, but considers the portrait "an idealization of her features, purified of contingencies and wrought into an inner image of feminine beauty." André Malraux writes that the painting "is doubtless the subtlest homage genius has paid to a living face."

Whatever it was, the picture had cast its magic spell for centuries. "If there is a strong connection between the paradisiacal woman in the painting and the genius who painted her, there is also a similar relationship between the painting itself and the visitor," noted Jean-Pierre Mohen of the Louvre. "The work actually produces a strange kind of rapture which is part of its greatness."

As Washingtonians and visitors from all parts arrived at the National Gallery, chief curator Perry Cott kept a careful vigil. He was nearly always present, watching from the sidelines as the enormous crowds passed through the museum and stood in hushed awe in front of the painting. He checked the thermostat readings hundreds of times, noting the tiniest change in his notebook.

Tens of thousands filed past the Mona Lisa. Some of the luckiest visitors were small children who were perched upon their father's shoulders where they were treated to a bird's-eye view of the masterpiece. The Gallery staff went out of their way to accommodate groups of visiting schoolchildren who arrived in big yellow buses holding hands and chaperoned by their grade school teachers. Many children returned to their classrooms to learn more about the artist who had painted the picture, and others were invited to draw their own Mona Lisa with crayolas.

Many of the city's elderly residents also came to gaze at the famous face. Among them, many were women. "It's the most exciting day of my life," announced one great-grandmother. Feeling that she did not have enough time to sufficiently admire the Mona Lisa, the woman moved to the back of the line to get a chance to see the masterpiece one more time.

Seven days into the exhibition, the climatic conditions inside the museum appeared satisfactory. On January 16, Perry Cott dispatched updated details to Madame Hours concerning the painting's status based on the readings of the two hygrothermograph recorders hidden in the flower pots near the white-capped Marines. Now preparing for the picture's New York debut, Madame Hours was temporarily residing at the Stanhope Hotel at Fifth Avenue near the Metropolitan Museum.

"*Chère amie*," Cott wrote Hours. "All goes well with 'the Lady,' no change that one can see. The temperature is always between 68–70 degrees Fahrenheit depending on the crowd (which is immense), and the humidity always around 50–51%." The preexisting warping of the poplar wood was still visible, but it had not worsened. If the temperature remained constant, Cott felt the condition of the Mona Lisa would remain stable.

The Mona Lisa mania gripping the United States prompted some Italians to feel their country's contributions had been unfairly overlooked. Italian Prime Minister Amintore Fanfani convened a press conference to correct "an important misconception" that Leonardo was Italian and not French. His pronouncement sparked more debate. After all, Italy didn't unite until 1861. Leonardo da Vinci may have been culturally Italian, but he was more accurately a Florentine. And while he started work on the Mona Lisa in his homeland, most experts believe the painting was executed between 1503 and 1506 during Leonardo's second stay in Florence. He is thought to have finished it in France, where he lived the last three years of his life under protection of the French king.

Be that as it may, Italian or French, Leonardo had triggered a cultural explosion in the United States more than four hundred fifty years after his death. French Ambassador Hervé Alphand reiterated this point by saying she was no longer a painting but a talisman. "The Mona Lisa is more than an extraordinary painting, she is the ideal woman, as well as the ideal work of art."

The crowds kept coming, and museum visitors snapped up tens of thousands of exhibition catalogues in the Gallery bookstore. Outside the museum street peddlers busily hawked Mona Lisa merchandise. Postcards featuring the masterpiece were printed with the caption "Mona Lisa, We salute the First Lady of the land, Mrs. John F. Kennedy, for bringing to America the First Lady of the world."

Walker had managed to keep his promise to Jackie, and the exhibition, despite its disastrous opening night, had exceeded all expectations. Now it was time for Mona Lisa to travel to New York

City for display in the halls of the august Metropolitan Museum. Walker's anxiety reached its human limits as he prepared to hand over the Mona Lisa to museum director James J. Rorimer. It would be an excruciating experience to pass responsibility for the masterpiece to someone else. "I made one enemy in life," Walker later said, "and that man was Jim Rorimer."

Manhattan Falls in Love

The weather could not have been more miserable for Mona Lisa's departure. John Walker had been encouraged when an afternoon of sunshine gave a brief respite to the gloomy wet cold, but on the morning she was scheduled to leave the National Gallery, an icy wave descended upon the city with wind gusts of thirty-six miles an hour. Cold air chilled the city as Walker anxiously prepared the painting for transport to the Metropolitan Museum of Art. At Jackie's request, Walker traveled with the painting to New York.

In the early morning of February 4, the Mona Lisa was gently removed from its frame. After close inspection and photographs were taken, Walker watched as curators prepared the picture to be packed inside its traveling case. Just like the arrangements made for her excursion from New York to Washington, on the return trip, her large wooden box was delicately placed inside the back of the Gallery's black van and secured with straps mounted to the floor. Behind the wheel was Hillary Brown, the museum's long-time driver. Inside the truck, seated next to the Mona Lisa's box once again was heavily armed Secret Service agent John Campion. As the small convoy left the museum's gates and traveled along Constitution Avenue, Walker watched anxiously as frigid gusts buffeted the well-armed procession.

Mona Lisa had generated the biggest blockbuster exhibition in the National Gallery's history, and the famous lady had completed her Washington tour with no apparent damage. "No tears were shed however over the departure of their glamorous feminine guest by the National Gallery guards," noted the *Post.* "Happily anticipating an end to the unusually large crowds, the guards had written on the blackboard in their locker room: "MONA GO HOME!" Walker didn't plan it so, but at the exact moment that the Mona Lisa was headed north from Washington, the other traveling masterpiece, Whistler's Mother, was headed south. The two convoys passed one another along the Jersey Turnpike. "The old lady was on her way down to Atlanta," noted the *New York Times*, "and the young woman was going up to New York, both by courtesy of President de Gaulle."

Unlike John Walker, Metropolitan Museum of Art Director James Rorimer did not remove every single piece of art near the location where the high-profile French visitor was to be installed. He also refused to move the Met's $2.3 million Rembrandt, *Aristotle Contemplating a Bust of Homer*, from its station in the museum's grand entrance hall. "There are many things in *Aristotle* that please me more than the Mona Lisa," he said.

Rorimer had designed a handsome installation inside the Gothic Room, the museum's largest space, featuring sweeping sixty-five-foot ceilings. He planned to hang the picture on the wrought-iron doorway in the center of the Medieval Sculpture Hall, a "solid chapel-like recess of steel and wood," which was also fireproof. Special spotlights had been mounted to focus on the picture. He had had a "dry run" with a painting by Lorenzo de Credi and had learned how to position the light for minimal reflection off the bulletproof glass.

Rorimer had worked in tandem with Madame Hours to position the hidden hygrothermograph recorders in an ideal location to measure the room's temperature and humidity, and Rorimer was confident that the Secret Service agents who now patrolled his museum would fully protect the painting. Instead of placing two marine guards to flank the picture, as they had at the National Gallery, Rorimer decided to use two regular museum guards. "I'm rather pleased," he said. "Marine dress uniforms are a little too colorful; they tend to distract attention from the exhibit. Our guards have nice drab uniforms."

The crowds were another issue altogether. "The accumulation of dust from scuffling shoes!" he exclaimed. "We'll have literally balls of dust . . . Well, we get them anyway," he added, "there'll just be more. I've never known anything so extraordinary as the degree of interest." He had written a blueprint with a plan for foot traffic that would lead visitors into the museum's main entrance where they would proceed in a more or less straight line to the Medieval Sculpture Hall. "They'll have to go four abreast part of the way, in the narrow exhibition hall south of the main staircase."

Rorimer had sent "spies" to Washington to see how Walker had hung the masterpiece and to gauge the reaction to it. His informants had gleefully reported that the painting was hung too high and was barely visible because of the shiny bulletproof glass. The lighting was abysmal, and visitors were allowed only four or five seconds to pause in front of the picture before they were pushed along.

Rorimer decided to change all that at the Metropolitan. "It's our desire not to hurry people," he said, insisting that guards let museum goers linger as long as was reasonable. He also wanted the visitors waiting in line to get an education. "We've put up little posters—enlargements of the hands and eyes of the Mona Lisa with captions—for them to look at and read as they pass by."

Madame Hours had returned to Paris shortly before the Mona Lisa left for New York and waited nervously for news from her office at the Louvre laboratory. On February 5, National Gallery curator Perry Cott wrote to inform her of the celebrated lady's status. He had examined her closely after removing the picture from its frame and bulletproof glass shield. "I examined the painting carefully and could detect no change in it from the time we examined it together," he told her, and he sent large color photographs taken immediately after the picture was inspected.

"We are now all breathing more easily. As you will have heard by now, the famous lady arrived safely in the Metropolitan Museum."

In truth, Madame Hours may have felt more confident in leaving her charge behind with the director of the Metropolitan. Rorimer was familiar with protecting valuable art under hazardous conditions. In the Army he served in the Monuments, Fine Arts, and Archives Section of the Western District's Seventh Army, where he tracked down and preserved significant works of art stolen by the Nazis, and he had supervised many directives on the care of Allied treasures that had been hidden throughout France and elsewhere. The atmospheric conditions for the Mona Lisa that had been demanded by Madame Hours were exactly what Rorimer had suggested to Louvre curators during the war just prior to the liberation of Paris. Rorimer was proud to say that he was the first Allied officer to enter the museum after the Nazis fled.

Like fellow museum director John Walker, Rorimer was a Harvard man who developed an early interest in art. His father was an interior designer in Cleveland, and Rorimer grew up appreciating architecture and the decorative arts. By the time he entered college he had already begun collecting rare ancient pottery.

At the Met, Rorimer became a medieval specialist and presided over a building boom at the museum that greatly expanded its space and collections. He supervised construction of the Cloisters (the branch of the museum featuring the art and architecture of medieval Europe) in such detail that he even built forms out of gunnysacks to guide the masons as they laid its stone walls. When Rembrandt's *Aristotle Contemplating a Bust of Homer* emerged from a private collection to go on auction in 1961, Rorimer bid $2.3 million to secure it for the Met, which made it one of the most expensive paintings in the world. "Ridiculous," clucked the *New York Herald Tribune* on behalf of many observers. "No picture is worth that much money."

Rorimer's dynamism and flair for showmanship was a boon to the Met, though, and under his leadership attendance soared. But Walker, who competed with Rorimer for the favor of the country's wealthiest art donors, thought Rorimer exaggerated his accomplishments. In one thank-you letter to Walker for the National Gallery's loan of eighteenth-century French drawings, Rorimer bragged that on a Sunday at the Met the drawings had been viewed by 60,000 people. Walker thought that number sounded preposterous because the Met was open only part of the day on Sundays, so he called the Pentagon to ask experts how long it would take for columns of soldiers to march by a particular point. "I found that if they never did anything but walk past, it would be the same as Jim Rorimer had claimed. Which of course had nothing to do with the truth at all," Walker said.

After the Mona Lisa was hung inside the large Medieval Sculpture Hall under the direction of James Rorimer, Walker undoubtedly felt a tinge of envy. Even the typically brutal art critics of *Connoisseur* magazine remarked on the stunning display, noting its beauty, simplicity, and importance. "As you drew near the beautiful antique doorway (a wrought-iron choir screen from the cathedral of Valladolid: a gift of the William Randolph Hearst Foundation) a reverent mood fell upon you, and you were inescapably conscious of the fact that you were there for the purpose of doing homage to a more-than-earthly queen of art and beauty."

Rorimer had more to work with in the sweeping space of the Medieval Sculpture Hall than Walker did in the noisy barrel-vaulted West Sculpture Hall at the National Gallery. At the Metropolitan, the painting hung at the perfect eye sight line, not too high and not too low. Displayed against a hanging of modern French green and red wool-and-rayon brocade, it was lit from the top, bottom, and sides. Bulletproof glass protected the painting's surface, but somehow the glare from the custom spotlights did not reflect as much as it had in Washington, distorting the visitor's view. The presentation was flawless.

At 10:00 A.M. on Thursday, February 7, the exhibition opened amid a citywide newspaper strike, but it still generated a "cultural blitzkrieg." Traffic was jammed and lines of museum-goers waited for hours in the bitter cold to get inside. The first citizen in line was Brooklyn taxi driver Joseph Lasky, a "self-admitted lover of the finer things," who arrived at the museum at 4:30 A.M. By the time the doors opened, a line extended down the museum steps and along Fifth Avenue.

The city had fallen in love with Mona. Bars and restaurants got in on the act by generating a new cocktail in honor of the famous visitor. Simply called "The Mona Lisa," the yummy concoction was made up of cognac on the rocks with a dash of dry vermouth. Shopkeepers sold Mona Lisa knick-knacks by the boxload, and the famous name suddenly appeared everywhere in cartoons and advertisements. Suddenly all things Mona Lisa were terribly in vogue; well-known hairdresser Michel Kazan created a new Madonna-like parted coiffure that was the talk of the town when he presented it at the Pierre Hotel ballroom for 200 international fashion editors.

Women up and down the eastern seaboard asked their hair dressers to give them "the Mona Lisa look." *Life* magazine printed an eye-catching full-page photograph of one model sporting the sleek sexy hair style. In Manhattan, the Mona Lisa hairdo created by Kazan became "the biggest thing since Cleopatra."

"Women will be aiming high for beauty this spring," noted the *Boston Herald.* "Jackie is not completely out of the running but sights have been set on no less a beauty than the Mona Lisa."

Mona Lisa had barely arrived in the Big Apple when a diplomatic row erupted over a party thrown by the Metropolitan Museum in her honor. The embarrassing flap was triggered by none other than Ambassador Alphand, who objected to sitting with U.N. Secretary-General U. Thant at the head table, insisting that the loan of the Mona Lisa was a strictly French-American gesture. The French Ambassador, aware of the disdain with which French President Charles de Gaulle regarded the United Nations, asked Thant to be moved. When Thant learned of the snub, he chose not to attend the dinner at all, while other U.N. officials also sent their regrets.

On February 7, Jackie Kennedy unexpectedly arrived in New York to help smooth out the situation by attending an important luncheon at the United Nations. On her right was seated U.N. Secretary-General Thant and seated on her left was Adlai Stevenson, chief American delegate to the United Nations. "As a roomful of diplomats from 110 nations watched, Mrs. Kennedy managed to make it clear that she, the President's wife, found the company of Thant and Stevenson about the best thing she could think of at the moment," wrote the St. Louis, Missouri, *Post-Dispatch*.

The moment had been artfully coordinated by President and Mrs. Kennedy to demonstrate American support for the embattled United Nations secretary. Jackie posed for photographers on her way inside the building, dressed in a sleeveless oyster-white dress and black mink coat. One newspaper also noted the First Lady's "Mona Lisa smile." Through her well-timed appearance, she avoided a nasty diplomatic fracas in the middle of the New York exhibition. Her surprise attendance "smoothed over one of the biggest protocol flaps in years," and ensured that global media attention remained focused on the Mona Lisa exhibition and Franco-U.S. goodwill. "In a single whisper-voiced appearance at the U.N.," added the *Post-Dispatch*, "sweeping out of her mink coat and into the delegates' dining room, the President's wife mended two badly battered diplomatic fences at once."

In the first seven days of the New York exhibition, more than 250,000 people viewed the painting, the highest recorded attendance in the museum's history. On Valentine's Day, Rorimer announced that because of the unprecedented demand and public response, the museum would remain open until 9:00 P.M. on week days. A festive ambiance filled the surrounding streets as thousands of New Yorkers descended on Fifth Avenue to find the back of the line. So many city dwellers came to see the portrait that *The New Yorker* calculated visitors would average only four seconds each to contemplate the masterpiece, noting that Leonardo's sfumato technique had taken him more than four years to paint the Mona Lisa.

Eclectic arguments erupted among museum visitors over Mona Lisa's true identity, renewing speculation that the Mona Lisa was in fact Leonardo's self-portrait. (In 1913, one expert claimed that while the lower portion of the subject's face is that of a woman, the upper portion was that of a man.) New York art lovers hunted for hidden coded messages and debated the real reasons behind the enigmatic smile. Director Rorimer and his staff even received passionate love letters addressed to the Mona Lisa and left for her at the Met.

Visitors may have been rushed as they were ushered past the painting's display, but museum goers expressed a certain satisfaction in the experience, one that reached a spiritual dimension. As they approached, their voices grew quiet, a churchlike stillness permeating the atmosphere. Near the masterpiece the crowds were transformed into pilgrims who, after waiting for hours, were allowed to "approach the sacred crypt and behold the holy relics," wrote author Donald Sassoon.

The First Lady's innate sense of the dramatic and the pageantry associated with the picture's unveiling had led many Americans to think of the Mona Lisa as a harbinger of peace, and a great many came to believe that she was "personally their own." Museum visitors earned the right to that sentiment, noted one critic, by the long outdoor wait in freezing weather for their chance to glimpse the masterpiece.

"The fact that the Lady resides in Paris," noted *Connoisseur* magazine, is, after all, a mere detail. "They will call on her there, who have seen her here, to see her again; those who have not, to make up for a great historical opportunity lost.

"By popular vote, she has been elected our Perennial First Lady of Art. Who would contest her this title? After so many centuries, may she not have grown tired of the Old World's rather perfunctory admiration?—the fresh heady incense must rise like a pleasant savour in her finely chiseled nostrils of palest ivory."

Between February 6 and March 4, 1963, more than 1,000,000 people came to see the famous face at the Metropolitan Museum of Art. The exhibition opened up the rarified world of fine art to those who had never experienced it before, and both the National Gallery of Art and the Metropolitan Museum continued to receive record crowds long after the exhibit closed.

As long lines snaked around the sidewalks of the Metropolitan Museum of Art, Walker was attending to the lengthy list of details concerning the painting's safe return to French officials. As early as February 8, he was compiling memorandums for the Gallery files concerning the exact details connected with the hand off.

He dictated list after list, as if committing the details to paper would make them reality. The question remained whether he could trust Rorimer to meet his obligations to fully protect the painting.

As if he were preparing a legal defense ahead of time, Walker noted in his official memo, "The responsibility for the painting will be that of the Metropolitan Museum until it is delivered to its cabin on the SS *United States* when the responsibility will shift to the French government."

Rorimer, whose career at the Met spanned thirty-six years, appeared to take his stewardship of the Mona Lisa in stride, treating it like any other object on loan for exhibition. Relaxed and at ease, he smiled and posed for photographs in the various press conferences and held one-on-one conversations with the press. Walker, on the other hand, felt as if real danger lurked around every corner. His anxiety grew so intense, in fact, that his private physician increased his prescription for mild tranquilizers to help him relax and get some sleep. The "Mona Lisa Anxiety pills" were a godsend for a man who was in a constant state of torment over the visitor from Paris.

Walker continued to press for absolute adherence to the plan coordinated with the French government and insisted that Rorimer fully understand that, following the closing of the exhibition on March 4, the picture was to remain in its frame until the morning of her departure. After inspection and packing, it would leave the Met and travel by motorcade to the point where the painting would be placed onboard the SS *United States* bound for Paris.

The red, white, and blue crowned ship was the fastest ocean liner ever built and was known by her nickname, the "All American Beauty." The ship stretched 990 feet with spacious accommodations for 2,000 passengers and 1,000 crew. Once the picture was safely tethered inside its suite, Secret Service responsibility for the Mona Lisa would cease. Walker felt it was imperative that the picture not be unpacked for inspection for receipt purposes inside the cabin. At all times aboard ship, the picture must stay safely packed inside its custom traveling case.

Walker intended to limit Rorimer's direct control by hiring a special trucking firm to handle movement of the masterpiece from the museum to the SS *United States*. Walker and museum administrator Ernest Feidler had investigated a roster of possibilities and decided on the Sofia Brothers trucking firm, which had a reputation for moving delicate objects. (The same firm had moved the historic painting *Aristotle Contemplating a Bust of Homer*, from the Parke-Bernet galleries to the Metropolitan after Rorimer purchased it at auction.) When Feidler contacted the firm, Theodore Sofia Jr., the company's vice president, assured him that he would personally escort the painting with a hand-picked crew.

Jackie insisted that Walker return to France aboard the SS *United States* with the painting and remain with the masterpiece until it was safely returned to the Louvre. Walker penned more than a dozen drafts of a receipt of discharge that he planned to give officials during the exchange onboard the ship that would formally pass responsibility back to Mona Lisa's French caretakers.

The very last chance for the public to view Leonardo's masterpiece was Monday, March 4. Museum staffers planned to close the doors promptly at 9:00 P.M. so that the painting would have two full days of rest before she would embark on her long ocean journey home. The end of the exhibition was marked by a special ceremony that was attended by museum directors Rorimer and Walker in addition to Edouard Morot-Sir, Cultural Counselor to the French Embassy, and Albert Beuret, representing the French Ministry of Cultural Affairs.

Walker delivered a poignant address to commemorate the occasion. Long a believer in the exclusivity of institutions of fine art, he publicly acknowledged that something extraordinary had occurred with Mona Lisa's American exhibition. He believed strongly that museums existed primarily for the connoisseur, for the satisfaction of people like himself. His words reflected just how much his ideas about a fine arts museum and its purpose had changed:

> The Mona Lisa has had a fantastic success in the United States. While it was in Washington and New York it drew more people than any World Series or football game or prize fight in history. What is the explanation?
>
> First of all the personality of this mysterious sitter has enthralled spectators since the day Leonardo immortalized her. Second, the painting is a milestone in the history of art, as influential for other painters as any single picture ever executed. And third, the events in its fascinating history from the time Francis the First persuaded Leonardo to make France his home and the portrait arrived at Amboise, down to its carefully planned and guarded trip to the United States, have captivated the imaginations of hundreds of thousands of people.
>
> But I think we should look a little deeper than these three explanations. I believe that the [nearly two million] people who stood in line, sometimes for hours on end, to spend a few minutes looking at the Mona Lisa were paying a tribute to art that goes far beyond this single picture.
>
> They wanted to see it because they knew it was a peak of artistic achievement, a summit of human creativity and they wanted their children to see it for the same reason. Perhaps afterwards they felt a little better to belong to the human species, perhaps they felt they shared a little in Leonardo's genius, the way the Catholic Church teaches that we share in the merits of the saints.
>
> The Mona Lisa was a catalytic agent as well. It caused a kind of aesthetic explosion in the minds of a certain percentage of these people. I used to go into the various galleries while the Mona Lisa was in Washington, and they were packed with visitors who had come to see one picture but had stayed to see the whole collection.
>
> Since the Mona Lisa has left, our attendance has been unusually high. This famous portrait stirred some impulse toward

> beauty in thousands of human beings, who had never felt that impulse before. Monsieur Malraux, the French Minister of Culture, who sent the picture to America deserves our heartfelt thanks for this brave gesture of friendship to this country.

Miraculously, everything worked according to plan. At 7:00 A.M. on the morning of March 7, museum curators removed the painting from its gilded frame and placed it inside its special traveling case. At 9:00 A.M., special riggers from the Sofia Brothers firm gingerly carried the crate from the museum storage entrance at 84th Street and Fifth Avenue to an unmarked van. Secret Service Agent Campion traveled in the back of the vehicle with the painting. The van slowly traveled to Pier 86 along the North River, and, at the dock, riggers carried the crate onboard the SS *United States*. Two special guards from the Louvre and the assistant director of the cabinet of the Minister of Cultural Affairs greeted her. The painting was situated in her luxury cabin and secured by special straps to the floor. Agent Campion then shook the hands of French officials and said his goodbyes.

At that precise moment, John Walker was handed three copies of a signed acknowledgment that read: "Received in Cabins M72, M74, and M75, onboard SS *United States*, at Pier 86, North River, West 46th Street, New York City, the painting Mona Lisa by Leonardo da Vinci, its frame, and the containers for both, all in the same condition as delivered to the National Gallery of Art on December 19, 1962. All responsibility of all officials of the government of the United States of America, the National Gallery of Art, and the Metropolitan Museum of Art for the painting, frame, and containers is hereby terminated."

The City of Light Beckons

On hearing that the masterpiece had been transferred to French custody, President John F. Kennedy sent the following message to His Excellency General Charles de Gaulle, President of the French Republic, on March 8, 1963:

Dear Mr. President:

I am informed that the Mona Lisa has been safely returned to French hands. No work of art ever exhibited in the United States has had a comparable impact. More than two million people, many standing in line for hours, saw the painting in its fifty-two days in Washington and New York. The visit of the Mona Lisa has produced the greatest outpouring of appreciation for a work of art in our history.

In these days marked with difficulties, I am personally most grateful for your generosity in confiding the Mona Lisa to my care. This act of friendship expresses the deeper undercurrents which have done so much to sustain our peoples throughout their history.

May I express the warm gratitude of the American people as well as my own personal appreciation for your kindness in lending the United States the most celebrated painting in the world.

Sincerely yours,
John F. Kennedy

After a five-day voyage on windswept and choppy seas, the masterpiece arrived at Le Havre dock on schedule on March 12, 1963. Under heavy guard and the cover of night the painting was quietly returned to its longtime habitat less than three months after it had been lifted from the walls of the Louvre.

The Mona Lisa was back home, but the painting was still under evaluation by Madame Hours and experts from the museum's laboratory. Walker had to wait three excruciating hours before he would be fully apprised of the painting's condition. Walker had been loaned a car and chauffeur by Jean Chatelain, Director of the French Museums, but he was so anxious about the Mona Lisa that he was unable to enjoy any sightseeing.

Thankfully, the Mona Lisa was given a clean bill of health. Museum records indicate that the "distortion of the panel was checked" and appeared consistent with photographs taken prior to the painting's departure for Washington. Madame Hours completed her written report, which was immediately dispatched to Minister André Malraux.

Madame Madeleine Hours, who had once been called Mona Lisa's "head nurse," declared that the great adventure had done no apparent harm. Gently installed in her special bulletproof case, the Mona Lisa returned to her spot on the wall. Suddenly, King Francis I, painted by the great Venetian artist Titian, no longer looked so lonely, his companion returned.

From Paris, Walker had the delightful duty of informing Jackie that the masterpiece was in fine condition and safely back on the walls of the Louvre. With a schoolboy's glee, he proudly declared that the Mona Lisa mission was over. Mrs. Foy received a handwritten letter from Walker in an international pouch that she then typed for him and forwarded to Evelyn Lincoln at the White House.

Dear Mr. President,

Tuesday, March 12, was one of the happiest days of my life. After three hours of inspection by the leading experts of the Louvre, a receipt was given to M. Malraux, on which I am getting a copy, saying that the Mona Lisa was returned in perfect condition. I immediately cabled the Gallery asking that they inform you that one of your anxieties, though a minor one, was ended!

I believe that the visit of the Mona Lisa was a triumphant success, only slightly marred by elevators and loud speakers at the National Gallery of Art, and by some protocol problems at the Metropolitan Museum!

Very sincerely yours,
John Walker

John Walker immediately flew home to Washington. Upon his return he wrote to Monsieur Jean Chatelain: "The visit of the Mona Lisa to the United States entailed many responsibilities and anxieties which we shared. I am glad, therefore, that all has ended happily."

On April 1, President Kennedy sent Walker a copy of President de Gaulle's letter of reply with the French leader's thoughtful musings on the exhibition:

> *As the Mona Lisa resumes her place in the Louvre, enhanced with newly acquired glory, I am deeply touched that you personally have conveyed to me the gratitude of the American people.*
>
> *In entrusting to your museums this most famous work of art, the people of France had felt that they were marking a predilection. With the inner understanding that comes from the heart, your fellow citizens did not fail to sense this and this constitutes for every Frenchman a satisfaction of a very high order.*

In late April, White House Press Secretary Pierre Salinger called a special press briefing in Palm Beach, Florida, to announce that Mrs. Kennedy was expecting her third child in August. The news created quite a stir among reporters. The last child born to a sitting president was sixty-eight years earlier when Mrs. Grover Cleveland gave birth to daughter Marion. Jackie's obstetrician, Dr. John Walsh, told journalists that the First Lady's White House duties were "the second hardest job in the U.S." and he recommended that she "give up official duties for the duration" of her pregnancy. The planned state visit to Italy in June in which she was to accompany President Kennedy was postponed. Lady Bird Johnson offered to step in for Jackie as needed and had already served as hostess for a state luncheon in honor of Princess Beatrix of the Netherlands.

Jackie withdrew from her public duties to spend more time with her children and prepare for the arrival of the new baby. "Caroline, 5, who graduates from kindergarten this year, is growing up," noted *Time* magazine. "The President, who used to call her 'Buttons,' now addresses her by her real name. In Washington she often drops in at the President's office and sits in one of the big black wooden chairs beside his desk—just to chat. In Palm Beach she strides hand in hand with her father on shopping sprees along Worth Avenue, and aboard the *Honey Fitz* she likes to sit with feet dangling over the side and swap stories with the crew." Two-year-old John Jr. was "at the talking age," and was spotted by reporters jumping in the White House south fountain on a warm spring day.

Jackie spoke on the telephone only occasionally with John Walker, but continued to work with him on the White House restoration project. She did, however, continue her correspondence with André Malraux, and sent him private letters via diplomatic pouch delivered through the American French Embassy.

That April, the *New York Times* announced that President Kennedy planned to create the nation's first federal advisory council on the arts. The council would be comprised of thirty private citizens who were widely recognized for their role in the arts, including practicing artists as well as civic and cultural leaders who would make recommendations for bolstering the cultural resources of the nation.

Kennedy arts advisor August Heckscher compiled names of candidates and drafted a resolution for creation of the council. At the request of the President, Heckscher completed a report with his recommendations entitled "The Arts and the National Government." The President's Advisory Council on the Arts was enacted by Executive Order 11112 and signed by President Kennedy on June 12, 1963.

Since Heckscher wanted to return to working at the Twentieth Century Fund research foundation, Jackie proposed White House aide Richard Goodwin as his successor. According to Arthur Schlesinger, Goodwin hesitated, but Jackie sent him a "beguiling and persuasive letter" that closed the deal. "Goodwin saw the special consultancy as a way of approaching the whole problem of the aesthetics of American society—the way our cities looked and the beauty of our environment, along with great encouragement of the arts."

Plans moved forward to make the Special Consultancy on the Arts a full-time permanent office. Meanwhile, Jackie completed restoration of the upstairs Yellow Oval Room, decorated in eighteenth-century style with Louis XVI furnishings. She considered the room her "personal domain."

"Indeed more than any other space," wrote author James A. Abbott, "the Yellow Oval Room best represented [the Kennedys] ideal backdrop for the presidency—inviting yet somewhat formal, inspired by history while fashionable and chic." The Yellow Oval Room, the "heart of the White House," fulfilled Jackie's every wish.

"I never dreamt anything so perfect could happen," she wrote John Loeb, who assisted in funding the restoration. "A million, million thanks! Shall we have a little statue of you on the mantelpiece?" she asked.

In mid-June, President Kennedy announced a "strategy of peace" to end the Cold War during an important address at American University. In July, the United States, the Soviet Union, and Britain initialed the Nuclear Test Ban Treaty in Moscow, which, despite the goodwill generated from the loan of the Mona Lisa, was abruptly rejected by President Charles de Gaulle.

But the month of August also brought great sorrow, as Patrick Bouvier Kennedy, born prematurely on August 7, 1963, died two days later. In a small private chapel, the President knelt as Richard Cardinal Cushing, Archbishop of Boston, said the centuries-old Mass of the Angels. The infant was buried at Holywood Cemetery. On August 11, Caroline Kennedy, age five, walked in a Cape Cod garden and picked larkspur, black-eyed susans, and pink trumpet flowers and took the bouquet to her mother's bedside.

On October 7, President Kennedy signed the Nuclear Test Ban Treaty, the first disarmament agreement of the nuclear age. In a speech delivered on October 19, the president said that the nation, nearly one year after the Soviet-American crisis in Cuba, was "stronger than ever before." America had been strengthened by the increased power of its arms and increased efforts for peace. The two, he said, had brought a pause in the Cold War. It was, he said, progress on the long journey ahead.

At the end of the month, Kennedy delivered his most important speech on the arts and culture at Amherst College during the groundbreaking ceremony for the Robert Frost Library. Calling Frost one of the "granite figures of our time," the President emphasized the critical importance of the artist in American life:

> If art is to nourish the roots of our culture, society must set the artist free to follow his vision wherever it takes him. We must never forget that art is not a form of propaganda; it is a form of truth.
>
> I look forward to an America which will not be afraid of grace and beauty, which will protect the beauty of our national environment, which will preserve the great old American houses and squares and parks of our national past, and which will build handsome and balanced cities for our future.

> I look forward to an America which will reward achievements in the arts as we reward achievements in business or statecraft. I look forward to an America which will steadily raise the standards of artistic accomplishment and which will steadily enlarge cultural opportunities for all of our citizens. And I look forward to an America which commands respect throughout the world not only for its strength but for its civilization as well.

On the morning of November 17, with a showman's relish, John Walker unveiled his newest acquisition, Nicholas Poussin's *The Assumption of the Virgin*, during a television show that linked the Louvre with the National Gallery. The trans-Atlantic connection of the two great museums was broadcast via *Relay*, the little cousin of *Telstar*, the same communications satellite that had beamed the magnificent pictures of the Mona Lisa and Jacqueline Kennedy to viewers in London and Paris.

The program, entitled "Museums Without Walls," was produced by the National Broadcasting Network and, in untested technology for the era, cut between shots of the National Gallery and the venerated Louvre. Many of the faces who had worked so hard for Mona Lisa's American odyssey were reunited. Dressed in a dark wool double-breasted suit with his hair neatly combed, Walker showed viewers the spectacular seventeenth-century French painting with its billowing clouds, swirling draperies, and flying cherubs.

As Walker enthusiastically described the painting's historical significance, he was joined by Ambassador Hervé Alphand and his wife Nicole. In Paris, Madame Madeleine Hours (dressed in

Christian Dior) conducted the tour of the Louvre alongside the new American Ambassador, Charles E. Bohlen, and his wife.

Walker took Parisian television viewers on a short stroll of the Gallery, pointing out Renoir's *Girl With a Watering Can*, Houdon's bust of Voltaire, and one of Walker's personal favorites, *Madame Henriot*. American viewers got the chance to see the prized treasures of the Louvre, including Poussin's self-portrait, Whistler's Mother, and, of course, Leonardo da Vinci's Mona Lisa, described by Madame Hours as "the mistress of the house."

The development of what Jackie hoped would someday constitute a cabinet-level office for the American arts inspired by her friendship with André Malraux resumed with the planned appointment of aide Richard Goodwin. As Goodwin was about to take over as White House Special Consultant on the Arts, he proposed to President Kennedy that the "aesthetics of American society" could be for Kennedy, and his legacy, what the conservation movement had been for President Theodore Roosevelt. "It's a good idea," Kennedy said. "Let's work on it." Goodwin was to be named arts advisor on November 25, following the President's return from Dallas, Texas.

Newsman Edward Folliard was traveling with the White House press corps on the morning of November 22, 1963. His editors at the *Post* had assigned him a routine feature covering the president's political swing through Dallas. Folliard was seated in a press bus, two blocks away from the car in which the President and Mrs. Kennedy were riding. Suddenly the press bus stopped. Folliard craned his neck out the window and saw the presidential car, standing motionless. Then, moments later, he watched as the limousine raced away.

Sensing what had occurred, Folliard made his way to Parkland Hospital. "There was utter confusion," he recalled. "I saw a priest hurrying down a corridor." At roughly 1:30 P.M., Mac Kilduff, the assistant White House Press Secretary, met with reporters and made the solemn announcement that the President was dead. "The ghastly tragedy came with appalling suddenness, transforming gayety into horror in a flash," Folliard told readers in the *Post*.

On Sunday, November 24, the newsman chronicled the somber requiem for the slain leader: "The mighty of the land filed into the White House yesterday for a mournful adieu to President John F. Kennedy. Atop the mansion, the flag was at half staff and drenched by rain. Black crepe garlanded the door under the North portico. In the great East Room lay the body of the 35th President, who was felled by an assassin's bullet Friday at the age of 46. The flag-draped coffin had been placed on a black catafalque, at either end of which were flickering candles. A crucifix lay at the base."

"The final journey of the martyred thirty-fifth president was watched by a million mourners," Folliard wrote on November 26. He went on to report: "They were stretched out from the Capitol to the White House, to St. Matthews' Cathedral, to Arlington. Jacqueline Kennedy, the widow, marched behind the horse-drawn artillery caisson that bore the body of her husband from the White House to the Cathedral.

"Behind her walked kings and princes, a queen, presidents and prime ministers, dignitaries of 91 countries in all—come to honor a man, 'not young, not old' who longed for and worked for a world 'where the strong are just and the weak secure and the peace preserved.'

"Mrs. Kennedy had managed to cover up her grief in public until this final day. But as she was walking out of St. Matthews, anguish triumphed over her stoicism. She wept and the black veil could not hide the tears. Caroline Kennedy, 6, put her two hands over her mother's right hand, trying to comfort her. Then the little girl withdrew a hand to wipe away her own tears."

"It was all gone now," wrote Arthur Schlesinger. "He gave the world for an imperishable moment the vision of a leader who greatly understood the terror and the hope, the diversity and the possibility of life on this planet . . . So the people of the world grieved as if they had terribly lost their own leader, friend, brother."

On the morning before the state funeral, Jackie telephoned White House Curator Jim Ketchum. She said that she needed him to take care of a special task. "While we are at the Capitol," she said, "will you please get someone to help you, go to the Yellow Oval Room, and remove the Cézannes from the wall. In their place hang the Bennet and Cartwright prints—and I'll tell you why."

Ketchum was taken aback when he heard her request. He could not immediately understand why she wanted the Cézannes, which she had brought into the White House with such care and enthusiasm, removed.

"This afternoon I'm going to be receiving President de Gaulle in this room," she explained, "and I want him to be aware of the heritage of the United States, and these are scenes from our own history."

Ketchum and the White House carpenter followed her wishes, and removed the two Cézannes. In their place were mounted a "strong stamp of America—prints of Washington, Baltimore and Philadelphia—in the room where the widow would receive," recalled White House usher J. B. West.

After the somber ceremony at Arlington, Mrs. Kennedy returned to the White House and entered the Yellow Oval Room, where she met, one at a time, President de Gaulle, Prince Philip of England, Emperor Haile Selassie of Ethiopia, and Ireland's President Eamond de Valera. "She gave an example to the whole world of how to behave," President de Gaulle said, following the emotional private visit.

The day after the burial of President Kennedy, John Walker, with his eyes swollen from tears, sent to Jackie four of the six Cézannes remaining in his care at the National Gallery. These included the breathtaking impressionist masterpieces known as *Gardanne*, *Houses on a Hill*, *Boathouse on a River*, and *Landscape with a Tower*. Cézanne's sunlit images captured the tranquil beauty of Aix-en-Provence, a small town in the south of France. The fluid, colorful canvasses depicted scenes from the countryside and evoked a sense of stillness. Walker hoped that gazing at the serene landscapes could grant the First Lady release—if only for a few brief seconds.

On Monday, December 2, amid a light sprinkling of snow, Jackie was preparing to leave. The family's personal possessions had been put into boxes so that they would be ready to be taken to the red brick Georgetown home lent to her by Averell Harriman until she could select a permanent residence. The seven-bedroom town house had a lovely block-long terraced garden with English boxwood and magnolia trees. Inside, Jackie and her two small children would be surrounded by Harriman's paintings by Matisse and van Gogh.

As a gentle snow blanketed the White House lawn, Jackie wrote her last letter to John Walker from the residence, reflecting on their endeavors to benefit the arts and the National Gallery. It was the only time she affectionately called the museum director by his seldom used nickname: "My Dear Johnny," she wrote, reminiscing about their projects together. She recalled their exchanges concerning the White House Cézannes and thanked him for parting with the paintings after having worked so hard to secure them for the museum.

> *. . . I was always so proud of you—as you made the National Gallery what it was by fighting tooth and nail for all the best to stay in it. You are the kind of person that Jack was, in another way. And you helped me so much with our committee. Occasionally when our objectives crossed—it amused me.*

She wanted him to know she never felt at odds with him.

Now, she said, it was time for her to return the four Cézannes. She had been moved by Walker's sacrifice to give up the paintings, but the new mistress of the White House had different ideas about art. When Jackie had presented the Cézannes in the Yellow Oval Room to Lady Bird Johnson as a housewarming gift, the new First Lady gave a little shriek and said, "But he wasn't an American painter, was he?" No, Jackie told her, before giving a brief description of how Walker had pushed the limits and "violated poor Mr. Loeser's will" in order to protect the paintings and obtain them for the Gallery.

Mrs. Johnson, a bit taken aback, hastily expressed concern that with the paintings in the White House, the American people would be deprived of seeing them in the National Gallery. Wanting to carry on the tradition of displaying American objects in the White House, Lady Bird seemed uncomfortable with the idea of keeping the four French master paintings.

Jackie told Walker that she preferred to return the Cézannes now instead of waiting for the Johnsons to do so because Walker had given them to her. On Wednesday, December 4, the four Cézannes were packed and removed from the executive mansion and returned to the National Gallery.

> *I have worked so hard for America, and brought its best here—so I suppose no one can understand that when you come up to this magnificent Louis XVI room, as Thomas Jefferson would have had it—to see those Cézannes and great impressionists on the walls is a delight and a* soulagement *beyond belief. I have seen it happen to so many people who come there. . . .*
>
> *Thank you dear Johnny—for all your help—now I am gone—but you can help the White House Historical Association. Never put*

us ahead of the National Gallery because then you would not be the great director that you are—but sometimes think of us and protect and augment our collection.

Good bye and thank you for
all all *that you have done,*

Affectionately,
Jackie

Epilogue: Final Bows

Jacqueline Kennedy was proven right: no harm came to the Mona Lisa, and the exhibit contributed to a widespread cultural awakening for many Americans. Six years after the exhibition, John Walker wrote in his memoir that he was wrong about the likelihood that the portrait would be damaged.

"The visit of the Mona Lisa proved one thing," he said. "If you are willing to spend the money, you can move the most fragile object back and forth across the ocean without damage, provided you take sufficient care and put into effect certain precautions."

It may seem inconceivable in today's world, but not one credible threat was made against the Mona Lisa from the moment the masterpiece left the Louvre until it was safely returned eighty-eight days later. Nearly 2,000,000 Americans came to see her. In many respects, the exhibition changed the nature of museums and their relationship with the public.

The word "blockbuster" entered the lexicon in the late 1970s as a term describing popular art exhibitions that delivered massive numbers of visitors and ticket sales. The term was first widely used in connection with the wildly successful "Treasures of Tutankhamun"

exhibition, which opened on November 17, 1976, at the National Gallery. By almost any measure, however, the phenomenon unleashed by the American visit of the Mona Lisa in 1963 surpassed the three-year national tour of ancient objects from King Tut's tomb.

The exhibition of the artifacts of the Egyptian boy king and the Mona Lisa shared a strong element of international cultural diplomacy, however. "Ambassador Tut became a force of moderation," noted Christopher Knight in the *Los Angeles Times*. "His glittering mask helped soften callused perceptions in the eyes of bedazzled Americans. Making Egypt less of a boogeyman, the golden teenager helped ease public suspicions about Arab motivations in negotiations with Israel." On the spring day in 1979 that Egypt and Israel signed a formal treaty ending three decades of war and establishing diplomatic relations, Knight observed, Ambassador Tut was in New York greeting enthusiastic crowds at the Metropolitan Museum. (King Tut's objects of the afterlife returned to America once again in 2005 to meet teeming throngs.)

The powerful cultural impact of the blockbuster exhibition in terms of education and aesthetic enjoyment is undeniable. But art officials caution that increased attendance and revenue alone are not enough to justify an art exhibition. One treatise on museum management states that public programs should encompass activities that enrich the visitor's experience, attract new audiences, and encourage return visits. The record crowds that descended on Washington, D.C. and New York to view the Mona Lisa proved that Jacqueline Kennedy understood these principles and, through her adept staging, she pioneered the modern phenomenon of the blockbuster museum exhibition. Mona Lisa's visit triggered a lingering national love affair with the arts in which culture was no longer the privileged domain of a few educated connoisseurs, but rather central in the life of all Americans.

The 1960s opened with a frenzy of plans to build an arts infrastructure (the Los Angeles Music Center was completed in 1964, for example, and New York's Lincoln Center in 1968) amid a growing belief that art was economically viable and beneficial for mankind, which suggested a faith and optimism at odds with the pervasive Cold War anxiety.

Mrs. Kennedy's vision for an American ministry of the arts inspired by André Malraux never came to pass, but she did see government support for the arts grow. In 1965, under the Lyndon Johnson administration, the National Endowment for the Arts and the National Endowment for the Humanities were created as independent federal agencies. They weren't run by cabinet-level officials as Jackie had envisioned, but they did provide much of the funding and support she had long sought for artists.

In her post-presidential life, Mrs. Kennedy became a leader in promoting the appreciation of America's heritage. She sought President Lyndon Johnson's support for the revitalization of Pennsylvania Avenue and continued her work to preserve Lafayette Square in Washington, D.C. According to John Carl Warnecke, the architect who worked closely with Jackie on the project, it was the first time in the modern period of design that the public saw new, large buildings designed in context with old, historic buildings. "She refused to give up," Warnecke recalled. "A lot of other people have taken credit for Lafayette Square, but she was the true savior." Later, working with the New York Municipal Arts Society, Jackie led a passionate campaign to preserve New York City's historic Grand Central Terminal from demolition.

Jackie continued her lifelong interest in the arts and letters when she joined Viking Press in 1975, and worked as a nonfiction book editor. "I'm drawn to books that are out of regular experience," she said in an interview with *Publishers Weekly*. "Books of other cultures, ancient histories. I'm interested in the arts in general, especially the creative process. I'm fascinated by hearing artists talk about their craft. To me, a wonderful book is one that takes me on a journey into something I didn't know before." In 1978, she was named associate editor at Doubleday. "As she had in the White House, Jackie quickly mastered the gamesmanship of publishing," noted one writer. During her stay at Doubleday, Jackie published many significant titles, including Joseph Campbell's acclaimed work, *The Power of Myth.*

She continued to devote her time to causes that were important to her, including the American Ballet Theater, the Municipal Arts Society, and the New York Public Library. She was the guiding benevolent force behind the creation of the John F. Kennedy Library and Museum in Boston, Massachusetts. Designed by renowned architect I. M. Pei, who also designed a new wing for the National Gallery, the library opened to the public in October 1979. The glass pavilion of the Presidential Library rises grandly from the edge of the Columbia Point Peninsula and offers a sweeping view of Boston Harbor.

In January 1994, at the age of sixty-four, Jackie was diagnosed with a form of cancer, non-Hodgkin's lymphoma. Her health soon faded and she made her last trip home from the hospital on May 18, 1994. Well-wishers and reporters gathered on the street outside her Fifth Avenue apartment before she died the following day. Her funeral was at St. Ignatius Loyola Roman Catholic Church in Manhattan, the same church where she was baptized in 1929. The *New York Daily News* captured the national outpouring of grief in a simple headline: "Missing Her."

The former First Lady chose to be buried in Arlington Cemetery with John F. Kennedy and their two children, the unnamed stillborn daughter who died in 1956, and Patrick Bouvier Kennedy.

"In a public sea she steered a private course . . . in the age of confession, she kept her own counsel," observed the *New York Times* at the time of her death.

Theodore Sorensen, Special Counsel to the President, closely observed the First Lady's impact: "By maintaining her own unique identity and provocative personality . . . by refusing to appear more folksy at political rallies or less glamorous in power nations, by carrying her pursuit of excellence and beauty into the White House dinners . . . she became a world-wide symbol of American culture and good taste, and offered proof in the modern age that the female sex can succeed by merely remaining feminine."

Hugh Sidey of *Time* magazine noted, "I would say that in some ways, Jackie was about as influential a woman in terms of culture as we've had in this century—intelligent, cultured, and with an eye and a sense of what needed to be done."

In 2001, Caroline Kennedy published a book of her mother's favorite poetry, observing, "Throughout her life, my mother took great pride in the role of poetry and the arts in my father's administration. She celebrated American arts and artists in the White House, believing as my father did, that America's artistic achievements were equal to her political and military power, and that American civilization had come of age."

John Walker and Jackie maintained a correspondence with one another for the rest of their lives. On October 6, 1965, she confided to him that she needed more time before the official portrait of President Kennedy was to be unveiled. "Thank you for writing me about the President's portrait," she wrote. "I have the feeling, however, that it is still too soon to hang any portrait of President Kennedy in the White House.

"Everyone knows that the White House Historical Association will be giving the portrait—and that means so much to me—but I still would rather have some more time pass by before anything is actually hung there.

"That day will be such an important one—and I know that I should be there—but, dear Mr. Walker, I do not think I could bring myself to go back to Washington yet. I do hope you will understand." She signed the letter as she did always in her notes to Walker, "Affectionately, Jackie."

In 1969, Walker retired as director of the National Gallery and passed the baton to his talented assistant, J. Carter Brown, who would lead the Gallery into a new era. Walker penned his memoirs, *Self-Portrait with Donors: Confessions of an Art Collector*, which detailed his relentless pursuit of masterpieces for the Gallery and his close relationships with Francis Watson, John Pope Hennessey, and Kenneth Clark.

In 1976, he was awarded the Gallery's medal for distinguished service from Paul Mellon. His last visit to the museum was in 1991 to celebrate the institution's fiftieth anniversary. Suffering from the long-standing effects of paralysis when he was a child, Walker arrived at the Gallery seated in what the *Guardian* newspaper called a "brilliant red wheelchair."

Until the end, Walker remembered the exhibition of the Mona Lisa as the most trying period of his professional life. In second place was the arduous task of securing Chester Dale's fine collection of nineteenth- and twentieth-century French paintings in perpetuity for the National Gallery. According to his successor, J. Carter Brown, Walker's pursuit of "CHESTERDALE" was so taxing that it turned his gray hair white and "left him on tranquilizers for the rest of his life." Ironically, in his last will and testament, Dale left Walker a sizeable sum of money. Surprised and deeply touched, Walker used the funds to purchase a home in Fisher's Island, New York. Walker affectionately called the property "Will O'Dale."

The two master paintings by Paul Cézanne, from the collection of Charles A. Loeser, cherished by Jacqueline Kennedy and protected by Director John Walker, endured travels of their own. On July 25, 1985, *House on the Marne* and *The Forest* were removed from the White House and returned to the National Gallery where they were periodically placed on display. Twenty years later, during the administration of George W. Bush, one of the pictures, *The Forest*, was returned to the White House where it remains today.

John Walker died on October 16, 1995, at the age of eighty-eight of cardiopulmonary arrest at his home in Amberley, Sussex, England. Shortly before his death, he had been hospitalized with a broken leg and a lung ailment. His only son, John Anthony, had died suddenly and unexpectedly in 1986; Lady Margaret died one year later in 1987. He was survived by his daughter Gillian, wife of noted filmmaker Albert Maysles, and three grandchildren.

André Malraux dedicated his autobiography *Anti-Memoirs*, published in 1968, to Jacqueline Kennedy. He died of lung cancer at the age of seventy-seven, and was buried at the cemetery of Verrieres-le-Buisson. Twenty years later, Malraux's body was exhumed and was reinterred in Paris at the Panthéon, the French burial site for national heroes. Over the years, many Malraux biographers have taken great pains to sort out the facts concerning

Malraux's life story, debating what was true and what was fabricated. "For the most part," Malraux claimed, "man is what he hides."

Edward Folliard continued working as a reporter for the *Washington Post* until his retirement in 1966. His career in journalism spanned more than fifty years through the extreme transitions of "The American Century."

In his oral history for the John F. Kennedy Presidential Library, Folliard said he believed that newspapermen were the link between government and the great "mass rank and file" of Americans. He considered his role as that of a public servant. "That's the way I've always thought of myself," he said.

Covering the assassination of President Kennedy was the most excruciating experience of his professional life. "Every big story I've ever covered, I've written under difficulty," he recalled. "That's the one story I just wish to God none of us had ever had to cover." Folliard later reflected on the leader whose life had ended so abruptly: "My admiration of Kennedy is without limit. I think he was probably the most brilliant President of our time."

Over the years, Folliard continued his close association with former Presidents Eisenhower and Truman. In 1969, President Nixon asked Folliard to accompany him on Air Force One to Independence, Missouri, on the occasion of Truman's eighty-fifth birthday. On April 22, 1970, Folliard was awarded the Presidential Medal of Freedom, the nation's highest civilian award, following a white-tie dinner at the White House. At the ceremony, President Nixon credited Folliard with playing a role in the reconciliation between himself and President Truman several years earlier.

Folliard died at his Washington home from cancer on November 25, 1976; he was seventy-seven years old. His lengthy obituary was printed on the front page of the *Washington Post*. When he won the Pulitzer Prize in 1947 for national reporting, the newspaper wrote: "Broadly speaking, good newspaper reporters fall into one of three categories—those whose primary value lies in their ability to uncover important news; those whose value lies primarily in their skill in writing the news, and finally those who have a special aptitude for interpreting the news, that is, for discerning and clarifying the meaning that underlies the superficial facts. Mr. Folliard is one of those rare and invaluable journalists who combines in themselves all three gifts."

The Mass of Christian Burial was conducted for the newsman at the Church of the Annunciation in Northwest Washington on November 29, where his casket was carried by his son, Michael, and fellow reporters from the *Post*. He was survived by his wife Mary Helen, two adult children, and eight grandchildren.

America was not the final stop for Leonardo da Vinci's Mona Lisa. The picture left the Louvre again in 1974; first on loan to the Museum of Art in Tokyo, where she was displayed from April through June 2, and then to the Pushkin Museum of Fine Art in Moscow, where she was exhibited for eleven days beginning on June 13. The question of how best to protect the picture was again the task of Madame Madeleine Hours of the Louvre.

Once the decision was made that the picture would travel by airplane, Madame Hours was confronted with a new set of problems including the possibility of rapid depressurization or fire aboard the aircraft. The first travel box made for her trip to America had aged, and the Klegecell panels and the rubber seals were no longer effective. The Centre d'Electronique de l'Armement was asked to design a new container that provided "an additional envelope" for Mona Lisa's safety. Inside the wood crate was added a layer of a bricklike material that could protect the Mona Lisa for thirty minutes before it could be damaged by flames.

Curators at the Louvre requested the same temperature and humidity be replicated in Japan as had been achieved in America to protect the fragile picture. A special glass box was constructed to display the painting in order to avoid any risk of overheating and excessive dryness due to the artificial lighting. The exhibition was flawless, and more than 1,000,000 visitors came to see Leonardo's masterpiece.

When it came time to leave, Madame Hours supervised the removal of the painting and its placement inside the custom *catafalque*. Tokyo authorities banned all traffic on the road leading to the airport in preparation for Mona Lisa's departure. The traveling case was delicately placed inside the aircraft and hooked by straps connected to the floor. Madame Hours watched with great emotion as the plane slowly taxied onto the runway as a long line of government officials stood under large black umbrellas and bowed, a final salute to the masterwork of the old Italian artist.

During the long flight from Tokyo to Moscow, Madame Hours was the only passenger. One hour before the aircraft reached the Ural Mountains and the European border, Mona Lisa and her escort experienced a frightening encounter: "I saw a bright red light like a rocket taking off from the ground, and suddenly, at our level there was a bright ball of fire. I thought it was an explosion or a flying saucer. I paused, having lost my breath, but tried to find an explanation. I then saw a capsule, a space ship, emerging from a cloud that seemed to be at our altitude. It disappeared as quickly as lightning into the dark sky."

Moments later the flight commander jumped from the cockpit and ran toward Madame Hours. "Did you see it?" he gasped. The pilot explained that he had been instructed to change course just minutes earlier. "The dear man was just as stupefied as I was," Madame Hours said of the Soviet spaceship that mysteriously crossed Mona Lisa's path.

Once the painting was returned to the Louvre, Madame Hours examined the Mona Lisa and found that she did not suffer from her travels. She experienced "some play" on the flexible frame on her back, but not enough to warrant concern, and she was returned to her bulletproof, temperature-controlled glass case.

The Mona Lisa's journey to Tokyo and Moscow would be her last. During a luncheon to celebrate the Louvre Museum's 200th anniversary in 1994, museum officials assured reporters that the Mona Lisa would never again leave the Louvre. "It's much too fragile," officials announced.

Scientific investigations in the twenty-first century have shed further light on details about the painting. As she sat for her portrait, Mona Lisa was apparently wearing a gauzy overdress common to women who were expecting a baby or nursing, and some of her hair was rolled up and tucked into a small bonnet that had an attached veil. The overdress and hat were lost from view over time as now-discolored layers of lacquer were added but they can still be seen in infrared photographs, according to French and Canadian researchers. "This remarkable painting is actually more remarkable than we believed," said John M. Taylor, an imaging scientist and conservator with the National Research Council of Canada.

French engineer and inventor Pascal Cotte, founder of Lumière Technology of Paris, developed a new high-tech multispectral camera capable of penetrating layers of varnish and paint, and announced that Mona Lisa once had eyelashes, eyebrows, a wider smile, and was painted with a fur-lined coat resting on her knees. Images of the scanned painting from the 240-megapixel camera "peeled away the centuries" and enabled new examination of the pigments on the painting's surface with scientific precision. Cotte's infrared images also revealed the artist's preparatory drawings hidden behind multiple layers of paint. "If you look at the left hand you see the first position of the finger, and he changed his mind for another position," Cotte told reporters.

The precise method of da Vinci's mastery of the wondrous smoky sfumato brush technique of applying paint, however, still continues to elude experts, and as Madame Hours once observed, it defies technical analysis.

In 2005, the Mona Lisa was given a new place of honor inside the Louvre. After a four-year renovation, the nineteenth-century Salle des États was redesigned to accommodate the enormous crowds and provide a superior display. Designed by architect Lorenzo Piqueras, the gallery is lit from the ceiling with natural light. The Mona Lisa now sits alone on a freestanding wall that divides the gallery. Before she was "wheeled away" to be hung inside her new home in the large rectangular wing, only 750 feet away, curators delicately wrapped the picture in tissue paper. Jean Habert, the

Louvre's chief curator of Venetian paintings, said the painting's every move is scrutinized and there is always a camera nearby. "She's like a living person," he said. "She was surrounded by photographers the second she re-opened. They were acting like the paparazzi—kneeling in front of her, craning to get the best spot, standing up, sitting down."

Journalists from around the world reported that the Florentine Lady never looked better. She now looked "positively rejuvenated, with the new ceiling allowing daylight in from above, and subtle spotlights getting rid of the greenish tinge of age."

The Mona Lisa still sits inside her bulletproof box mounted on the walls of the Louvre where she is seen by millions of museum visitors each year. Inside the box, the temperature is kept at a constant 68°F and 55 percent humidity. Once a year, officials at the Louvre delicately remove the painting from her isothermic container, and her condition is closely examined. In 2009, the Louvre expects as many as 9,000,000 visitors will come to see her, easily ensuring that she is the most observed woman in history.

Acknowledgments

In 2003 I was in the middle of writing *The Culture Broker: Franklin Murphy and the Transformation of Los Angeles.* Purely by accident, I stumbled on some of the correspondence written by First Lady Jacqueline Kennedy and National Gallery Director John Walker concerning the exhibition of the Mona Lisa. My encounter with these letters launched a five-year hunt to locate all the available primary materials associated with the historic exhibition.

From the start, my visits to the Gallery Archives at the National Gallery of Art in Washington, D.C., and the John F. Kennedy Library in Boston were riveting experiences. There is endless excitement in the search to reconstruct what went before, as Arthur Schlesinger beautifully described it. Writers pursue history, he said, because of the thrill of the hunt, because exploring the past is such fun and because a nation must know its history.

I would like to express my profound appreciation to Caroline Kennedy for her gracious permission to quote from the correspondence of Jacqueline Kennedy and John Walker. I'm deeply indebted to Maygene F. Daniels, chief of the Gallery Archives at the National Gallery of Art, for her invaluable and gracious assistance through all the stages of research and writing of this book. I greatly appreciate Anne G. Ritchie, senior archivist, for her kind efforts in locating all of the pertinent documents and photographs connected with the exhibition. Many thanks to the fine staff of the Gallery Archives including Jean Henry.

The documents and photographs from the John F. Kennedy Presidential Library are an indispensable record of the Mona Lisa story. I'm extremely grateful to research archivist Stephen Plotkin for his skillful and exceptional expertise. I greatly appreciate the insights and knowledge of audiovisual archivist Maryrose Grossman. Roy Meachum's vivid memories of Edward Folliard made an important contribution. Very special thanks are owed to French translator Brian Quinn of Quinn Translation Services in Los Angeles and to my researcher based in Paris, Sara Watson. I must extend my deep appreciation to journalist Ellen Beck, who somehow found the missing Mona Lisa photos from all corners.

I gratefully acknowledge Larry Ashmead, Gina De Roma Bowles, Karen Chappelle, Nicholas A. Curry, Catherine Davis, Carol Easton, Joseph Alexander Gallego II, Uri Herscher, Ashley Mendoza, Jack Miles, Dorota Shortell, Victoria Steele, William Strachan, Roger Vincent, Frank and Carla Vincent, and David Wilk.

My deepest thanks to my literary agent, Betsy Amster, for finding this book its perfect home. Most of all, my gratitude must go to my talented editor Wendy Francis for her extraordinary commitment to this project. As I write this, Wendy is about to give birth to her first child, a baby boy. I am grateful to Kate Burke, Alex Camlin, Kevin Hanover, Trent Knoss, Ashley St. Thomas, and Collin Tracy of the Perseus Books Group.

This book is dedicated to the members of my Los Angeles book club, the Women's Literary Society, including Stacie Hirsch, Jeanne MacDonald, Meena Nainan, Kim Nemoy, Esq., Dr. Deborah Lynn Shyer, and Abigail Walsh, Esq. No group of women has ever delighted or tortured me more.

Lastly, I would like to acknowledge my cherished friend T. Sumner Robinson (1945–2003), maverick journalist, Internet pioneer, and mentor.

NOTES

The material for this book has been drawn primarily from the private records, office files, correspondence, and memoirs of the principals in the story. At the John F. Kennedy Presidential Library and Museum in Boston, documents connected with the exhibition are located in the President's Office Files, National Security Files, White House Central Files, the White House Social Files, and the various White House Staff Files as well as interviews conducted under the auspices of the Library's Oral History Program.

At the Gallery Archives at the National Gallery of Art in Washington, D.C., information pertaining to the exhibition can be found in the Secretary-General Counsel Exhibition Files, Administrator Attendance-Special Exhibitions Files, Central Subject Files, Publications Special Exhibitions Files, Press Office Exhibition Files, Press Office Scrapbooks, and the General Curatorial Subject Files and General Curatorial Exhibition Files. At the archives of the Metropolitan Museum of Art in New York, items related to the exhibition are housed in the Mona Lisa Exhibition Files and the museum's exhibition scrapbooks. Although this book focuses on the American side of the exhibition, additional relevant documents are located at the archives at the Musée du Louvre, in Paris, France.

AUTHOR'S NOTE

In France, the painting is known as *La Joconde*, and in Italy the work is known as *La Gioconda*. The painting's popular title in English is the Mona Lisa.

"stirred some impulse": Folliard, Edward, "Escorting Mona Lisa to America," *National Geographic* (June 1963): 847.

CHAPTER ONE

"love it so at Merrywood": *New York Times*, January 14, 1962, 51; also see "Less Than Merry at Merrywood," *Time*, May 11, 1962.

"floating on air": Letter, Jacqueline Kennedy to John Walker, undated, Research Files, Kennedy/Onassis, Gallery Archives, National Gallery of Art, Washington, D.C.

"frenzy of excitement": Ibid.

a ruse that he later admitted: Walker, John, *Self-Portrait with Donors: Confessions of an Art Collector* (Boston: Little, Brown, 1974); See Walker, John, "My Most Infamous Intrigue: The White House Cézannes," Research Files, Loeser Collections (Cézanne Paintings), Gallery Archives, National Gallery of Art, Washington, D.C.

outdoor scenes Cézanne had created: Shapiro, Meyer, *Paul Cézanne* (New York: Harry N. Abrams, 2004), 88.

appeared before a national television audience: "20th Birthday of National Gallery of Art," *Accent*, 1961. Audiovisual Archives Code TNC 57, John F. Kennedy Library (JFKL); Press Release, Office of the White House Press Secretary, Transcript, Mrs. Kennedy's Remarks on Behalf of the National Gallery of Art, March 19, 1961, Research Files, Kennedy/Onassis, Gallery Archives, National Gallery of Art, Washington, D.C.; also see *Washington Post,* March 18, 1961, C7; *Washington Post*, March 19, 1961, F1; *Washington Post,* March 20, 1961, B5; "National Gallery of Art Hailed by Mrs. Kennedy," *New York Times*, March 20, 1961.

Rotate the pictures periodically: Press Release, Office of the White House Assistant Social Secretary for the Press (concerning the installation of the Cézannes in the Green Room), May 3, 1961, Research Files, Loeser Collections (Cézanne Paintings), Gallery Archives, National Gallery of Art, Washington, D.C.

"greatness, to our walls": Letter, Jacqueline Kennedy (JBK) to John Walker, March 8, 1961, White House Social Files, Folder, John Walker, JFKL.

Jackie wrote to Matilda Loeser Calnan: White House Memo written by Dean Rusk, "Cross Reference Sheet" (concerning the Loeser Cézannes), White House Social Files, Folder, John Walker, JFKL.

"Mr. Loeser is one of a number": Press Release, May 3, 1961.

"suffering from *ennui*": Letter, JBK to John Walker, May 5, 1961, Research Files, Kennedy/Onassis, Gallery Archives, National Gallery of Art, Washington, D.C.; also White House Social Files, JFKL.

"These flowers were to have gone": Letter, Tish Baldridge to John Walker, undated, Research Files, Kennedy/Onassis, Gallery Archives, National Gallery of Art, Washington, D.C.

"watching everything from a chair": Bowles, Hamish, ed., *Jacqueline Kennedy: The White House Years; Selections from the John F. Kennedy Library and Museum* (New York, Metropolitan Museum of Art, 2001), 4.

"She had a fantastic desire": Ibid., 3.

"inside and out": Alphand, Nicole, "Malraux: Chevalier servant de La Joconde," *La Nouvelle Revue des Deux Mondes* (May 1976): 325–329.

"authentic French beauty": Salinger, Pierre, *With Kennedy* (New York: Doubleday, 1966), 98.

"Her dearest wish was to hear": Alphand, Nicole, "Malraux: Chevalier servant de La Joconde," 325–329.

"must not feel obligated to keep his promise": Ibid.

"get a towel and rub his head": Lincoln, Evelyn, *My Twelve Years with John F. Kennedy* (Boulder, CO: Black Pebbles Publishing, 2003), 265.

congenial pleasantries during discussions: "La Presidente," *Time*, June 9, 1961.

"irritating, intransigent, insufferably vain": Sorensen, Theodore C., *Kennedy* (New York: Perennial Library, 1988); Smith, Marie, *Entertaining in the White House* (New York: MacFadden-Bartell, 1967), 197.

"dynastic complexities of the later Bourbons" and "knew more French history": Schlesinger, Arthur M. Jr., *A Thousand Days: John F. Kennedy in the White House* (Boston: Houghton Mifflin, 1965), 350.

"taken over by a profound emotion": Alphand, Nicole, "Malraux: Chevalier servant de La Joconde," 325–329.

"What a destiny": Todd, Oliver, *Malraux: A Life* (New York: Knopf, 2005) 361.

"What did you do before": Smith, Sally Bedell, *Grace and Power: The Private World of the Kennedy White House* (New York: Random House, 2004), 206.

"intellectual crush" and "Malraux was her prize": Baldridge, Letitia, *A Lady, First: My Life in the Kennedy White House and the American Embassies of Paris and Rome* (New York: Viking, 2001), 190; Smith, Sally Bedell, 206.

linking of Jupiter with Prometheus: "The Last Renaissance Figure," *Time*, December 6, 1976.

"tattled of neglect": "Paris at the Cleaners," *Time*, September 14, 1962.

loved glory even more: Lacouture, Jean, *André Malraux* (New York: Pantheon, 1975), 412.

"I thought I was in heaven": Smith, Sally Bedell, 207.

"five diamond pins": "Tribute to Louis XIV," *Time*, June 9, 1961.

"I have more confidence": Sulzberger, C. L., *The Last of the Giants* (New York: Macmillan, 1970), 759.

"packed their pages with so many bouquets": *New York Times*, June 3, 1961, 7.

"solidified Mrs. Kennedy's position": Wertheimer, Molly Meijer, ed., *Inventing a Voice: The Rhetoric of American First Ladies of the Twentieth Century* (Lanham, MD: Rowman and Littlefield, 2004), 258.

"conquering the skeptical city": Schlesinger, *A Thousand Days*, 352.
"I am the man who accompanied": Schlesinger, *A Thousand Days*, 356.
"He spoke of the larger purposes of culture": Anthony, Carl Sferrazza, *As We Remember Her: Jacqueline Kennedy Onassis in the Words of Her Family and Friends* (New York: HarperCollins, 1997), 168.
"Culture is the sum of all the forms": "The Rise of Mass Culture," *Time*, May 25, 1962.
"He was far more interested in Jackie": Bowles, 9.
"Now for all your thoughtfulness": Letter, JBK to Minister Malraux, June 21, 1961, White House Social Files, Folder, André Malraux, JFKL; Todd, 361.
"Queen of Rummage sales": Baldridge, *A Lady, First*, 177.
"Off to the dungeons with them": West, J. B., with Mary Lynn Kotz, *Upstairs at the White House: My Life with the First Ladies* (New York: Coward, McCann, and Geoghegan, 1973), 229.
"Everything in the White House": *Life*, September 1, 1961, 56; also see Sidey, Hugh, "Editing the First Lady, *Life* Magazine Goes to the White House," *White House History*, no. 13 (Summer 2003), 9.
Fourteen prominent Americans: The Fine Arts Committee for the White House consisted of Mr. Henry F. du Pont (Chairman), Mr. Charles Francis Adams, Mrs. C. Douglas Dillon, Mrs. Charles W. Englehard, Mr. David E. Finley, Mrs. Albert D. Lasker, Mr. John S. Loeb, Mrs. Paul Mellon, Mrs. Henry Parish II, Mr. Gerald Shea, Mr. John Walker, Mrs. George Henry Warren and Mrs. Charles B. Wrightsman; see Abbot, James A. and Elaine M. Rice, *Designing Camelot: The Kennedy White House Restoration* (New York: Van Nostrand Reinhold, 1998), 22; also see Thayer, Mary Van Rensselaer, *Jacqueline Kennedy: The White House Years* (Boston: Little, Brown, 1967), 284.
"At last we have a list": Letter, JBK to Walker, June 29, 1961, Research Files, Kennedy/Onassis, Gallery Archives, National Gallery of Art, Washington, D.C.
"It is my greatest hope": Perry, Barbara A., *Jacqueline Kennedy: First Lady of the New Frontier* (Lawrence: University Press of Kansas, 2004), 151.
Scottish artist David Martin: Bowles, 23.
"a magnificent portrait of Ben Franklin": Adler, Bill, *The Eloquent Jacqueline Kennedy Onassis: A Portrait in Her Own Words* (New York: HarperCollins, 2004), 126–127; "First Lady Rallies Wealth to Her Cause," *Washington Post*, September 5, 1962; "The Franklin Portrait: Thereby Hangs a Tale," *Washington Post*, December 22, 1987; Bradlee, Benjamin C., *Conversations with Kennedy* (New York: W. W. Norton, 1975), 123; Anthony, Carl Sferrazza, *First Ladies: The Saga of the Presidents' Wives and Their Power, 1961–1990* (New York: William Morrow and Co., 1991), 32.
Heckscher based a claim for federal support: Heckscher, August, "The Nation's Culture: New Age for the Arts," *New York Times*, September 23, 1962; also

see Larson, Gary O., *The Reluctant Patron: The United States Government and the Arts 1943–1965* (Philadelphia: University of Pennsylvania Press, 1983), 10; Heckscher, August, *The Public Happiness* (New York: Atheneum, 1962).

"what kind of shape": Anthony, *As We Remember Her*, 164; also see Bradford, Sarah, *America's Queen: A Life of Jacqueline Kennedy Onassis* (New York: Penguin, 2000), 235; Anthony, *First Ladies*, 38, note 16.

"No support of the museums on a regular basis": Quote attributed to Vivian Crespi in Anthony, *As We Remember Her*, 164.

"The arts had been treated as a stepchild": Ibid., 165.

"We are bombarded every week by requests": August Heckscher, Recorded Interview by Wolf von Eckhardt, December 10, 1965, Oral History Program, JFKL; also see Perry, 149; Anthony, *First Ladies*, 38–39.

"She was an original and difficult to decipher": Cassini, Oleg, *In My Own Fashion: An Autobiography* (New York: Simon and Schuster, 1987), 304.

"Sometimes she seemed to draw back": Anthony, *First Ladies*, 38–39; also see Heckscher Recorded Interview, JFKL.

"Man of the Year": "A Way with the People," *Time*, January 5, 1962.

"I'm going to be a television star": West, 281.

"Yes, these two chairs": Jacqueline Kennedy White House Tour, Online Transcript, website JFKL.

"This must be scholarly": Note, JBK to Walker, January 27, 1962, Research Files, Kennedy/Onassis, Gallery Archives, National Gallery of Art, Washington, D.C.

"eliminate the purple prose": Letter, JBK to John Walker, January 30, 1962, Research Files, Kennedy/Onassis, Gallery Archives, National Gallery of Art, Washington, D.C.

"What I would really love": Letter, JBK to John Walker, March 30, 1962, Research Files, Kennedy/Onassis, Gallery Archives, National Gallery of Art, Washington, D.C.

"I would be so grateful" and "worthy of Euripides": Note, JBK to Schlesinger, February 14, 1962; memo from Lorraine Pearce, March 5, 1962, Papers of Arthur M. Schlesinger, Jr. (#206), Subcollection 3, Writings, Box W–7, Jacqueline B. Kennedy, Correspondence, 1961–65, JFKL; also see Perry, 114–118.

"At last our guidebook is a reality": JBK to John Walker, undated, Research Files, Kennedy/Onassis, Gallery Archives, National Gallery of Art, Washington, D.C.

"too provincial," "official flavor," "full red carpet treatment," and "He was deeply touched": See Papers of Arthur M. Schlesinger, Jr. (#206), Series 10, Subject Files, 1961–1964, Box WH–15, Folder, André Malraux, JFKL.

"She was a completely disciplined creature": Baldridge, *A Lady, First*, 186.

"Mrs. Kennedy is dying to personally take Malraux": Letter, Baldridge to Mr. Gerard de la Villesbrunne, April 24, 1962, White House Social Files, Folder, André Malraux, JFKL.

"taste in telling touches": Bowles, 69.

"Jack and Jackie actually shimmered": Baldridge, *In the Kennedy Style: Magical Evenings in the Kennedy White House* (New York: Doubleday, 1998), 90.

"I think this is the most extraordinary collection": Lincoln, Anne H., 98–99; also see "Far from the Briar Patch," *Time*, May 11, 1962; the White House dinner for the Nobel Prize winners took place on April 29, 1962.

CHAPTER TWO

"I am one of the few people": Walker, *Self-Portrait with Donors*, 7; Walker was diagnosed with poliomyelitis, a disease that also afflicted President Franklin D. Roosevelt, Ibid., 6.

"My curiosity about the works": Walker, John, "Secrets of a Museum Director," *The Atlantic Monthly*, February 1972; also see Kopper, Philip, *America's National Gallery of Art: A Gift to the Nation* (New York: Harry N. Abrams, 1991), 171.

"I was, and still am, an elitist": Walker, *Self-Portrait with Donors*, 28.

"Can life offer any greater pleasure": Walker, John, "Secrets of a Museum Director."

a handsome panther bracelet designed by Cartier: Mulvaney, Jay, *Jackie: The Clothes of Camelot* (New York: St Martin's, 2001), 103.

"Some paintings are in the Gallery" and Malraux museum tour: "Malraux Takes Over National Gallery Tour," *New York Times*, May 12, 1962; *Washington Post*, May 11, 1962, C3; also see Lebovics, Herman, *Mona Lisa's Escort: André Malraux and the Reinvention of French Culture* (Ithaca, NY: Cornell University Press, 1999), 10. Interestingly, the Copley family were loyal to the crown and the artist painted the picture in London after his Tory family fled the revolution.

"combination of orchestra conductor and stage manager": Sulzberger, 486.

"You should lend us": *Paris Match*, December 22, 1962, 44–45.

"I learned a great deal": *New York Times*, May 12, 1962, 1.

At 11:00 A.M.: "Draft Schedule Visit of André Malraux," Papers of Arthur M. Schlesinger, Jr. (#206), Series 10, Subject Files, 1961–1964, Box WH–15, Folder, André Malraux, JFKL.

"Trust was currency": Anderson, Jim, "End of an Era," *American Journalism Review*, November 1, 2002.

"If France's culture was imperiled": Cate, Curtis, "Malraux at the Bastilles of Culture," *New York Times*, May 6, 1962.

"Wouldn't it be a wonderful thing," "Perhaps a loan," and "France feels that these masterpieces": "Mona Lisa, Other Louvre Works May be Shown at National Gallery," *Washington Post*, May 12, 1962, A1; Folliard, "Escorting Mona Lisa to America," 838. Also see Thayer, 192–196; Sassoon, Donald, *Becoming Mona Lisa: The Making of a Global Icon* (New York: Harcourt, 2001), 241.

"tall and gangling": *Washington Post*, November 26, 1976, A1.

"Here's a question": Salinger, 141.

"From a Hollywood standpoint": Folliard, Edward, "Mellon wants Connoisseurs to Aid Gallery," *Washington Post*, February 25, 1935; "Art of Mellon Stored in City, Ready for Gift," *Washington Post*, February 24, 1935; "Gallery Dedication to Make Capital a World Art Center," *Washington Post*, March 16, 1941; "Freedom that Produces Art Shall Go On, Roosevelt Tells 7,962 at Gallery Opening," *Washington Post*, March 18, 1941; "Mellon Treasure House Marking 20th Year," *Washington Post*, March 12, 1961. The new National Gallery was designed by celebrated architect John Russell Pope.

While Mellon did not live to see: Davis, Margaret Leslie, *The Culture Broker: Franklin D. Murphy and the Transformation of Los Angeles* (Berkeley: University of California Press, 2007), 244.

"This became almost an obsession with me": Folliard, "Escorting Mona Lisa to America," 838.

"She had a total mastery of detail": West, 226.

"Wrinkles take on wrinkles": Baldridge, *A Lady, First*, 186.

"spring fare with French flair": Baldridge, *In the Kennedy Style*, 107.

"Prince of Carnegie Hall": Baldridge, *In the Kennedy Style*, x.

"It would be so difficult": Issac Stern to Mrs. Kennedy, July 16, 1961, letter as featured in "Jacqueline Kennedy: The White House Years, Selections from the John F. Kennedy Library and Museum," Corcoran Gallery, Washington, D.C., 2002.

new crimson velvet–upholstered stage designed by Lincoln Kirsten: Abbott, James A. and Elaine M. Rice, *Designing Camelot: The Kennedy White House Restoration* (New York: Van Nostrand Reinhold, 1998), 65.

"How strange to give a book" and "List very good but ask": "Jacqueline Kennedy Entertains: The Art of the White House Dinner," Exhibition, JFKL, 2006.

"All she needed to do was fill": Alphand, Hervé, *L'Etonnement d'être: journal 1939–1973* (Paris: Fayard, 1977); also see Leaming, Barbara, *Mrs. Kennedy: The Missing History of the Kennedy Years* (New York: The Free Press, 2001), 195.

"I worked carefully on the guest list": Anthony, *As We Remember Her*, 168.

For her formal gown: Cassini, Oleg, *A Thousand Days of Magic: Dressing Jacqueline Kennedy for the White House* (New York: Rizzoli, 1995), 153.

The eighteenth-century sapphire and diamond starburst diamond pin: Mulvaney, 189; also see Media Slide Show, website JFKL. Note conflict in sources whether dress was designed by Guy Douvier for Christian Dior or by Oleg Cassini; see Bowles, 99, and Cassini, *A Thousand Days of Magic*, 122–123.

"The total sensual appeal": Wertheimer, 254.

"Could you write a toast" and "Would you give strict instructions": Papers of Arthur M. Schlesinger, Jr. (#206), Series 10, Subject Files, 1961–1964, Box WH–15, Folder, André Malraux, JFKL.

"center of attention": Baldridge, *In the Kennedy Style*, 104.

"I suppose all of us wish to participate" (President Kennedy's toast): Lincoln, Anne H., 118.
"You know, these are the moments": Baldridge, *In the Kennedy Style*, 109.
"Malraux himself understood": Leaming, 196.
In a moment caught on film, Malraux whispered a promise: Bowles, 99.

CHAPTER THREE

"It did not seem appropriate": Zöllner, Frank, "John F. Kennedy and Leonardo's Mona Lisa: Art as the Continuation of Politics," in Kersten, Wolfgang, ed., *Radical Art History: Internationale Anthologie* (Zurich: ZIP, 1997), 470.
"SOB": Miller, John J. and Mark Molesky, *Our Oldest Enemy: A History of America's Disastrous Relationship with France* (New York: Doubleday, 2004), 216–217; and Rusk, Dean, *As I Saw It* (New York: Penguin, 1990), 268.
"Gaullism": Miller, 216; supporters say Gaullism enabled France to become a mediator between the superpowers during the Cold War.
"When it gets to New York": Todd, 370.
On Sunday, Malraux and his wife joined the President: "Draft Schedule of Events," Papers of Arthur M. Schlesinger, Jr. (#206), Series 10, Subject Files, 1961–1964, Box WH–15, Folder, André Malraux, JFKL.
"It is such an important occasion": Anthony, *First Ladies*, 68.
That evening Johnson delivered a rousing speech: "Defiance of Man's Fate," Remarks by Vice President Lyndon B. Johnson Prepared for Delivery in Response to Andréé Malraux, 50th Anniversary Dinner, French Institute, Tuesday, May 15, 1962, Papers of Arthur M. Schlesinger, Jr. (#206), Series 10, Subject Files, 1961–1964, Box WH–15, Folder, André Malraux, JFKL.
"Culture is the free world's": "The Rise of Mass Culture," *Time*, May 25, 1962.
on June 3, 1962, a chartered Air France jet crashed: *Washington Post,* June 4, 1962, 1; also see "The Day Atlanta Died," at http://ngeorgia.com/feature/orly.html.
Whistler's Mother: The formal title of the painting is *Portrait of the Artist's Mother: Arrangement in Gray and Black, No. 1,* but is widely known under its popular name, Whistler's Mother, and was painted by James McNeill Whistler in 1871.
"Just as one places on a tomb": Letter, André Malraux to JBK, August 3, 1962, White House Social Files, Folder, André Malraux, JFKL.
"fiery as his red hair": Walker, *Self-Portrait with Donors*, 155.
Walker confided to Jackie how difficult it was: Letter, JBK to Walker, undated, Research Files, Kennedy/Onassis, Gallery Archives, National Gallery of Art, Washington, D.C.
Chesterdale called Walker with daily demands: Walker, *Self-Portrait with Donors*, 154.
"Mr. Chester Dale, the president of our board of trustees": Letter, Walker to

Malraux, June 4, 1962, 7A2, Central Files, Subject Files, Mona Lisa (from Director's Office), Gallery Archives, National Gallery of Art, Washington, D.C.

"very preliminary step" and "Before the art loan": *Washington Post*, June 12, 1962, B1.

"age of vandalism": Walker, *Self-Portrait with Donors*, 54–55.

"You are the kindest, nicest, most thoughtful": Letter, Walker to JBK, June 11, 1962, White House Social Files, Folder, John Walker, JFKL.

"I am sure curators of the French museums": Letter, Mrs. Albert D. Lasker to Walker, June 21, 1962, 7A2, Central Files, Subject Files, Mona Lisa (from Director's Office), Gallery Archives, National Gallery of Art, Washington, D.C.

"I spoke to André Malraux": Letter, Nicole Alphand to Walker, July 28, 1962, 7A2, Central Files, Subject Files, Mona Lisa (from Director's Office), Gallery Archives, National Gallery of Art, Washington, D.C.

"A wife in any career is important": Walker, *Self-Portrait with Donors*, 35.

It was also the same time that the great art: Davis, 261–272.

The best of these were destined: Kopper, 174; Davis, 244–245.

"Their wealth, inherited or accumulated": Walker, *Self-Portrait with Donors*, xi. Along with the Gallery's first director, David Finley, Walker assisted in landing the great works of art collected by Samuel Kress, Joseph Widener, and Lessing J. Rosenwald. With great emotion Walker witnessed the gallery dedication by President Roosevelt on March 17, 1941. Ten years later, the museum had transformed into a thriving arts institution and a vital part of the nation's cultural identity. Following David Finley's retirement in 1956, Walker was named the museum's second director.

Walker's most "nefarious activity" as director (the story of the Cézannes): Walker, John, "My Most Infamous Intrigue: The White House Cézannes," Research Files, Loeser Collections (Cézanne Paintings), Gallery Archives, National Gallery of Art, Washington, D.C. Even though the Cézannes were not displayed in exact accordance with Loeser's will, Walker felt the collector would have been satisfied to see the lovely Cezanne's displayed on the walls of Jackie's White House.

"breathless with the news": Thayer, 195.

On October 10, Jackie asked Walker (details of the October meeting): Walker, *Self-Portrait with Donors*, 62; Letter, John F. Kennedy to John Walker, October 10, 1962, White House Social Files, Folder, John Walker, JFKL.

To Walker's surprise, instead of reacting: Letter, JBK to Walker, December 2, 1963, Research Files, Kennedy/Onassis, Gallery Archives, National Gallery of Art, Washington, D.C.

"ultimate cultural statement": Wertheimer, 247.

CHAPTER FOUR

"a secret, self-dubbed think tank": Knebel, Fletcher, "Washington in Crisis: 154 Hours on the Brink of War," *Look*, December 18, 1962.

"fell upon the Louvre like a bomb": Hours, Madeleine, *Une vie au Louvre (A Life in the Louvre)*, Translation by Sarah Watson (Paris: édition Robert Laffont, 1987), 179 (translation by Brian Quinn).

"Pictures, like people, lead two lives": Hours, Madeleine, *Secrets of the Great Masters: A Study in Artistic Techniques* (Paris: Robert Laffont, 1964), 19.

The flimsy poplar panel (details concerning condition of painting and its travels): Please see Hours, *Une vie au Louvre*, 179–195; Mohen, Jean Pierre, Michel Menu, and Bruno Mottin, *Mona Lisa: Inside the Painting* (New York: Harry N. Abrams, 2006), 20, 24–27, 32; "Noted Dames Returned," *Washington Post*, April 6, 1919. Also see Hours, Madeleine, "Étude analytique des tableaux de Léonard de Vinci au Laboratoire du musée du Louvre," in *Leonarado: saggi e ricerche,* 13–26, Achille Marazza, ed. (Rome, 1954): Hours-Médian, Madeleine, *Á la découverte de la peinture par les méthods physiques* (Paris, 1957); and Hours, *Secrets of the Great Masters.*

The Mona Lisa rested safely on the walls of the Louvre until: "Tourist Damages the Mona Lisa: Stone Breaks Glass in Louve—Paint Slightly Chipped," *New York Times*, December 31, 1956.

The rarefied world of fine art had played (the background of Madeleine Hours): Hours, *Une vie au Louvre*, 14–15, 19–22, 38, 42–61.

"Our tactics had backfired": Ibid., 180.

"black mood": Salinger, 249.

The night before, the CIA had examined aerial photographs: Chang, Laurence and Peter Kornbluh, eds., *The Cuban Missile Crisis: A National Security Archive Documents Reader* (New York: The New Press, 1992), iv.

"By the President's own definition": Watson, Mary Ann, *The Expanding Vista: American Television in the Kennedy Years* (New York: Oxford University Press, 1990), 77.

During the next few days, Salinger kept a tally: Salinger, 250; Chang, xxi. Also present were White House advisors McGeorge Bundy, Ken O'Donnell, and Theodore Sorensen.

"My Dear Mr. President": Letter, Walker to JFK, October 18, 1962, 7A2, Central Files, Subject Files, Mona Lisa (from Director's Office), Gallery Archives, National Gallery of Art, Washington, D.C.

"My only excuse": Walker, *Self-Portrait with Donors*, 62.

"This town is a sieve": Salinger, 253.

Although Walker's opening night dinner: See National Gallery of Art, Past Exhibitions, 1962, Old Master Drawings from Chatsworth, website National Gallery of Art.

"wanted her and the children to be there": Bradford, 239.

Jackie did her best to keep: Ibid., 240.

After the filming, Caroline showed up carrying: Ibid., 241.

To increase security, Hours decided (details concerning experimental packing case): Hours, *Une vie au Louvre,* 179–195; *Paris Match*, December 22, 1962, 44–45; Mohen, 20, 24–27, 32; Todd, 366.

"After listening to her": Walker, *Self-Portrait with Donors*, 63.

"Dear Mr. Walker": Letter, JBK to John Walker, November 29, 1962, Research Files, Kennedy/Onassis, Gallery Archives, National Gallery of Art, Washington, D.C.

CHAPTER FIVE

On December 3, John Walker sent a three-page (details of French stipulations): Letter, Walker to JBK, December 3, 1962 and 'Protocole: a soumettre à l'approbation du Gouvernement français et du Gouvernement des Etats-Unis, December 1, 1962 (form of Procedure to be submitted for the approval of the French Government and the Government of the United States), White House Social Files, Folder, John Walker, JFKL.

After reviewing Walker's list: JBK handwritten note added to John Walker letter of December 3, 1962, White House Social Files, Folder, John Walker, JFKL.

One disgraced government official: "She's Packed and Pampered—The Toast of Past and Today," *Life*, January 4, 1963, 17.

Secret chambers where unseen guards: "Safeguarding the Treasures of the Louvre," *Washington Post*, February 15, 1914.

"The unbelievable news item seems true": "Mona Lisa: One of the Most Fragile Paintings in the World SHOULD NOT LEAVE THE LOUVRE," *Le Figaro*, December 3, 1962 (translation by Sara Watson).

"endangering the world's most famous painting": *Le Figaro*, December 7, 1962, 11 (translation by Sara Watson).

"Indignant letters against the proposed journey": "Mona Lisa," *New Yorker*, December 15, 1962, 177.

Critics accused the culture minister: "Sea Trip Risks May Keep Mona Lisa at Home," *Washington Post*, December 11, 1962, A1.

"curved like a warped bicycle wheel": Ibid.

"one does not ask a pretty woman": *Newsweek*, December 17, 1962.

"this surreal army": Hours, *Une vie au Louvre*, 43.

Fearing its seizure: Edsel, Robert M., *Rescuing Da Vinci: Hitler and the Nazis Stole Europe's Great Art America and Her Allies Recovered It* (Dallas: Laurel Publishing, 2006), i, 60, 61. The Chateau at Chambord and the Chateau de Sourches near Le Mans stored many masterworks. For further details about Mona Lisa's hidden locations during the war, also see Hours, *Une vie au Louvre.*

"We listened with passion": Hours, *Une vie au Louvre*, 60–61.

"Why, then, [will] the French permit": Associated Press, "'Mona Lisa' Waits Release From Vault," *Christian Science Monitor*, December 21, 1962, 3.

The outcry against the exhibition: "The Mona Lisa Endangered: Our Report Upsets the Americans," *The Parisien Libéré*, January 3, 1963 (translation by Sara Watson).

"elaborate care and protection": *Washington Post*, December 13, 1962, A1, A19, A20.

"Air Force One": Walsh, Kenneth T., *Air Force One: A History of the Presidents and Their Planes* (New York: Hyperion, 2003), 63.

"as offering the safest, smoothest": "Sub Due to Bring 'Pieta' Of Michelangelo to U.S.," *Washington Post*, October 20, 1962. The Pietà and its traveling crate was estimated to weigh 4,000 kilograms, or approximately 8,818 pounds.

In fact, four different itineraries: "The Passenger of Cabin 79 is Afraid of Rolling," *Paris Match*, December 22, 1962.

But on Saturday, December 8 (Mona Lisa announcements): "London Reports Mona Lisa Due," *Washington Post*, December 10, 1962; "France May Lend U.S. 'Mona Lisa'," *New York Times*, November 30, 1962; "France Will Loan Mona Lisa to U.S.," *New York Times*, December 7, 1962, 28.

At the National Gallery, Walker received: *Washington Post*, December 10, 1962, B1.

"Is it possible": "The Mona Lisa Endangered: Our Report Upsets the Americans," *Parisien Libéré*, January 3, 1963 (translation by Sara Watson).

"Knowing the Americans": "People," *Time*, December 21, 1962.

"Taze probably hasn't had": Memo, Letitia Baldridge to JBK, undated, approximately December 10, 1962; JBK quote from handwritten note added to memo, White House Social Files, Folder, John Walker, JFKL.

CHAPTER SIX

On the weekend of December 8: *Washington Post*, December 10, 1962, A2.

"It is understood here that he virtually promised": *Washington Post*, December 11, 1962, A1.

"the final word must come from Paris": *Washington Post*, December 11, 1962, A1.

"cheery look": "Peace on Earth," *Time*, December 21, 1962.

Before the questions were to begin (JFK press conference): News Conference No. 46, President John F. Kennedy, State Department Auditorium, Washington, D.C., December 12, 1962, website JFKL; "Transcript of President Kennedy's Conference with Newsmen," *Washington Post*, December 13, 1962, A14.

According to *Time* magazine, the one hundred-plus reporters: "Peace on Earth," *Time*, December 21, 1962.

"I wanted to see it one last time": *Washington Post*, December 14, 1962, A1.

"For centuries his companion": Ibid.

Less than eighteen hours earlier along (details on parkway crash): *Washington Post*, December 15, 1962, A1, A6; *Paris Match*, December 22, 1962, 44–45.

Monsieur Jean Chatelain (Mona Lisa's escorts): According to John Walker's files, three French museum officials accompanied the painting: Jean Chatelain, Director of the French Museums; Mr. Tournois, Assistant Director of the laboratory of the Louvre; and Mr. Maurice Serullaz, Chief Curator of the Louvre. 7A2, Central Files, Subject Files, Mona Lisa (from Director's Office), Gallery Archives, National Gallery of Art, Washington, D.C.

"as near as he could get": *Washington Post*, December 15, 1962, A1, A6.

"I wanted to write you a note": Letter, John Walker to Edward Folliard, December 14, 1962, 7A2, Central Files, Subject Files, Mona Lisa, Gallery Archives, National Gallery of Art, (from Director's Office), Washington, D.C.

The superliner's butchers, pastry makers, and table cooks: *Life*, January 4, 1963, 16.

He remembered the old song: "Mona Lisa and a White House Correspondent," *America*, January 5, 1963. "That gave [Edward Folliard] the idea of having a dream a night," his colleague Walter Abbott reported.

"I think I owe the Americans a visit" (Folliard and Mona Lisa encounter): Folliard, Edward, "Dream Interview Finds Mona Lisa Feel She Owes Americans a Visit," *Washington Post*, December 16, 1962.

"whipped, whined and whistled": Root, Waverly, "Paris Fears for Mona Lisa's Safety in Storm at Sea," *Washington Post*, December 17, 1962.

"perfectly secured": Ibid.

"Could there be a more convincing emblem": Adlow, Dorothy, "Mona Lisa, Amity Role," *Christian Science Monitor*, December 15, 1962.

Always attuned to the deep power of symbols: Watson, 16; also see Wertheimer, 249.

"Never before had a work of art directly": Zöllner, 472.

"Nobody suspected back then": Cassini, *A Thousand Days of Magic*, 33; also see Wertheimer, 249.

Letters written by August Heckscher and John Walker: Letter, John Walker to Mrs. Frederick F. Powers, January 29, 1963, 4A16, Secretary-General Counsel, Exhibition Files, Box 5, Gallery Archives, National Gallery of Art, Washington, D.C. Walker wrote: "Other incidental expenses are being defrayed through funds made available by a private donor. I think, therefore, it would be fair to say that the exhibition has been virtually [supported] without any additional expense to the American taxpayer." Letter, August Heckscher to Eugene W. Sutherland, May 3, 1963, White House Staff Files of August Heckscher, Series 2, Arts File, Box 13, Folder Mona Lisa, JFKL. Heckscher wrote: "The French government financed all transportation costs of the Mona Lisa from France to the United States and back. The National Gallery in Washington paid all costs of display and transportation from New York to Washington, through contribution of an anonymous private donor. The Metropolitan Museum in New York paid its display costs. Any remaining costs were handled by our government." One theory is that on her own initiative, Mrs. Kennedy may have made arrangements for the donation of funds to the National Gallery through her close ties with Paul and Rachel Lambert (Bunny) Mellon.

CHAPTER SEVEN

Under Walker's specific directions (details of Walker's preparation): "Sculpture at Gallery Moved for Mona Lisa," *Washington Post*, December 14, 1962; See 7A2, Central Files, Subject Files, Mona Lisa, Boxes 39 and 40, Gallery Archives, National Gallery of Art. Washington, D.C.

"At a glance, he recognized that the drawing": Walker, John, "A Note on President Kennedy," April 1, 1964, Research Files, Walker, Gallery Archives, National Gallery of Art, Washington, D.C. "It is not generally known that President Kennedy had considerable discrimination in the visual arts," Walker wrote. Walker only mentions the surname Wildenstein, but it was most likely Daniel Wildenstein (1917–2001), who represented the third generation of the Wildenstein family.

"On December 19, 1962, a motor convoy": Letter, Walker to Commissioner Michael J. Murphy, December 14, 1962, 7A2, Central Files, Subject Files, Mona Lisa, Boxes 39 and 40, Gallery Archives, National Gallery of Art, Washington, D.C.

"Everything seems to be progressing well": Letter, Walker to Mme. Hervé Alphand, December 13, 1962, 7A2, Central Files, Subject Files, Mona Lisa (from Director's Office), Box 39, Gallery Archives, National Gallery of Art. Washington, D.C. Robert Lehman was a longtime trustee of the Metropolitan Museum: "When a portion of Robert Lehman's collection was exhibited at the Orangerie in Paris in 1956, it garnered accolades from French critics who might not have expected the scion of an American investment banking family to display such refined taste and robust instincts in the field of fine art." For details on The Robert Lehman Wing, which opened in 1975, see [www.metmuseum.org].

According to Madame Hours, at the moment (atmospheric readings): Memorandum for the File, L. D. Hayes, December 10, 1962, 7A2, Central Files, Subject Files, Mona Lisa, Boxes 39 and 40, Gallery Archives, National Gallery of Art, Washington, D.C.

"I hope all will go well": Letter, Madeleine Hours to John Walker, December 15, 1962, 7A2, Central Files, Subject Files, Mona Lisa, Box 39, Gallery Archives, National Gallery of Art, Washington, D.C.

When she was 24 years old (Folliard's encounters with Mona Lisa): Folliard, Edward, "Dream Interview Finds Mona Lisa Feels She Owes Americans a Visit," *Washington Post*, December 16, 1962, A1; "Queenly Welcome Awaits Mona Lisa at New York and in Nation's Capital," *Washington Post*, December 18, 1962, A1.

"As long as Chester was alive": Walker, *Self-Portrait with Donors*, 172.

"When I think of him I have so many blocks": Ibid., 154.

CHAPTER EIGHT

"She is Here!" (Mona Lisa's arrival): "Queenly Welcome Awaits Mona Lisa at New York and in Nation's Capitol," *Washington Post*, December 18, 1962, A1; "Jubilation—Mona Lisa Slated to Arrive Tonight," *Washington Post*, December 19, 1962, A1; "Unseen Mona Lisa Gets Dizzy Welcome," and "Mona Lisa's Trip here from Paris Completed," *Washington Post*, December 20, 1962; "Well-Chaperoned 'Mona Lisa' Arrives for U.S. Visit," *New York Times*, December 20, 1962, 1.

Four uniformed French line crew members (Mussorgsky): "Pictures at an Exhibition" was composed in 1874, based on ten drawings and watercolors produced by his recently deceased friend; see Frankenstein, Alfred, "Victor Hartmann and Modeste Mussorgsky," July 1939, *Musical Quarterly*.

"It looked exactly like the back": "Unseen Mona Lisa Gets Dizzy Welcome," *Washington Post*, December 20, 1962, A16.

"leave a deep imprint on the cultural history": Winship, Frederick, "Mona Lisa Given Queen's Welcome," *Greensburg Independent News*, December 19, 1962, Scrapbook, Metropolitan Museum of Art, New York.

"The most important single work of art" (Walker's remarks): *Washington Post*, December 20, 1962, A1; Press Release, Ambassade de France, Release Nos. 905–906, December 19, 1962, 14A4, Press Office Exhibition Files, Box 2, Gallery Archives, National Gallery of Art, Washington, D.C.; also see Walker's notes, 7A2, Central Files, Subject Files, Mona Lisa (from Director's Office), Gallery Archives, National Gallery of Art, Washington, D.C.

"I've nothing to declare except a hangover": *Washington Post*, December 20, 1962, A1.

"nestled in a special cradle": *Washington Post*, December 20, 1962, A1.

"I've traveled with kings": *Washington Post*, December 20, 1962, A1.

"France asked us to treat Lisa": Folliard, "Escorting Mona Lisa to America," 844.

The Secret Service had served similar: "Secret Service Guard Assigned to Mona Lisa," *Los Angeles Times*, December 19, 1962.

His code name, known only to other agents: See Historical Resources, Archives, Reference Desk, Code Names, website JFKL.

"To find a scholar and administrator": National Gallery of Art Press Release, "Chief Curator Retires," June 24, 1999, Research Files, Cott, Gallery Archives, National Gallery of Art, Washington, D.C.; also see Walker, *Self-Portrait with Donors*, 42.

"I think the Prendergast is a jewel": Letter, Walker to John F. Kennedy, December 20, 1962, 7A2, Central Files, Subject Files, Mona Lisa (from Director's Office), Gallery Archives, National Gallery of Art, Washington, D.C.; also see President's Office Files, Box 139, JFKL. Sadly, Walker did not know it at the time, but he had assisted Kennedy in selecting the final Christmas present the President would give to his wife.

At Jackie's suggestion, Walker offered: 14A4, Press Office Exhibition Files, Box 2, Gallery Archives, National Gallery of Art, Washington, D.C.

"The French to whom ceremony is no trifle": *Washington Post*, December 22, 1962, A1.

"She's covered with mold!": Hours, *Une vie au Louvre*, 183.

"If anyone on the curatorial staff": Memo, Walker to Campbell, Sullivan, and Cooke; "Mona Lisa—Authorization to Go Into Vault X," December 26, 1962, 7A2, Central Files, Subject Files, Mona Lisa, Box 40, Gallery Archives, National Gallery of Art, Washington, D.C.

"our Days of Trial": Letter, J. Carter Brown to Letitia Baldridge, January 11, 1963, 7A2, Central Files, Subject Files, Mona Lisa, Box 39, Gallery Archives, National Gallery of Art, Washington, D.C.

"Nineteen sixty two closed for Jackie": Bradford, 242.

"*tout va bien*": Telegram, Hours to Directour Musée du Louvre, Paris, January 3, 1963, 7A2, Central Files, Subject Files, Mona Lisa, Box 39, Gallery Archives, National Gallery of Art, Washington, D.C.

"This is my suggestion for the Mona Lisa text": August Heckscher, Memorandum for Arthur Schlesinger, Jr., January 4, 1962, White House Staff Files of August Heckscher, Series 2, Arts File, Box 13, Folder Mona Lisa, JFKL.

"Never before had any president sought": Schlesinger, *A Thousand Days*, 730–733.

Relay, the second U.S. communications satellite: *Washington Post*, August 6, 1961, A4; March 1, 1962, A6; May 4, 1962, A7; July 8, 1962, A1; July 11, 1962, A1; December 14, 1962, A1; January 6, 1963, A8; January 9, 1963, A8; January 10, 1963, A3.

It was left to Walker to orchestrate: Walker, John, "Categories for Invitations, Evening of Jan. 8," 14A3, Press Office Exhibition Files, Box 1, Gallery Archives, National Gallery of Art, Washington, D.C.

Once Jackie had submitted her lengthy list (invitation list): Walker, John, "Invitation List for the Dinner at the French Embassy, Tuesday Jan. 8," 7A2, Central Files, Subject Files, Mona Lisa, Box 39, and 14A3, Press Office Exhibition Files, Box 1, Gallery Archives, National Gallery of Art, Washington, D.C.

A team of genealogists later discovered: Gherardini and Kennedy: Martin, Judith, "A Mona Lisa-Kennedy Connection," *Washington Post*, November 2, 1974, E1; also see "The Renaissance Lives on in Tuscany," *National Geographic* (November 1974): 9.

"There will be need for Director Walker's humor": *Washington Post*, December 20, 1962, A1.

CHAPTER NINE

"very slightly more ": Todd, 368.

Hours expressed concern over the temperature: Memo, Perry B. Cott to NGA Administrator, January 7, 1963, 7A2, Box 39, Central Files, Subject Files, Mona Lisa, Gallery Archives, National Gallery of Art, Washington, D.C.

The Gallery's administrator was asked (details concerning temperature): Ibid.

He was also concerned that the huge throng (plan for audio speakers): Letter, Frank H. McIntosh to John Walker, January 15, 1963, 7A2, Box 39, Central Files, Subject Files, Mona Lisa, Gallery Archives, National Gallery of Art, Washington, D.C.

"My wife and I sincerely regret": Telegram, Nat King Cole to the Trustees of the National Gallery, January 7, 1963, 4A16, Secretary-General Counsel Exhibition Files, Box 5, Gallery Archives, National Gallery of Art, Washington, D.C.

Mindful of the rarity of the occasion: Walker, Notice to All Employees, January 7, 1963, 7A2, Box 39, Central Files, Subject Files, Mona Lisa, Gallery Archives, National Gallery of Art, Washington, D.C.

"In Vault X of the National Gallery of Art": "'Mona Lisa' Waits Release From Vault," *Christian Science Monitor*, December 21, 1962.

"We had discussed what Jackie should wear": Cassini, Oleg, *A Thousand Days of Magic*, 181.

"were hosts at a dinner and a tableau": "Keep Smiling," *Time*, February 15, 1963.

The celebration to honor the unveiling (details of the Embassy dinner): "Invitation L'Ambassaduer de France et Madame Hervé Alphand pirnet the President et Mrs. Kennedy, Monday, January 8 at 7:30," 7A2, Central Files, Subject Files, Mona Lisa, Gallery Archives, National Gallery of Art, Washington, D.C.; "Keep Smiling," *Time*, January 18, 1963; "Dinner at French Embassy Precedes Mona's Welcome," *Washington Post*, December 19, 1962.

"De Gaulle stayed in France": Sassoon, 242.

Rapoport recalled that Madame Alphand: See [rapo.com].

"It was a wonderful dinner" (recollections from Madame Hours): Hours, *Une vie au Louvre*, 185–190. She also added: "As for little brother Ted, she introduced me to him as a senator, despite his young age! It was a united family with overflowing charm."

"Thanks for a nice dinner Ed!": Thayer, 198.

"The Mona Lisa, first lady of the world": *Washington Post*, January 9, 1963, A1, A5.

"It was a long awaited reunion": *Life*, January 18, 1963, 38–39.

Malraux and Kennedy speeches: Papers of Arthur M. Schlesinger, Jr. (#206), Series 10, Subject Files, 1961–1964, Box WH–15, Folder, André Malraux, JFKL; also see website JFKL.

"television straddled the Atlantic via's America's": "Relay Beams Da Vinci Smile to Europe's TV," *Chicago Daily Tribune*, January 10, 1963.

On international scholar noted: Zöllner, 473.

"I was exhausted and my face" (encounter between JFK and Madame Hours): Hours, *Une vie au Louvre*, 186–187.

"I feel worse!": Walker, *Self-Portrait with Donors*, 66.

At that moment the white-capped Marine (details of the bayonet incident and its aftermath): Hours, *Une vie au Louvre*, 188–190.

"Madame, had you been killed": Oral History of Catharine Bonner, Conducted by John J. Harter, National Gallery of Art Oral History Program, June 2, 1989, 103–107, 32A4, Oral History Program, Gallery Archives, National Gallery of Art, Washington, D.C. (Bonner was a longtime administrative employee); also see Lebovics, 12–13.

"attended by the entire listing": "Debut is Cataclysmic," *Daily News*, January 9, 1963, Mona Lisa Exhibition Scrapbook, Gallery Archives, National Gallery of Art, Washington, D.C.

"Everything went wrong that night": Oral History of Catharine Bonner, Conducted by John J. Harter, National Gallery of Art Oral History Program, June 2, 1989, 32A4, Oral History Program, Gallery Archives, National Gallery of Art, Washington, D.C., 103–107.

"the world's most powerful nation": *New York Times*, January 9, 1963, A1; also see Todd, 368–369.

"I want to thank you for all you": Letter, Walker to Malraux, January 9, 1963, 7A2, Box 40, Central Files, Subject Files, Mona Lisa, Gallery Archives, National Gallery of Art, Washington, D.C.

"Last night I suddenly heard Jackie": Schlesinger, Arthur M. Jr., *Journals 1952–2000* (New York: Penguin, 2007), 187; also see Schlesinger, *A Thousand Days*, 671.

"Dear Jackie": Walker to JBK, January 11, 1963, 7A2, Box 40, Central Files, Subject Files, Mona Lisa, Gallery Archives, National Gallery of Art, Washington, D.C.

"I am taking the veil": Adler, 105.

The last occasion when the Gallery had seen: *Washington Post*, December 22, 1962, A1; "Paintings from the Berlin Museums," March 17–April 25, 1948; see website National Gallery of Art.

"Dear John": Letter, JBK to John Walker, January 15, 1963, White House Social Files, Folder, John Walker, JFKL; also Research Files, Kennedy/Onassis, Gallery Archives, National Gallery of Art, Washington, D.C.

"The most powerful nation in the world": Cassini, *A Thousand Days of Magic*, 178. "Success changes people, and I saw Jackie change as she grew in confidence, as did the President. When the whole world is applauding, I think its natural," Cassini said.

"She had dreaded coming to the White House": Schlesinger, *A Thousand Days*, 671.

CHAPTER TEN

"Unfortunately, Ernie Feidler had great": Letter, John Walker to Donald D. Shepard, January 14, 1963, 7A2, Box 40, Central Files, Subject Files, Mona Lisa, Gallery Archives, National Gallery of Art, Washington, D.C.

"The late Andrew W. Mellon": Folliard, Edward, "Culture Booming in the National Capitol," *America*, January 26, 1963.

"I'm frozen stiff": *Washington Post*, January 10, 1963, A1, B1.

"It is not a knock-out at first glance": Ibid.

"The American interest is not always the French interest": "Monsieur No," *Time*, January 18, 1963.

"Mr. Minister, we in the United States": "Remarks of the President at Ceremony in Honor of the Mona Lisa at the National Gallery of Art, Washington, D.C., January 8, 1963," 7A2, Box 40, Central Files, Subject Files, Mona Lisa, Gallery Archives, National Gallery of Art, Washington, D.C.; also see website JFKL.

"No French newspaper has remarked": Lebovics, 24.

"So tangled are the strains and stresses": *New Republic*, January 19, 1963, 29–30.

"Think of people seeing it generations from now" and Green Room restoration: Letter, JBK to Averell and Marie Harriman, June 22, 1962, Harriman Papers, Library of Congress; also see Smith, Sally Bedell, 343; *Washington Post*, January 23, 1963, D1.

"The Yellow Oval Room was the most completely": See Abbott, 173.

On January 14, alarming news came (Klee burglary): *Tampa Florida Times*, January 14, 1963, Mona Lisa Exhibition Scrapbook, Gallery Archives, National Gallery of Art, Washington, D.C.

"most comprehensive smile in the folios": "'Mona Lisa' Waits Release From Vault," *Christian Science Monitor*, December 22, 1962.

"The enthusiasm and adoration showered": Exhibition Catalogue, "On the Occasion of the Exhibition of the Mona Lisa by Leonardo da Vinci, Lent to the President of the United States and the American People by the Government of the French Republic, 1963," Central Files, Subject Files, Mona Lisa, Gallery Archives, National Gallery of Art, Washington, D.C.

"There is a quality to the brush work": *San Antonio Texas News*, January 13, 1963, Mona Lisa Exhibition Scrapbook, Metropolitan Museum of Art, New York.

"The fine and well-pumiced gesso" and "Portrait of Mona Lisa" (Catalogue description): Exhibition Catalogue. Walker's Exhibition Catalogue added: "The artist labored more than four years to paint the small picture. Mona Lisa's smile, which has been the object of countless explanations, resulted according to Vasari, Leonardo's contemporary, from the fact that Leonardo 'retained musicians who played and continually jested' in order to amuse the portrait's sitter."

"The work actually produces a strange": Mohen, 12; Mohen serves as general curator of the French Center for Museum Research and Restoration and the Louvre.

"*Chère amie*": Letter, Perry B. Cott to Madame Madeleine Hours, January 16, 1963, 17A3, General Curatorial Subject Files, Mona Lisa, Box 6, Gallery Archives, National Gallery of Art, Washington, D.C.
"an important misconception": Lebovics, 20, 22.
"The Mona Lisa is more than an extraordinary": Todd, 369.
Postcards featuring the masterpiece: Perry, 132.
"I made one enemy in life": John Walker, Interview by Anne G. Ritchie, October 23, 1990, National Gallery of Art, Oral History Program, 71–72.

CHAPTER ELEVEN

The weather could not have been more miserable (weather report): "Wet Weather Swept Away by Icy Wave," *Washington Post*, February 4, 1963.
"MONA GO HOME!": *Washington Post*, January 10, 1963, B1.
"The old lady was on her way": *New York Times*, February 11, 1963, 6.
"There are many things in Aristotle": Dudley, Earl, "Mona Lisa Begins NY City Visit, Vies with Rembrandt," *Schenectady Gazette*, February 7, 1963, Mona Lisa Exhibition Scrapbook, Metropolitan Museum of Art, New York.
"We'll have literally balls of dust": "Mona Lisa," *New Yorker*, February 9, 1963.
Rorimer had sent "spies" (Rorimer's preparations at the Metropolitan Museum): "N.Y. Readies for Visitor," *Christian Science Monitor*, January 16, 1963, 7; "New York Smiles Back at 'Mona Lisa'," *Christian Science Monitor*, February 8, 1963; "Mona Lisa Opens Run in New York," *New York Times*, February 8, 1963; also see Mona Lisa Exhibition Scrapbook, Metropolitan Museum of Art, New York.
"We are now all breathing more easily": Letter, Perry B. Cott to Madame Madeleine Hours, February 5, 1963, 17A3, General Curatorial Exhibition Files, Mona Lisa, Box 6, Gallery Archives, National Gallery of Art, Washington, D.C.
In the Army he served in the Monuments: Deitch, Joseph, "NY Readies for Visitor," *Christian Science Monitor*, January 16, 1963, 7.
He supervised construction of the Cloisters: "Double Loss," *Time*, May 20, 1966.
"Ridiculous": "It Cost $2.3 Million; Moving Bill $63," *New York Herald Tribune*, November 17, 1961.
"I found that if they never did anything": John Walker, Interview by Anne G. Ritchie, October 23, 1990, National Gallery of Art, Oral History Program, Gallery Archives, National Gallery of Art, Washington, D.C.
"As you drew near the beautiful antique": *Connoisseur*, May 1963, 66.
"self-admitted lover of the finer things": "Mona Lisa Opens Run in New York," *New York Times*, February 8, 1963; *Philadelphia Inquirer*, February 8, 1963, 1.
"the biggest thing since Cleopatra": *Life*, January 4, 1963, 18.

"Women will be aiming high for beauty": "Famed Mona Lisa Inspires Hairdo," *Boston Herald*, January 8, 1963, Scrapbook, Metropolitan Museum of Art, New York.

The moment had been artfully coordinated: Grant, Donald, "Mrs. Kennedy Mends Two Fences At Luncheon with Stevenson, Thant," *St. Louis Post Dispatch*, February 8, 1963, Scrapbook, Metropolitan Museum of Art, New York.

"smoothed over one of the biggest protocol flaps": "First Lady Helps End Protocol Rift," *Chicago Illinois News*, February 8, 1963, Scrapbook, Metropolitan Museum of Art, New York.

"In a single whisper-voiced appearance": Grant.

In the first seven days of the New York exhibition: "Memo to the Press," Metropolitan Museum of Art, March 5, 1963, Archives, Metropolitan Museum of Art, New York.

On Valentine's Day, Rorimer announced: "Metropolitan Museum Will Remain Open Mondays through Fridays Until 9 PM as a Result of Great Interest in Mona Lisa," News for Release, February 15, 1963, Metropolitan Museum of Art, 14A3, Press Office Exhibition Files, Box 1, Gallery Archives, National Gallery of Art, Washington, D.C.

So many city dwellers came to see the portrait: "Mona Lisa," *New Yorker*, February 9, 1963.

"approach the sacred crypt": Sassoon, 245.

"The fact that the Lady": *Connoisseur*, May 1963, 66.

"The responsibility for the painting": John Walker, Memorandum for the Files, February 8, 1963, 4A16, Secretary-General Counsel Exhibition Files, Box 5, Gallery Archives, National Gallery of Art, Washington, D.C.

Walker speech: John Walker, "Statement at Closing of Mona Lisa Exhibition at the Metropolitan Museum," March 6, 1963, 7A2, Box 39, Central Files, Subject Files, Mona Lisa, Gallery Archives, National Gallery of Art, Washington, D.C.

Walker penned more than a dozen drafts of a receipt: "Receipt, March 7, 1963," 4A16, Secretary-General Counsel Exhibition Files, Box 5, Gallery Archives, National Gallery of Art, Washington, D.C.

CHAPTER TWELVE

"I am informed that the Mona Lisa": Letter, JFK to de Gaulle, March 8, 1963, President's Office Files, Series 9, Countries, Box 116, Folder 14, JFKL.

"Dear Mr. President": Letter, Walker to JFK, March 18, 1963, 7A2, Box 39, Central Files, Subject Files, Mona Lisa, Gallery Archives, National Gallery of Art, Washington, D.C.

"The visit of the Mona Lisa to the United States": Letter, Walker to M. Jean Chatelain, March 28, 1963, 7A2, Box 39, Central Files, Subject Files, Mona Lisa (from Director's Office), Gallery Archives, National Gallery of Art, Washington, D.C.

"As the Mona Lisa resumes her place": Letter, Charles de Gaulle to JFK, March 19, 1963, President's Office Files, Series 9, Countries, Box 116, Folder 14, JFKL.

"the second hardest job in the U.S.": "Big Year for the Clan," *Time*, April 26, 1963.

The council would be comprised of thirty: "President Planning to Create Council of Advisers in Arts," *New York Times*, April 1, 1963.

The President's Advisory Council on the Arts was enacted: Executive Order 11112, see [www.presidency.ucsb.edu]. In furtherance of the administration's goal of positioning the arts to assume their rightful place "among other concerns of government," Executive Order 11112 was signed by the president on June 12, 1963. Also see Larson, 152–180.

"beguiling and persuasive letter": Bowles, 10.

"Indeed more than any other space": Abbott, 173.

"I never dreamt anything so perfect": Thayer, 252.

"A million, million thanks!": Ibid.

But the month of August also brought: Folliard, Edward, "Kennedy Baby is Buried in Boston After Rites at Cardinal's Residence," *Washington Post*, August 11, 1963, A1.

On August 11, Caroline Kennedy: "Flowers for Caroline's Mommy," *Washington Post*, August 12, 1963, A1.

The two, he said, had brought a pause: Folliard, Edward, "President Warns of Perils Despite Cold War Pause," *Washington Post*, October 20, 1963, A1.

"If art is to nourish the roots": "Remarks At Amherst College, President John F. Kennedy," Amherst, Massachusetts, October 26, 1963, see website JFKL; also see Folliard, Edward, *Washington Post*, October 27, 1963, A1.

The trans-Atlantic connection of the two great museums: "National Gallery's Latest Acquisition to Have D.C. Paris TV Debut Today," *Washington Post*, November 17, 1963, A1.

As Goodwin was about to take over: Anthony, *As We Remember Her*, 170: "I hoped one day to have a minister for the arts in the cabinet," Jackie said later. "Much groundwork would have to be done before that would be possible." The president's arts consultant, August Heckscher, left his post in June 1963 after he issued his findings on how the administration could best initiate a formal link between the federal government and the cultural arts. Official presidential action on the recommendations had been delayed.

"It's a good idea": Bowles, 11.

Newsman Edward Folliard was traveling (Folliard in Dallas): Edward Folliard, recorded interview by William M. McHugh, March 30, 1967, John F. Kennedy Library Oral History Program, JFKL; also see Folliard's features in the *Washington Post*, November 23, A1 and A2, November 24, A1, and November 26, A1.

"It was all gone now": Schlesinger, *A Thousand Days*, 1030–1031.

"While we are at the Capitol": West, 312–313.

"She gave an example to the whole world": Anthony, *First Ladies*, 104.

On Monday, December 2 (Harriman home): "Moving Out," *Time*, December 13, 1963.

"My Dear Johnny": Letter, JBK to John Walker, December 2, 1963, Research Files, Kennedy/Onassis, Gallery Archives, National Gallery of Art, Washington, D.C. On Wednesday, December 4, 1963, the four Cézannes were returned to the National Gallery. *House on the Marne* and *The Forest* remained displayed on the walls of Jackie's beloved Yellow Oval Room until 1985, when, after twenty-four years, they were returned to the National Gallery. In December 2005, one of Jackie's pictures, *The Forest*, was returned to the White House where it remains to this day. See "Loeser Cezanne Paintings Summary Chronology," Research Files, Loeser Collections (Cézanne Paintings), Gallery Archives, National Gallery of Art, Washington, D.C.

EPILOGUE

"The visit of the Mona Lisa": Walker, *Self-Portrait with Donors*, 63.

"Ambassador Tut became a force of moderation": Knight, Christopher, "The Boy Shill: How King Tut Evolved from Cold War Cultural Ambassador to Today's Corporate Pitchman," *Los Angeles Times*, August 28, 2005, E35.

"She refused to give up": "Once in Camelot," *Time*, May 30, 1994.

"As she had in the White House": Keogh, Pamela Clarke, *Jackie Style* (New York: HarperCollins, 2001), 204.

"Missing Her": *New York Daily News*, 1.

"In a public sea she steered a private": *New York Times*, May 21, 1994, 1.

"By maintaining her own unique identity": Sorensen, x.

"I would say that in some ways": Keogh, 14.

"Throughout her life, my mother took": Kennedy, Caroline, *The Best Loved Poems of Jacqueline Kennedy Onassis* (New York: Hyperion, 2001).

"Thank you for writing me about the President's portrait": Letter, JBK to John Walker, October 6, 1965, Research Files, Kennedy/Onassis, Gallery Archives, National Gallery of Art, Washington, D.C.

"brilliant red wheelchair": "John Walker: A Washington Love Affair with Great Art," *Guardian*, October 20, 1995.

"left him on tranquilizers" and "Will O'Dale": *New York Times*, October 17, 1995, D–25.

John Walker died on October 16, 1995: *Washington Post*, October 17, 1995, B1, D4.

He died of lung cancer at the age of seventy-seven: "André Malraux, 75, Dies in Paris; Writer, War Hero, de Gaulle Aide," *New York Times*, November 25, 1976.

Twenty years later, Malraux's body: Lebovics, ix.

"For the most part": Todd, x.

"That's the one story I just wish": Edward Folliard, recorded interview by William M. McHugh, March 30, 1967, John F. Kennedy Library Oral History Program, JFKL.

In 1969, President Nixon (details of his relationship with President Nixon) and "Broadly speaking": *Washington Post*, November 26, 1976, A1, B13; also November 27, 1976, A14.

The picture left the Louvre again (Mona Lisa's trip to Tokyo): Hours, *Une vie au Louvre*, 256–269.

"an additional envelope": Ibid., 158. "Of course we couldn't protect her from the hazards of all possibilities, Madam Hours said, "including the possibility of an explosion [aboard the aircraft]."

Madame Hours watched with great emotion: Ibid., 264.

"I saw a bright red light like a rocket": Ibid., 264.

"Did you see it?": Ibid., 265.

Once the painting was returned to the Louvre, and "some play": Mohen, 27–28.

French engineer and inventor (French and Canadian researchers): "New Look at 'Mona Lisa' Yields Some New Secrets," *New York Times*, September 27, 2006.

Images of the scanned painting: "Mona Lisa Had 'Wider Smile' and 'Eyebrows,'" *The Economic Times*, October 24, 2007; "25 Secrets of Mona Lisa Revealed," at [LiveScience.com]; also see Mohen, 94–110.

"wheeled away": *International Herald Tribune*, April 6, 2005, 11.

"She's like a living person": "Fans Hail Mona Lisa's New Setting," *BBC News*, April 6, 2005.

Mona Lisa temperature: "Techniques That Might Smile Upon Mona Lisa," *New York Times*, January 1, 2005.

Selected Bibliography

ORAL HISTORIES

Hervé Alphand, recorded interview by Adalbert de Segonzac, October 14, 1964, John F. Kennedy Library Oral History Program.

Catharine Bonner, interview by John J. Harter, June 2, 1989, National Gallery of Art, Oral History Program.

Edward Folliard, recorded interview by William M. McHugh, March 30, 1967, John F. Kennedy Library Oral History Program.

August Heckscher, recorded interview by Wolf von Eckhardt, December 10, 1965, John F. Kennedy Library Oral History Program.

Letitia Baldrige Hollensteiner, recorded interview by Mrs. Wayne Fredericks, April 24, 1964, John F. Kennedy Library Oral History Program.

Jacqueline Kennedy Onassis, interview by Joe B. Frantz, January 11, 1974, Lyndon B. Johnson Library Oral History program, JFKL.

John Walker, interview by Anne G. Ritchie, October 23, 1990, National Gallery of Art, Oral History Program.

BOOKS, ARTICLES, DISSERTATIONS

Abbott, James A. and Elaine M. Rice. *Designing Camelot: The Kennedy White House Restoration*. New York: Van Nostrand Reinhold, 1998.

Adler, Bill. *The Eloquent Jacqueline Kennedy Onassis: A Portrait in Her Own Words*. New York: HarperCollins, 2004.

Alphand, Hervé. *L'Etonnement d'être: journal 1939–1973*. Paris: Fayard, 1977.

Anthony, Carl Sferrazza. *As We Remember Her: Jacqueline Kennedy Onassis in the Words of Her Family and Friends*. New York: HarperCollins, 1997.

Anthony, Carl Sferrazza. *First Ladies: The Saga of the Presidents' Wives and Their Power, 1961–1990*. New York: William Morrow and Co., 1991.

Baldridge, Letitia. *A Lady, First: My Life in the Kennedy White House and the American Embassies of Paris and Rome*. New York: Viking, 2001.

Baldridge, Letitia. *In the Kennedy Style: Magical Evenings in the Kennedy White House*. New York: Doubleday, 1998.

Baldridge, Letitia. *Of Diamonds and Diplomats: An Autobiography of a Happy Life*. New York: Ballantine, 1968.

Boorstin, Daniel J. *The Creators: A History of Heroes of the Imagination*. New York: Vintage, 1993.

Boorstin, Daniel J. *The Image: A Guide to Pseudo Events in America*. New York: Vintage, 1991.

Bowles, Hamish, ed. *Jacqueline Kennedy: The White House Years; Selections from the John F. Kennedy Library and Museum*. New York: Metropolitan Museum of Art, 2001.

Bradford, Sarah. *America's Queen: A Life of Jacqueline Kennedy Onassis*. New York: Penguin, 2000.

Bradlee, Benjamin C. *Conversations with Kennedy*. New York: W. W. Norton, 1975.

Cassini, Oleg. *A Thousand Days of Magic: Dressing Jacqueline Kennedy for the White House*. New York: Rizzoli, 1995.

Cassini, Oleg. *In My Own Fashion: An Autobiography*. New York: Simon and Schuster, 1987.

Chang, Laurence and Peter Kornbluh, eds. *The Cuban Missile Crisis: A National Security Archive Documents Reader*. New York: The New Press, 1992.

Dallek, Robert. *An Unfinished Life: John F. Kennedy, 1917–1963*. Boston: Little, Brown, 2003.

Davis, Margaret Leslie. *The Culture Broker: Franklin D. Murphy and the Transformation of Los Angeles*. Berkeley: University of California Press, 2007.

Edsel, Robert M. *Rescuing Da Vinci: Hitler and the Nazis Stole Europe's Great Art America and Her Allies Recovered It*. Dallas: Laurel Publishing, 2006.

Folliard, Edward. "Escorting Mona Lisa to America." *National Geographic*, June 1963: 838–847.

Heckscher, August. *The Public Happiness*. New York: Atheneum, 1962.

Hours, Madeleine. *Secrets of the Great Masters: A Study in Artistic Techniques*. Paris: Robert Laffont, 1964.

Hours, Madeleine. *Une vie au Louvre (A Life in the Louvre)*. Paris: édition Robert Laffont, 1987.

Kennedy, Caroline, ed. *The Best-Loved Poems of Jacqueline Kennedy Onassis*. New York: Hyperion, 2001.

Keogh, Pamela Clarke. *Jackie Style*. New York: HarperCollins, 2001.

Kersten, Wolfgang, ed. *Radical Art History: Internationale Anthologie*. Zurich: ZIP, 1997.

Kloss, William. *Art in the White House: A Nation's Pride*. New York: Harry N. Abrams, 1992.

Kopper, Philip. *America's National Gallery of Art: A Gift to the Nation*. New York: Harry N. Abrams, 1991.

Lacouture, Jean. *André Malraux*. New York: Pantheon, 1975.

Larson, Gary O. *The Reluctant Patron: The United States Government and the Arts 1943–1965*. Philadelphia: University of Pennsylvania Press, 1983.

Leaming, Barbara. *Mrs. Kennedy: The Missing History of the Kennedy Years*. New York: The Free Press, 2001.
Lebovics, Herman. *Mona Lisa's Escort: André Malraux and the Reinvention of French Culture*. Ithaca, NY: Cornell University Press, 1999.
Lincoln, Anne H. *The Kennedy White House Parties*. New York: Viking, 1967.
Lincoln, Evelyn. *My Twelve Years with John F. Kennedy*. Boulder, CO: Black Pebbles Publishing, 2003.
Lowe, Jacques. *Jacqueline Kennedy Onassis: A Tribute*. New York: Jacques Lowe Visual Arts Project, 1995.
Miller, John J. and Mark Molesky. *Our Oldest Enemy: A History of America's Disastrous Relationship with France*. New York: Doubleday, 2004.
Mohen, Jean Pierre, Michel Menu, and Bruno Mottin. *Mona Lisa: Inside the Painting*. New York: Harry N. Abrams, 2006.
Mulvaney, Jay. *Jackie: The Clothes of Camelot*. New York: St. Martin's, 2001.
Pallanti, Giuseppe. *Mona Lisa Revealed: The True Identity of Leonardo's Model*. New York: Rizzoli, 2006.
Perry, Barbara A. *Jacqueline Kennedy: First Lady of the New Frontier*. Lawrence: University Press of Kansas, 2004.
Rusk, Dean. *As I Saw It*. New York: Penguin, 1990.
Salinger, Pierre. *With Kennedy*. New York: Doubleday, 1966.
Sassoon, Donald. *Becoming Mona Lisa: The Making of a Global Icon*. New York: Harcourt, 2001.
Schlesinger, Arthur M. Jr. *A Thousand Days: John F. Kennedy in the White House*. Boston: Houghton Mifflin, 1965.
Schlesinger, Arthur M. Jr. *Journals: 1952–2000*. New York: Penguin, 2007.
Shapiro, Meyer. *Paul Cézanne*. New York: Harry N. Abrams, 2004.
Smith, Marie. *Entertaining in the White House*. New York: MacFadden-Bartell, 1967.
Smith, Sally Bedell. *Grace and Power: The Private World of the Kennedy White House*. New York: Random House, 2004.
Sorensen, Theodore C. *Kennedy*. New York: Perennial Library, 1988.
Suarès, J. C. and J. Spencer Beck. *Uncommon Grace: Reminiscences and Photographs of Jacqueline Bouvier Kennedy Onassis*. Charlottesville, NC: Thomasson-Grant, 1994.
Sulzberger, C. L. *The Last of the Giants*. New York: Macmillan, 1970.
Thayer, Mary Van Rensselaer. *Jacqueline Kennedy: The White House Years*. Boston: Little, Brown, 1967.
Todd, Oliver. *Malraux: A Life*. New York: Knopf, 2005.
Walker, John. *Self-Portrait with Donors: Confessions of an Art Collector*. Boston: Little, Brown, 1974.
Walsh, Kenneth T. *Air Force One: A History of the Presidents and Their Planes*. New York: Hyperion, 2003.
Watson, Mary Ann. *The Expanding Vista: American Television in the Kennedy Years*. New York: Oxford University Press, 1990.

Wertheimer, Molly Meijer, ed. *Inventing a Voice: The Rhetoric of American First Ladies of the Twentieth Century*. Lanham, MD: Rowman and Littlefield, 2004.

West, J. B., with Mary Lynn Kotz. *Upstairs at the White House: My Life with the First Ladies*. New York: Coward, McCann, and Geoghegan, 1973.

White, Theodore Harold. *The Making of the President*. New York: Atheneum, 1988.

INDEX

DA